CANTO GENERAL

Pablo Neruda. (Courtesy of the Archivo Fotográphia Fundacion Pablo Neruda)

A CENTENNIAL BOOK

One hundred distinguished books
published between 1990 and 1995
bear this special imprint
of the University of California Press.
We have chosen each Centennial Book
as an exemplar of the Press's great publishing
and bookmaking traditions as we enter
our second century.

UNIVERSITY OF CALIFORNIA PRESS

Founded in 1893

PABLO NERUDA

CANTO GENERAL

Translated by
Jack Schmitt

Introduction by
Roberto González Echevarría

UNIVERSITY OF CALIFORNIA PRESS
Berkeley   Los Angeles   Oxford

A WAKE FOREST STUDIUM BOOK

WFS

Pro Humanitate

Canto General © Tundacion Pablo Neruda

University of California Press
Berkely and Los Angeles, California

University of California Press
Oxford, England

Copyright © 1991 by The Regents of the University of California

Library of Congress Cataloging-in-Publication Data

Neruda, Pablo, 1904–1973.
  [Canto general. English]
  Canto general/Pablo Neruda : translated by Jack Schmitt.
    p.   cm.—(Latin American literature and culture : 7)
  Translation of: Canto general.
  Includes bibliographical references.
  ISBN 0-520-05433-4
  1. America—Poetry.   I. Schmitt, Jack, 1932–   .   II. Title.
III. Series: Latin American literature and culture (Berkeley,
Calif.) : 7.
PQ8097.N4C1713   1991
861—dc20   90-39070
                                                   CIP

Printed in the United States of America

1 2 3 4 5 6 7 8 9

The paper used in this publication meets the minimum require-
ments of American National Standard for Information Sciences —
PErmanence of Paper for Printed Library Materials, ANSI
Z39.48-1984 ∞

CONTENTS

Acknowledgments   xvii
Introduction by
    Roberto González Echevarría   1

I A LAMP ON EARTH   13

    I. *Amor America* (1400)   13
       Vegetation   14
    II. Some Beasts   16
    III. The Birds Arrive   17
    IV. The Rivers Come Forth   19

       Orinoco   19
       Amazon   20
       Tequendama   20
       Bío-Bío   20

    V. Minerals   21
    VI. Man   24

II THE HEIGHTS OF MACCHU PICCHU   29

    I. From air to air, like an empty
       net   29
    II. If the lofty germ is carried
       from flower to flower   30
    III. Like corn man was husked in
       the bottomless granary   31
    IV. Mighty death invited me many
       times   32
    V. It was not you, solemn death,
       iron-plumed bird   33
    VI. And so I scaled the ladder of
       the earth   33
    VII. O remains of a single abyss,
       shadows of one gorge   35
    VIII. Rise up with me, American
       love   36
    IX. Sidereal eagle, vineyard of mist   37
    X. Stone upon stone, and man,
       where was he?   38

Contents

XI. Through the hazy splendor   40

XII. Rise up to be born with me,
my brother   41

III THE CONQUISTADORS   43

I. They Come Through the
Islands (1493)   43

II. Now Its Cuba   44

III. They Reach the Gulf of Mexico
(1519)   45

IV. Cortés   46

V. Cholula   47

VI. Alvarado   48

VII. Guatemala   48

VIII. A Bishop   49

IX. The Head on the Spear   49

X. Homage to Balboa   50

XI. A Soldier Sleeps   51

XII. Ximénez de Quesada (1536)   52

XIII. Rendezvous of Ravens   54

XIV. The Agonies   55

XV. The Red Line   56

XVI. Elegy   57

XVII. The Wars   58

XVIII. Discoverers of Chile   59

XIX. The Combatant Land   60

XX. Land and Man Unite   61

XXI. Valdivia (1544)   62

XXII. Ercilla   64

XXIII. The Spears Are Buried   64

XXIV. The Magellanic Heart (1519)   65

I Awaken Suddenly in the
Night Thinking about
the Far South   65

I Remember the Solitude
of the Strait   65

The Discoverers Appear
and Nothing Is Left of
Them   66

Only Destruction Prevails   67

Contents

Memorial to the Old
Discoverer   67
Magellan   67
He Reaches the Pacific   68
All Have Perished   68

XXV. Despite the Fury   68

IV THE LIBERATORS   71

The Liberators   71
I. Cuauhtemoc (1520)   73
II. Brother Bartolomé de Las
Casas   74
III. Advancing in the Lands of
Chile   77
IV. The Men Rise Up   78
V. Chief Caupolicán   79
VI. The Civil War   80
VII. Impaled   81
VIII. Lautaro (1550)   82
IX. The Chief's Training   82
X. Lautaro Among the Invaders   83
XI. Lautaro Against the Centaur
(1554)   84
XII. Pedro de Valdivia's Heart   85
XIII. The Protracted War   86
XIV. (Interlude) The Colony Covers
Our Lands (1)   88
XV. The Haciendas (2)   89
XVI. The New Proprietors (3)   90
XVII. Commoners from Socorro
(1781)   91
XVIII. Tupac Amaru (1781)   92
XIX. Insurgent America (1800)   93
XX. Bernardo O'Higgins Riquelme
(1810)   94
XXI. San Martín (1810)   97
XXII. Mina (1817)   99
XXIII. Miranda Dies in the Fog (1816)   101
XXIV. José Miguel Carrera (1810)   102

Episode   102

Contents

	Chorus	103
	Episode	103
	Chorus	104
	Exodus	105
	Chorus	106
	Antistrophe	107
XXV.	Manuel Rodríguez	108
	Cueca. Life	108
	Cueca. Passion	109
	Cueca. And Death	109
XXVI.	Artigas	110
XXVII.	Guayaquil (1822)	112
XXVIII.	Sucre	114
	The Flags	115
XXIX.	Castro Alves from Brazil	115
XXX.	Toussaint L'Ouverture	116
XXXI.	Morazán (1842)	117
XXXII.	Journey Through the Night of Juárez	118
XXXIII.	The Wind over Lincoln	119
XXXIV.	Martí (1890)	121
XXXV.	Balmaceda from Chile (1891)	122
XXXVI.	To Emiliano Zapata with Music by Tata Nacho	125
XXXVII.	Sandino (1926)	127
XXXVIII.	1. Toward Recabarren	129
	2. Copper	130
	3. Night in Chuquicamata	131
	4. The Chileans	132
	5. The Hero	133
	6. Trades	133
	7. The Desert	134
	8. Nocturne	134
	9. The Wasteland	135
XXXIX.	Recabarren (1921)	136
	Envoi (1949)	140
	Father of Chile	140
XL.	Prestes from Brazil (1940)	141
XLI.	Pronounced in Pacaembú (Brazil, 1945)	144

Contents

XLII. The Tyrants Again 146
XLIII. The Day Will Come 147

V THE SAND BETRAYED 149

Perhaps, perhaps oblivion 149

I. The Hangmen 150

Doctor Francia 150
Rosas (1829–1849) 152
Ecuador 154
García Moreno 154
America's Witches 156
Estrada 156
Ubico 156
Gómez 156
Machado 157
Melgarejo 157
Bolivia (22 March 1865) 158
Martínez (1932) 159
The Satrapies 160

II. The Oligarchies 161

Promulgation of the
Funnel Law 163
Election in Chimborongo
(1947) 164
The Cream 165
Celestial Poets 166
Exploiters 167
Fops 168
The Favorites 169
The Dollar's Lawyers 170
Diplomats (1948) 172
The Bordellos 174
Procession in Lima (1947) 175
Standard Oil Co. 176
Anaconda Copper Mining Co. 177
United Fruit Co. 179
Lands and Men 180
The Beggars 181
The Indians 182
The Judges 185

Contents

III. The Corpses in the Plaza (28 January 1946, Santiago de Chile)   186

    The Massacres   186
    The Nitrate Men   187
    Death   188
    How Flags Are Born   189
    I Invoke Them   189
    The Enemies   190
    They Are Here   191
    Forever   191

IV. Chronicle of 1948 (America)   192

    Paraguay   192
    Brazil   193
    Cuba   194
    Central America   194
    Puerto Rico   195
    Greece   196
    The Torments   197
    The Traitor   197
    I Accuse   198
    The Victorious People   199

V. González Videla, Chile's Traitor (Epilogue) 1949   200

VI AMERICA, I DO NOT INVOKE YOUR NAME IN VAIN   203

    I. From Above (1942)   203
    II. An Assassin Sleeps   204
    III. On the Coast   204
    IV. Winter in the South, on Horseback   204
    V. Crimes   205
    VI. Youth   205
    VII. Climates   206
    VIII. Varadero in Cuba   206
    IX. The Dictators   206
    X. Central America   207
    XI. Hunger in the South   207
    XII. Patagonia   208
    XIII. A Rose   208

Contents

XIV. Life and Death of a Butterfly 208
XV. The Man Buried in the Pampa 209
XVI. Sea Workers 209
XVII. A River 210
XVIII. America 210
XIX. America, I Do Not Invoke
Your Name in Vain 212

VII CANTO GENERAL OF CHILE 213

Eternity 213

I. Hymn and Homecoming (1939) 214
II. I Want to Return to the South
(1941) 215
III. Melancholy Near Orizaba
(1942) 216
IV. Ocean 219
V. Saddlery 219

Pottery Shop 220
Looms 220

VI. Floods 221

Earthquake 221

VII. Atacama 222
VIII. Tocopilla 223
IX. Peumo Tree 224

Quila Bamboo 225
Drimis Winterei 225

X. Untilled Zones 225
XI. House Wrens 226

Red-Breasted Meadowlark 227
Chucao Tapaculo 227

XII. Botany 228
XIII. Araucaria Pine 229
XIV. Tomás Lago 230

Rubén Azócar 231
Juvencio Valle 231
Diego Muñoz 232

XV. Rider in the Rain 232

Contents

XVI. Chile's Seas   232

XVII. Winter Ode to the Mapocho
River   235

VIII THE EARTH'S NAME IS JUAN   **237**

    I. Cristóbal Miranda (Shoveler,
Tocopilla)   237

    II. Jesús Gutiérrez (Agrarian)   238

    III. Luis Cortés (from Tocopilla)   239

    IV. Olegario Sepúlveda
(Shoemaker, Talcahuano)   240

    V. Arturo Carrión (Seaman,
Iquique)   241

    VI. Abraham Jesús Brito (People's
Poet)   242

    VII. Antonio Bernales (Fisherman,
Colombia)   243

    VIII. Margarita Naranjo ("María
Elena" Nitrate Works,
Antofagasta)   245

    IX. José Cruz Achachalla (Miner,
Bolivia)   246

    X. Eufrosino Ramírez (Casa Verde,
Chuquicamata)   247

    XI. Juan Figueroa ("María Elena"
Iodine Works, Antofagasta)   248

    XII. Master Huerta (from the "La
Despreciada" Mine,
Antofagasta)   248

    XIII. Amador Cea (from Coronel,
Chile, 1949)   250

    XIV. Benilda Varela (Concepción,
University City, Chile, 1949)   250

    XV. Calero, Banana Worker (Costa
Rica, 1940)   251

    XVI. Catastrophe in Sewell   252

    XVII. The Earth's Name Is Juan   253

IX LET THE WOODCUTTER AWAKEN   **255**

    I. Let the Woodcutter Awaken   255

    II. But they found a house guest
besides   258

Contents

III. Beyond your lands, America, I
also wend my way   261

IV. But if you arm your hordes,
North America   266

V. Let none of this come to pass   269

VI. Peace for the coming twilights   270

X   THE FUGITIVE   273

I. The Fugitive (1948)   273

II. It was the grape autumn   275

III. And so I turned to the night
again   275

IV. A young couple opened a door   276

V. Again, another night, I went
farther   277

VI. Window of the hills! Valparaíso   279

VII. It was the dawning of saltpeter
on the pampas   280

VIII. I love, Valparaíso, everything
you enfold   281

IX. I've ranged the far-famed seas   282

X. And so, from night to night   283

XI. What can you do, scoundrel,
against the air?   284

XII. To all, to you   285

XIII. American sand, solemn   286

XI   THE FLOWERS OF PUNITAQUI   289

I. The Valley of Stones (1946)   289

II. Brother Pablo   290

III. Hunger and Rage   291

IV. They Steal Their Land   292

V. Toward the Minerals   292

VI. The Flowers of Punitaqui   293

VII. Gold   295

VIII. Gold's Road   296

IX. I Went Beyond the Gold   297

X. The Poet   298

XI. Death in the World   299

XII. Mankind   299

xiii

Contents

XIII. The Strike   300

XIV. The People   301

XV. The Letter   303

XII **THE RIVERS OF SONG**   **303**

I. Letter to Miguel Otero Silva, in
Caracas (1948)   303

II. To Rafael Alberti (Puerto Santa
María, Spain)   307

III. To González Carbalho (in Río
de la Plata)   312

IV. To Silvestre Revueltas, from
Mexico, on His Death
(Oratorio Minor)   314

V. To Miguel Hernández,
Murdered in the Prisons of
Spain   316

XIII **NEW YEAR'S CHORALE FOR THE COUNTRY
IN DARKNESS**   **319**

I. Greetings (1949)   319

II. The Men from Pisagua   321

III. The Heroes   323

IV. González Videla   325

V. I Didn't Suffer   326

VI. In These Times   327

VII. They Spoke to Me Before   328

VIII. Chile's Voices   328

IX. The Liars   329

X. They Shall Be Named   330

XI. The Forest's Worms   330

XII. Homeland, They Want to
Parcel You Out   331

XIII. They Receive Orders Against
Chile   332

XIV. I Recall the Sea   332

XV. There's No Forgiving   333

XVI. You Will Struggle   334

XVII. Happy New Year to My
Country in Darkness   335

Contents

XIV THE GREAT OCEAN   **337**

      I. The Great Ocean   337
     II. Births   339
    III. The Fish and the Drowned
         Person   341
     IV. The Men and the Islands   342
      V. Rapa Nui   342
     VI. The Statue Builders (Rapa Nui)   344
    VII. The Rain (Rapa Nui)   345
  VIII. The Oceanics   347
     IX. Antarctica   348
      X. Children of the Seacoast   349
     XI. Death   350
    XII. The Wave   351
   XIII. The Seaports   352
   XIV. The Ships   356
    XV. To a Ship's Figurehead (Elegy)   357
   XVI. The Man Aboard the Ship   359
  XVII. The Enigmas   360
XVIII. Stones of the Seaboard   361
   XIX. Gongorine Mollusca   363
    XX. The Battered Birds   364
   XXI. Leviathan   366
  XXII. Phalacrocorax   367
XXIII. Not Only the Albatross   368
XXIV. Marine Night   369

XV I AM   **373**

      I. The Frontier (1904)   373
     II. The Slingman (1919)   374
    III. The House   375
     IV. Travel Companions (1921)   376
      V. The Student (1923)   377
     VI. The Traveler (1927)   378
    VII. Far from Here   379
  VIII. The Plaster Masks   379
     IX. The Dance (1929)   380
      X. The War (1936)   381
     XI. Love   382

Contents

XII.	Mexico (1940)	383
XIII.	On Mexico's Walls (1943)	384
XIV.	The Return (1944)	387
XV.	The Wood Line	388
XVI.	Combative Kindness	389
XVII.	The Steel Gathers (1945)	390
XVIII.	Wine	391
XIX.	Fruits of the Earth	392
XX.	Great Happiness	393
XXI.	Death	394
XXII.	Life	395
XXIII.	Testament (I)	395
XXIV.	Testament (II)	396
XXV.	Dispositions	397
XXVI.	I Am Going to Live (1949)	398
XXVII.	To My Party	398
XXVIII.	I End Here (1949)	399
	Notes	401

INTRODUCTION

NERUDA'S *CANTO GENERAL*, THE POETICS OF BETRAYAL

Neruda's *Canto general*, one of the highest poetic achievements of the century, was published in 1950 in a special edition printed in Mexico City, with drawings by the great muralists Diego Rivera and David Alfaro Siqueiros.[1] The poet was then forty-six and already a much-admired figure of international stature. Like the *Divine Comedy*, Neruda's *Canto general* was a work written in the middle of the poet's life journey, when his personal past and work were already a considerable weight on him and his poetic persona a deep mirror upon which to look at himself. The vast poem was a return to origins and a rebirth, a sweeping recollection dragging, along with the memories of Neruda's intimate and poetic self, the natural and collective history of Latin America. This is the Whitmanian thrust of the *Canto general*. In the poem, Neruda draws a balance of his personal and creative life as well as of the history of the New World at the century's midpoint. He gathers here his *vanguardista* experience, particularly the surrealist, and tempers it with the keen historical awareness forced on him by the political catastrophes of the 1930s and 1940s. It is an awareness that undermined much of the creative élan of the avant-garde, that sobered up artists and intellectuals who felt that art itself could be a salvation for the woes of the modern world.

While these same developments produced an existentialist gloom in post-war Europe and some regions of Latin America and the United States, neither Neruda nor Carpentier (or Borges, for that matter) fell prey to its doleful allure. It was instead a heady *mundonovismo*, based on the New World's ever-

I

renewed promise of a fresh start, that nourished the hope of Neruda and other Latin Americans; the hope that out of the ruins of Europe and Western civilization in general, Latin America would emerge as a new, vital force, untainted by the errors and sins of the Old World. At the core of the *Canto general* is an effort to create an American myth, a version of American history that can constitute the cipher of American destiny; in short, a story about origins which is at the same time about principles, in all of the various meanings of the word: as beginning, as rule, as enduring guide in all orders of life, not the least of which is the ethical and the political. Because Neruda is a romantic, that myth had to have as protagonist his own poetic self, the individual whose suffering and vision the myth will legitimize. Hence, his own journey through life is a foundational story woven into the fabric of the poem, as is the evolution of the poetic voice within its fictive time.

Neruda's life is inscribed throughout the *Canto general*: the poetic voice dates and details what he saw or experienced (e.g., an event as momentous as the ascent to Macchu Picchu) and later becomes the object of the last section of the poem, "I am." Although this prominent presence of the I as agent, and at times victim, is part of the *Canto*'s romantic foundation, it is also a component of the real story that is incorporated into the poem's fiction, as Neruda's life was very well known to the public, particularly the Latin American public, by the time he wrote the *Canto general*. Even the process of its writing had become public knowledge. This was not poetry contrived in a garret or ivory tower, away from the pressures of everyday life, but instead one written in the midst of a very dramatic life whose adventures were being closely followed by almost everyone.

A succinct version of Neruda's life—as known by most in Latin America—could be told as follows. He was born in Parral, in southern Chile, on July 12, 1904. His name was Ricardo Eliecer Neftalí Reyes Basoalto. Neruda's father, José del Carmen Reyes Morales, was a railroad worker and his mother, Rosa Basoalto, a primary school teacher. She died of tuberculosis less than two months after the poet was born. In 1906, José married again, this time to Trinidad Candia Marverde, a loving and tender woman who was the only mother Neruda was to know. The family moved to Temuco, set on the verge of the rain forest in southern Chile, where the poet spent his childhood and adolescence. Neruda was writing poetry at an early age, against his father's will, publishing a few poems in local newspapers and student magazines. In October 1920, to conceal his vocation, Ricardo assumed the pseudonym Pablo Neruda. The first name could be a homage to Paul Verlaine; the last was taken from Czechoslovakian writer Jan Neruda. In his memoirs, Neruda claims that he simply picked the name out of a magazine. In 1921, now eighteen, he moved to Santiago, the capital, and enrolled at the Instituto Pedagógico, where he planned to become a French teacher. For the next few years, he wrote for various journals and befriended a number of bohemian poets. He published *Crepusculario*, his first book, in 1923 and *Veinte poemas de amor y una canción desesperada* in 1924. This was the first time poetry in Spanish celebrated love in the language of everyday life, with unfettered expressions of desire for women whose beauty was not ethereal. *Veinte poemas* would make Neruda famous in the entire Spanish-speaking world. These love poems were and are known by heart by people of all social classes in Latin America and Spain. With very few close rivals, they are the most popular love poems ever written in Spanish.

Following every young Latin American writer's ambition to travel to Europe, Neruda sought a post in Chile's diplomatic corps. When a position finally materialized in 1927, however, it was as Consul *ad honorem* to Rangoon. Neruda had to rush to a map to find out where he was going, but he did accept the post. Between 1927 and 1932, when he returned to Chile, Neruda served as consul in Rangoon, Colombo, and Singapore. In the Orient, Neruda suffered his season in hell. Lonely, displaced, surrounded by the chaos and misery wrought by crumbling European empires, he delved deep into himself and wrote his first major book of poems (although *Veinte poemas* was no small accomplishment), *Residencia en la tierra*. This book revolutionized Spanish-language poetry. The poems, akin in their torrent of images to the surrealist poetry being written in Europe, show that Neruda had been reading Proust, Joyce, and other European "novelties," including perhaps the surrealists, while in the Orient. But the poems of *Residencia* were more powerful than anything the surrealists or any other avant-garde poets ever produced. This is so perhaps because they were closer to the romantic origin of the avant-garde. At the time, Neruda (who communicated mostly in English while in the Orient) had also been reading English romantic poetry and probably Whitman. These poems presented a world in ruins, a "godless apocalypse" as Amado Alonso put it in his fundamental book on Neruda, in a chaotic language that appeared to reflect inchoate passions, fears, and desires.[2] Only Quevedo, in the seventeenth century, had projected a world of such desolation in such powerful images. *Residencia* did not find a publisher until 1933, though most of the poems had been written in the 1920s.

In 1930, Neruda was married in Java to María Antonieta Haagenar Vogelzanz, a woman of Dutch ancestry, with whom he had a daughter. Their marriage only lasted until 1936, by which time Neruda had found his next great passion, Delia del Carril, an Argentine.

Back in Chile in 1932, Neruda was named consul in Buenos Aires. During the following year, he met Federico García Lorca, who was on tour at the time, and they became close friends and collaborators. But Neruda did not stay long in the Argentinian capital. In 1934, he was named consul in Barcelona, and in 1935, he was transferred to Madrid. The next few years, spent in the Spanish capital in the company of the Spanish poets known as the Generation of '27 (Lorca, Pedro Salinas, Rafael Alberti, Vicente Aleixandre, Luis Cernuda, Manuel Altolaguirre), were among Neruda's happiest and most productive. He became a kind of leader of the group, editing the journal *Caballo verde de la poesía*, taking under his wing the great shepherd-poet Miguel Hernández, and participating in literary gatherings and events. It was the frenzied time of the Second Republic, which was accompanied by a tremendous flowering in Spanish arts and intellectual life in general. It did not last. In July 1936, Spanish troops led by José Sanjurjo and Francisco Franco staged a right-wing revolt that led to the Spanish civil war. The events that followed marked Neruda forever. While he had been involved in political activities before, particularly during his years as a student, the Spanish civil war transformed him, as it did many other writers in and out of Spain. Politics would take a central place in Neruda's life and works from this moment on, and he would increasingly become a public figure. His influence in the cultural and political debates in the Spanish-speaking world remained considerable until his death.

Lorca's assassination and other appalling atrocities committed by the Fascists propelled Neruda into political activity as well as into a feverish period of creativity. He was dismissed as consul because of his political involvements, which freed him to travel to Barcelona and Paris to help organize a massive congress of artists against fascism. The event took place in Valencia, Barcelona, and Madrid in 1937. In October of that year, Neruda returned to Chile, where he rallied artists and intellectuals to the defense of the Spanish Republic. He also published *España en el corazón* in 1937, his first book of explicitly political poems. This book about the Spanish civil war would later be published at the frontlines in Barcelona, printed on paper made by the soldiers from captured flags, rags, bloodied gauze, and other trophies of war. In 1939, a more sympathetic Chilean government sent Neruda to Paris as consul for Spanish Emigration, with the mission of aiding refugees from the beaten Spanish Republic by finding countries that would take them. It was a bitter time, darkened by the gloom of defeat and by the impending European war. Fascism, victorious in Spain, was also on the march in Italy and Germany. Hundreds of European artists and intellectuals emigrated to the New World. Many Latin Americans living in Paris, like the great Cuban novelist Alejo Carpentier, made haste to return home.

In 1940, Neruda returned to Chile and then moved to Mexico, where he had been named consul general. His return to the New World coincided with the emigration to Latin America of many Spanish intellectuals fleeing the revanchist and vindictive Franco regime. Many settled in Mexico, which as a result enjoyed a moment of intellectual and artistic splendor. Many of these Spaniards were Neruda's friends from the Madrid years. By this time, his popularity was immense, not only as a poet but as a cultural and political figure. When he left the Mexican capital to return again to Chile in 1943, he was given a farewell banquet attended by more than 2,000 guests. In that same year, Neruda published the *Canto general de Chile*, which would eventually become the *Canto general*. On his way back to Santiago, he was honored by the governments of Panama and Peru and visited the pre-Incan ruins at Macchu Picchu. In 1944, he published *Alturas de Macchu Picchu*, which would also be integrated later into the *Canto general*.

Politics and poetry took a frenetic turn in the next few years. In 1944, Neruda was elected senator, and in 1945, he became a member of the Chilean Communist party. He campaigned, as head of propaganda, in favor of presidential candidate Gabriel González Videla, who, though not a Communist (he was on the Partido Radical slate), was supported by the party. González Videla won the presidency but backed away from many of his promises and outlawed the Communists. In 1947, Neruda published an open letter in Caracas accusing the Chilean president of betrayal. An order for his arrest was issued, on charges of contempt and treason (he was still a senator). Neruda went into hiding, pursued by the police. During this period, which lasted a year, it was widely known that he was writing the *Canto general*. Neruda's adventures while in hiding, and his escape on horseback through the Andes to Argentina in 1949, became an international intrigue. The Chilean government even released news of his death. Neruda surfaced in Paris bearing the passport of his friend, the great Guatemalan novelist Miguel Angel Asturias, with whom he had met in Buenos Aires. Neruda arrived back in Mexico in 1950, where he published the *Canto general*, an event of continental repercussions both poetically and politically.

Neruda then began a series of extended trips through Eastern Europe, as a sort of roving cultural ambassador representing his party, and at the same time initiated a radical change in his poetry, toward a simpler mode of expression. In 1953, he published anonymously a collection of love poems, *Versos del capitán*, dedicated to his new muse, Matilde Urrutia, a Chilean he had met in Mexico, who became his companion (they eventually married) until the end of his days.[3] His *odas elementales* appeared in 1954. Three volumes of *odas elementales* were published in the 1950s. These were poems in which the poet wished to look anew at the humblest elements of reality, to isolate with his gaze objects and beings normally left out of the purview of poetry. A celebration of matter in its various forms, the odes were widely acclaimed and marked a truly new poetic mode for Neruda.

In 1959, still in his role as itinerant poetic and political conscience of the Americas, Neruda traveled to Cuba and, as a result, wrote *Canción de gesta*, a poem in praise of the Revolution. But Neruda's next volumes of poetry, *Cantos ceremoniales* (1961) and *Memorial de Isla Negra* (1964), turned inward and backward, to his childhood, to his life on the Chilean coast. In 1971, Neruda returned to Europe, now as Chilean ambassador to France, representing the government of his longtime friend Salvador Allende, who had finally been elected president. It was a time of hope, of revolutionary plenitude, soon crowned by Neruda's long-expected Nobel Prize in literature.

But Neruda was gravely ill with cancer. He returned to Chile in 1972, where he witnessed the downfall of Allende's regime, brought about in part by the destabilizing efforts of the Nixon administration. Neruda died on September 23, 1973. Though the terminal illness was the direct physical cause of death, he was clearly debilitated by the deep sorrow of Allende's demise and the dark hour enveloping his beloved motherland. The two events— Allende's downfall and Neruda's death—will forever be linked in the memory of Latin Americans, not as dramatically but perhaps as indelibly as Lorca's murder and Franco's victory in Spain. It gave Neruda's life, which he had so forcefully shaped to match his poetry, a meaningful ending, both as literature and as politics.[4]

What does *Canto general* mean? It means, of course, "general song," perhaps in opposition to Whitman's *Song of Myself.* General song would be, then, the song of all. But it is also the song of or about everything, meaning both the objective, concrete world of what we call the real and the history of the world—the entire history of the world. This is consistent with the sweep of the poem, which begins in pre-Hispanic America, or prehistoric America, when humanity is just about to emerge from the clay, and moves along until it reaches the here and now of the poet writing in 1949. Perhaps a good translation would be "The Song of All," meaning not only history and the concrete world but also the mind of man, his beliefs and ethics, his fears and aspirations. In this there is a kind of medieval vestige, both in the title *Canto general* and in the actual poem. I am thinking, of course, of Alfonso the Wise's *Generale Storia*, the vast historical summa the Spanish king commissioned in the thirteenth century, which was *generale* because it comprised both the actual history of the world and the mythological versions created to express it up to his own time, including classical mythology and Christianity. A usage of *general* closer to our own and Neruda's time, but still tinged with a certain medievalism, is Gonzalo Fernández de Oviedo's *Historia general y natural de las Indias* and Garcilaso de la Vega, El Inca's *Historia general del Perú.* In these colonial histories, *general* meant that the book encompassed the natural and cultural history of America. In a sense, histories such as these are the only worthy antecedents of Neruda's *Canto general*, if one excludes Andrés Bello's *Silvas americanas.* One should not be put off by the scholasticism Neruda would share with these authors. There is a medieval ring to the epic thrust of Neruda's poem (*Chanson de Roland, Niebelungenlieder*), a certain gothicism in the upward movement of "Heights of Macchu Picchu," and even a medieval Manichaeism in Neruda's portrayal of historical and political figures. It is a Manichaeism garnished by a bestiary (particularly in the description of tyrants) that smacks also of medieval literature and art in general. But mostly, the medievalism is evident in the overall faith that holds the entire poetic enterprise together: Neruda's faith in the ultimate redemption of humanity, even if such a salvation is to come through the agency of something as worldly as historical materialism. Be that as it may, the point is that "General Song" is to be taken as a song about the totality of the human, a summa-like poem whose analogs and perhaps sources are medieval. This does not explain "song," of course. But it should be clear by now that "song" harks back to national epics, like the *Song of Roland*, and expresses a clamor, a celebration, a chant. One way of translating the title would be *General Chant*, meaning the chant sung by all in unison to celebrate the world and, particularly, the future of the world.

It is a solemn celebration, a chant in a major key. The *Canto*'s deep resonances come from its long, sonorous lines, occasionally broken by shorter ones for emphasis, and by its avalanche of metaphors. Neruda's poem is a tropological cornucopia. Everything is in a state of flux, everything is in the process of becoming something else or looking like something else. The analog here is America's proliferating nature ("In fertility time grew"). There is no conventional rhyme, meter, or strophic arrangement, and although the history recounted begins before the beginning of history, it does not flow chronologically from there until the end. The *Canto* establishes its own inner rhythms. There is something sacramental in Neruda's poetic language, like the words of a religion in the process of being founded, of a liturgy establishing its rituals and choosing its words. The grandiose tropes of his verse emerge as if not only to give names to things but to anoint them. There are really no antecedents in Spanish for this kind of poem, or even book, except perhaps in those colonial histories mentioned, or in Bello. But Bello's neo-classical rhetoric gets in the way too often. The closest modern parallel to the *Canto general* in the Hispanic world is in painting, particularly in Mexican muralism and Picasso's *Guernica*. Like the Mexican muralists, whose works he saw often and whom he knew personally and who illustrated the first edition of the *Canto*, Neruda's poem is monumental, in the sense that it covers a vast span of history and focuses on transcendental persons and deeds as well as on the humble masses. One has the sense of being in a crowd when viewing one of Rivera's great murals. The self is dwarfed by the size and by the transcendence of the historical figures; one is properly reduced to being a member of the mass of spectators or victims (they are sometimes both). The same is true of Neruda's poem. His is not a voice one can hope to imitate, emulate, or compete with. Neruda's voice has biblical resonances, while ours can only be part of the general clamor, hurrah, or wail; only as part of the throng's roar or cry can we hope to reach the resonance, the volume, and the tone of the voice in *Canto general*.

The *Canto* does have a recognizable plot, which leads from the prehistoric to a finale that pays homage to the Soviet Union and the Communist party, which appear as the restorers of broken promises, with a transition at the center provided by the ascent to Macchu Picchu. "The Heights of Macchu Picchu," like all the literature of ascent (Petrarch's to the Windy Mountain, for instance), is a poem of conversion. It is here that Neruda's vision is refocused by the presence of these ruins, testament to a utopia in the past, an allegiance of a collectivity with nature to create beauty and justice. It is an allegiance also marred by violence, abuse, and betrayal. It is also here that the poet meets death, in a descent to the region of the dead reminiscent of Homer, Virgil, and Dante. From here, the poem moves toward the present and a possible restoration of the original allegiance. This eventually takes the form of a homage to humble people and in the concluding sections, of a dedication to his party, including a paean to Stalin. The chiliastic scheme of *Canto general* has been made ironic by the intervening years, of course. When Neruda wrote the poem, he knew that Stalin had had to punish ("but he punishes too"; "punishment is needed") to bring about change, but he had no idea of the atrocities he had committed; these were revealed years later. As we pick up the morning paper today, fully forty years after Neruda wrote his poem, and see pictures of masses protesting the abuses of communism in Eastern Europe and witness the overall collapse of the Communist party throughout the world, Neruda's vision becomes increasingly obsolete. One is repulsed by his homilies to Stalin, and his praise of the party sounds, at best, naive. Yet, we have long ago ceased to believe in Dante's visions (not a few crimes against humanity have been committed in the name of the Christianity he saw as the fulfillment of prophecy), and we still read his poem with reverence for the cohesion of his world-view as reflected in the poetic world he created. It is difficult, this close to the revelations of Stalin's abuses, to have the same distance from Neruda's vision. But there is an inherent naiveté in the poet's stance which we must grant to enjoy his enormous accomplishment, even if we recognize that there are parts of the *Canto* that are very weak because of their dated rhetoric.

Canto general aspires to create an American myth, or what James E. Miller calls, following Wallace Stevens, a "Supreme Fiction."[5] Such a myth or fiction is about origins, about tradition, or, more to the point, about the lack of origins or tradition. In his remarkable essay, "A Literature of Foundations," Octavio Paz maintains that "American literature, which is rootless and cosmopolitan, is both a return and a search for tradition. In searching it, it invents it. But invention and discovery are not terms that best describe its purest creations. A desire for incarnation, a literature of foundations."[6]

How can a foundation myth be created in a modern poem? The *Canto general* contains various interwoven stories, all of them foundational. One is the history of Latin America from pre-Columbian days to the present; another is Neruda's own history, his personal life and emergence as poetic voice; then, there is what one could call natural history, which he drew from the naturalists' second discovery of America, that is, from the many naturalists who traversed Latin America in the eighteenth and nineteenth centuries, charting its natural phenomena, establishing its natural uniqueness.[7] All these narratives vie for preeminence, each aspires to become the master story that contains all others, by situating itself as the origin or beginning of the American continent. It is possible to write an interpretation of the *Canto general* allowing one of these narrative strands to be the guiding principle. They are all persuasive. In one of the most influential and perceptive pieces ever written on Neruda, Saúl Yurkiévich maintains that there are essentially two, conflicting, stories that cannot coalesce.[8] One tells the natural history of the New World and is coeval with the personal history of the poet, told in an irrational, mythic language, free from the temporal or historical dimension. It is a vision of the poet's subconscious that shares the inchoate creativity of the natural world. This is the language inherited from *Residencia*. The second story is prosaic, rational, political history, cast in time and often in the language of personal testimony. This story excludes myth, the irrational, the poetic, and wishes to be political action aimed at the future. It is impossible to deny the validity of Yurkiévich's proposal, and it would be naive to believe Neruda when he claims that there is a coalescence of voices in the poem. There is no such harmony, but only because the foundational story in *Canto general* is one of disruption.

Critics have attempted to fix the point at which Neruda conceived the *Canto general*, as if finding that originary moment would yield a key to a global interpretation of the poem. Emir Rodríguez Monegal, whose reading of Neruda rests on a psychoanalytic model, proposes that the poem was conceived in the wake of the death of Neruda's father, in 1938.[9] Others have placed that moment of illumination at the time when Neruda climbed to Macchu Picchu on his journey home from Mexico in 1943.[10] It is undeniable that these events must have had a decisive impact on the elaboration of the Canto, but neither can, by itself, explain its creation or serve as a key to its interpretation. Unless we hold to a terribly crude notion of artistic creation, it is difficult to think that a complicated and ambitious artistic project such as the Canto general can be conjured in a flash of psychological release or mystical revelation. It is true that poets and other artists are themselves deluded into recollecting that a specific moment or incident served as catalyst in the creation of a given masterpiece. These are usually productive errors that criticism can exploit, but carefully, for they tend to belong to the very fictive fabric of the literary work, as a kind of coda or meta-end. It is highly doubtful, also, that even if we hit on such a privileged moment, it would provide a key for the interpretation of the work.

In my view, the foundational story of the Canto general is one of betrayal. Betrayal is important because it sets up the mood of the Canto, which is one of outrage, and its promise, which is one of restoration. Betrayal is not original sin; it is an evil act committed by men in full knowledge of their own doings. Like the flood in Vico's system, which provides a second beginning after which history is man-made (as opposed to Genesis), betrayal is a beginning of history for which man is responsible. It is also violence committed against a given communal text, which sets up a rupture in history and in the interpretation of words, the shared words of the community. Break and restoration appear as the fundamental political and poetic acts; it is a rebonding of words and acts and a reconstitution of the collectivity. The fundamental events that led to the composition of the Canto general are González Videla's betrayal of his campaign promises, Neruda's letter accusing the president of treason, and the poet's trial for contempt, which led to his protracted persecution, during which he finished the poem.

These incidents took place at the very beginning of the so-called cold war. The alliance between the United States and the Soviet Union during World War II was quickly broken by their radical political differences, so the air was full of mistrust and accusations and counteraccusations of betrayal of the ideals that had forged the alliance in the first place. This was a time, of course, when Communist parties sought to ally themselves with other "progressive" groups to attempt to gain power by electoral means. Neruda, who was, needless to say, a very prominent member of his party, helped forge a coalition with the Radical party to which González Videla, who had also been a senator, belonged. Neruda was named campaign manager and, along with his party, worked hard to elect González Videla, who made promises to the Communists and signed a program outlining broad and drastic political reforms. On taking power, González Videla reneged on his promises and the program. Encouraged by the United States, who had an economic and stra-

9

tegic interest in Chile's nitrate and copper, he persecuted Communists, undermined labor unions, established a tight censorship of the press, and generally allowed the old Chilean landed oligarchy to exercise enormous influence on his government. At this point, Neruda wrote his "Letter to My Friends in Latin America," also known as the "Intimate Letter to Millions of Men," accusing the Chilean president. The letter was published in Caracas's *El Nacional*, on November 27, 1947. González Videla brought charges of contempt against Neruda for accusing the president of his own country and government abroad. Neruda then delivered, on January 6, 1948, a blistering speech against González Videla in the Chilean Senate, generally known by the Zola title, "Yo acuso." But the accusation against Neruda had been upheld by the Supreme Court, and an order for his arrest was issued. It was then that Neruda went into hiding and finished writing the *Canto general*. In his letter, Neruda says that the Communist party had granted him a leave of one year to finish writing his poem: "just two months ago the leaders of the Chilean Communist party called me to ask that I devote more time to my poetic work. To this end they offered me the isolation and solitude necessary for a year to push forward, particularly, my *Canto general*."[11] Two months later, however, in the speech against González Videla, Neruda still refers to the poem as *Canto general de Chile*: "If I wanted to insult the President of the Republic, I would do it within my literary work. But if I am obliged to deal with his case in the vast poem that I am now writing, entitled *Canto general de Chile*, singing the earth and the episodes of our country's history, I will also do it honestly, and with the purity that I have always displayed in my political activities."[12] It is clear that the transition toward the more ambitious poem took place during the time at which the events surrounding the charges and countercharges were made. From a poem about Chile, the *Canto* became a poem about the whole of Latin America, a myth of origins.

Myths are often a story of violence, physical, sexual, and psychological, involving members of the same family or clan. The consanguinity of all involved is of the essence. The reason for this is that the myth will establish the existence of one in contrast to the other, and to separate the one from itself, an upheaval of some sort must occur. In Neruda's *Canto general*, that violence against itself takes the form of treason, of betrayal. Treason can only take place if there has been a pledge of oneness, of fealty to a given corpus or body. It is an act against that covenant guaranteeing unity. Hence, treason or betrayal fulfills the quality of being against one in the process of splitting itself into another. Betrayal is the foundation of difference, of noncoincidence of the self with the self, of the word with the world. It is the beginning or, at least, one beginning of time. It is a separation as painful as birth and as laden with guilt and remorse as that physical act is portrayed in theogonies. González Videla's betrayal was the spark that organized in Neruda's mind the vast poetic project. Neruda says the following about González Videla in his *Memoirs*: "González Videla swore to see that justice was carried out" (171). Notice the vocabulary: he *swore*. He later says, "In the fauna of our America, the great dictators have been giant saurians, survivors of a colossal feudalism in prehistoric lands. The Chilean Judas was just an amateur tyrant, and on the saurian scale would never be anything but a poisonous lizard" (172). Notice Judas. But more significant still is the vocabulary of Neruda's letter accusing González Videla and the text of his speech in the Senate. Needless to say, the term "treason" plays a prominent role in both, but in the letter in particular, significant emphasis is placed on the president's violation of his promise to adhere to a written and published program: "These reforms were discussed in an open convention of organized democratic forces and the September 4 Program—such was the name given to this fundamental document—was sworn and signed by Mr. González Videla, in one of the most solemn acts in the political life of the country" (291). And later, "González Videla distributed millions of copies of this Program, with the statement he swore at the Democratic Convention, with a facsimile of his signature at the foot of the document" (293). It is González Videla, not Neruda, who has broken the written and signed promise, who has violated the covenant sealed by the fundamental document, by the bonding text. The president has surrendered ("entregado," 307) the motherland, including a secret map of the coast to United States authorities. Neruda, however, has been victimized by slander and persecution. He is the propitiatory victim that can restore the bonding. He says in the speech, "I am proud that this persecution should single me out. I am proud because the people who suffer and struggle thus have an open perspective as to who has remained loyal to his public duties and who has betrayed them" (332). Broken promises, surrendered documents and secrets, lies and slander, the whole business has to do with the misuse of language, with the tarnishing of words, with the cleft between words and actions. The basic story is set: the traitor is guilty of violence against the charter; the victim restores, or attempts to restore, words to their pristine, full meaning. This is the myth that underlies the *Canto general*, that bridges the gap between the atemporal world of the subconscious and nature and the historical present.

Neruda did take revenge on González Videla in his poem, bestowing on him a kind of negative immortality, giving him a relative grandeur. Hence, history can be "gonzalized," and all of the betrayals visited on Latin America become incarnate in this mere "lizard." The *Canto general* is a litany of perfidies committed in the name of promises for justice, a lament and a cry for retribution. Betrayal is the leitmotiv of that litany, the culmination of which is betrayal of the land itself ("The Sand Betrayed"), the very ground, the clay out of which humanity emerged innocent, uncorrupted, clean. The contingency of the political story that opened the poet's eyes is the germ of a vast historical and poetic vision. González Videla's betrayal merely recalls and brings to the fore the founding treasons of American history: betrayal of the original inhabitants of the New World, a series of repeated assaults against the people, after many broken promises at the time of the Conquest (the advent of justice supposedly brought about by Christianity, which was the Europeans' justification for the invasion) and political independence (with its pledge of freedom, equality, and democracy). These are not calamities visited on humanity by an angry god but wicked acts committed against the collective by evil men. It is here that the prophetic mode of Neruda's poetry enters, as an effort to reestablish links between beneficial events in a near future with promises broken in the past. The utterance of the words themselves is already the beginning of a restoration. The poem will cover the gap of the break created by treason, will reactivate the good promises forgotten in the intervening years.[13] This prophecy is, however, dependent on betrayal, the break at the origin that must be bridged by figures, by the figural quality of poetic language. This is the *Canto general*'s foundational myth, its "Supreme Fiction."

The translation the reader holds is, I believe, a truly remarkable poetic achievement in its own right. It is one of the most sustained efforts of poetic translation I know, fully comparable to Robert Fitzgerald's powerful renditions of Homer and Virgil. It is a labor of love. Jack Schmitt has given himself over to the task with the devotion and the passion that Neruda demanded. It has taken him through a sort of conversion, renewing his life. Before beginning to translate Neruda, Schmitt was an American academic, a Hispanist with a respectable career. On or about the middle of the poet's life journey, where Neruda stopped to write his *Canto*, Schmitt decided to translate *Arte de pájaros* and Raúl Zurita's *Anteparaíso*. The result was not only the masterful translations of those books we now treasure but a radical transformation in Schmitt's academic and personal life. Since then, he has been living in Chile as much as his teaching duties at California State University, Long Beach, will allow. He has bought a house there and married a Chilean woman. He has toured Chile's rich landscape in a mystical pursuit of the country's essence. His Spanish has acquired a distinctly Chilean accent, with no traces of his Minnesota childhood. Yet, for all these transformations away from his North American roots, Schmitt has discovered within him a rich poetic vein in his native English. It is for me a source of continuous wonder how this professor of Spanish and Portuguese can turn Neruda into English and make him sound original, powerful, authentic. The danger, which other translators of Neruda seldom escaped, was to translate Neruda into Whitmanian English. It seems to me that this has not happened in Schmitt's case, that he has found a Nerudian idiom in English that does not depend on Whitman, though it does not exclude him (it is not possible). Could this have happened had Schmitt been a professor of English? I doubt it. I think that part of the secret of Schmitt's success, if it can be fathomed, is his relative innocence in terms of American literature. Schmitt has gone directly to the source of Neruda's power: his ability to elevate everyday language to poetic discourse. By everyday language I mean not only the names of things but the language of human emotion in the presence of things and events. In Schmitt's Neruda, as in Neruda himself, we witness the prosaic being anointed by a language that suddenly acquires liturgical rhythms and accents but continues to be ours. Such is the way I hear Schmitt's translation. I hope the reader is able to share this emotion.

Balazuc-Hamden   Roberto González Echevarría
Summer 1989

I

A
LAMP
ON
EARTH

I

Amor
America
(1400)

Before the wig and the dress coat
there were rivers, arterial rivers:
there were cordilleras, jagged waves where
the condor and the snow seemed immutable:
there was dampness and dense growth, the thunder
as yet unnamed, the planetary pampas.

Man was dust, earthen vase, an eyelid
of tremulous loam, the shape of clay—
he was Carib jug, Chibcha stone,
imperial cup or Araucanian silica.
Tender and bloody was he, but on the grip
of his weapon of moist flint,
the initials of the earth were
written.
           No one could
remember them afterward: the wind
forgot them, the language of water

was buried, the keys were lost
or flooded with silence or blood.

Life was not lost, pastoral brothers.
But like a wild rose
a red drop fell into the dense growth,
and a lamp of earth was extinguished.

I am here to tell the story.
From the peace of the buffalo
to the pummeled sands
of the land's end, in the accumulated
spray of the antarctic light,
and through precipitous tunnels
of shady Venezuelan peacefulness
I searched for you, my father,
young warrior of darkness and copper,
or you, nuptial plant, indomitable hair,
mother cayman, metallic dove.
I, Incan of the loam,
touched the stone and said:

Who
awaits me? And I closed my hand
around a fistful of empty flint.
But I walked among Zapotec flowers
and the light was soft like a deer,
and the shade was a green eyelid.

My land without name, without America,
equinoctial stamen, purple lance,
your aroma climbed my roots up to the glass
raised to my lips, up to the slenderest
word as yet unborn in my mouth.

Vegetation   To the lands without name
or numbers,
the wind blew down from other domains,
the rain brought celestial threads,
and the god of the impregnated altars
restored flowers and lives.

In fertility time grew.

like a thick-tailed meteor
pulsing toward the archipelago.

And at the end of the enraged
sea, in the ocean rain,
the wings of the albatross rise up
like two systems of salt,
establishing in the silence
with their spacious hierarchy
amid the torrential squalls,
the order of the wilds.

IV

**The
Rivers
Come
Forth**

Lover of the rivers, assailed
by blue water and transparent drops,
like a veined tree your specter
of a dark goddess that eats apples:
when you awakened, naked,
you were tattooed by the rivers,
and in the wet heights your head
filled the world with fresh dew.
Water trembled on your waist.
You were shaped by fountainheads
and lakes glistened on your brow.
From your maternal density you gathered
the water like vital tears,
dredged the sandy riverbeds
through the planetary night,
traversing harsh dilated stones,
shattering on your way
all the salt of geology,
cutting forests of compact walls,
sundering the quartz's muscles.

Orinoco

Orinoco, on your banks
of that timeless hour,
let me as then go naked,
let me enter your baptismal darkness.
Scarlet-colored Orinoco,
let me immerse my hands that return

to your maternity, to your flux,
river of races, land of roots,
your spacious murmur, your untamed sheet
come whence I come, from the poor
and imperious wilds, from a secret
like blood, from a silent
mother of clay.

Amazon

Amazon,
capital of the water's syllables,
patriarchal father, you're
the secret eternity
of fecundation,
rivers flock to you like birds,
you're shrouded by fire-colored pistils,
the great dead trunks impregnate you with
        perfume,
the moon can neither watch nor measure you.
You're charged with green sperm
like a nuptial tree, silverplated
in wild springtime,
you're reddened by woods,
blue between the moon of the stones,
clothed in iron vapor,
leisurely as an orbiting planet.

Tequendama

Tequendama, do you remember
your lonely passage through
the solitary heights—thread
in the wilds, slender will,
celestial line, platinum arrow—
do you remember, step by step,
opening walls of gold until you
fell from the sky into the terrifying
theater of empty stone?

Bío-Bío

So talk to me, Bío-Bío,
yours are the words that
roll off my tongue, you gave me
language, the nocturnal song

fused with rain and foliage.
You, when no one would heed a child,
told me about the dawning
of the earth, the powerful peace
of your kingdom, the hatchet buried
with a quiver of lifeless arrows,
all that the leaves of the cinnamon laurel
have told you for a thousand years—
and then I saw you embrace the sea,
dividing into mouths and breasts,
wide and flowering, murmuring
a tale the color of blood.

V

Minerals
Mother of metals, they burned you,
bit you, martyred you,
corroded you, then
defiled you, when the idols
could no longer defend you.
Vines climbing toward the hair
of the jungle night, mahogany,
maker of the arrows' shaft,
iron amassed in the flowering loft,
imperious talons of my homeland's
surveillant eagles,
unknown water, malevolent sun,
cruel sea spray,
preying shark, teeth
of the antarctic cordilleras,
serpent goddess dressed in plumes
and rarefied by blue poison,
ancestral fever inoculated
by migrations of wings and ants,
quagmires, butterflies
with acid stingers, woods
approaching the minerals,
why did the hostile chorus
not defend the treasure?

Mother of the dark
stones that would color
your lashes with blood!

Turquoise,
from its epochs, from the larval gloam,
begat for the jewels of the priestly
sun alone, copper slept
in its sulphuric strata,
and antimony advanced layer by layer
to the depths of our star.
Coal glittered with black radiance
like the antithesis of snow,
black ice cysted in the secret
motionless tempest of the earth,
when the flash of a yellow bird
entombed streams of sulphur
at the foot of the glacial cordilleras.
Vanadium clothed in rain
to enter the chamber of gold,
tungsten sharpened knives
and bismuth braided
medicinal hair.

Disoriented glowworms,
still on high, kept
trickling drops of phosphorus
into the seams of abysses
and iron peaks.

They're the vineyards of meteors,
the subways of sapphires.
On the plateaus the toy soldier
sleeps in clothing of tin.

Copper establishes its crimes
in the unburied darkness
charged with green matter,
and in the accumulated silence
the destructive mummies sleep on.
In the Chibcha tranquility
gold moves slowly from opaque oratories
toward the warriors,
transforms into red stamens,
laminated hearts,
terrestrial phosphorescence,
fabulous teeth.
Then I sleep with the dream
of a seed, of a larva,

and with you I descend
the steps of Querétaro.
Awaiting me were
stones from an indecisive moon,
the fishlike gemstone opal,
the tree petrified in a church
frozen by amethysts.

How, oral Colombia, could you
know that your barefoot stones
concealed a tempest
of enraged gold,
how, homeland
of the emerald, could you foresee
that the jewel of death and the sea,
the chilling splendor,
would climb the throats
of the invading dynasts?

You were pure notion of stone,
rose trained by salt,
malignant buried tear,
siren with dormant arteries,
belladonna, black serpent.
(While the palm dispersed its column
of high ornamental combs,
salt kept stripping
the mountains' splendor,
transforming raindrops on the leaves
into a suit of quartz
and transmuting spruces
into avenues of coal.)

I raced through cyclones to danger
and descended to the emerald light—
I ascended to the tendril of rubies,
but I was silenced forever on the statue
of nitrate stretched out on the desert.
In the ash of the raw-boned
altiplano, I saw how
tin raised
its coral branches of poison
until it spread out, like a jungle,
the equinoctial mist, until it covered
the signet of our cereal monarchies.

VI

Man

The mineral race was
like a cup of clay, man
made of stone and atmosphere,
clean as earthen jugs, sonorous.
The moon kneaded the Caribs,
extracted sacred oxygen,
crushed flowers and roots.
Man roamed the islands,
weaving bouquets and garlands
of sulphur-colored seaweed
and trumpeting the conch
on the shore of the sea spray.

The Tarahumara, wearing spurs,
made fire of blood and flint
in the spacious Northeast,
while the universe was being born
again in Tarascan clay:
myths of the amorous lands,
moist exuberance whence
sexual mud and melted fruits
were to be the posture of the gods
or pale walls of vessels.

Like dazzling pheasants
the priests descended
the Aztec steps.
Triangular stones
sustained the infinite
lightning of their vestments.
And the august pyramid,
stone upon stone, agony upon air,
within its domineering structure,
tended like an almond
a sacrificed heart.
In a thundering cry
blood ran down
the sacred stairway.
But thronging multitudes
wove fiber, nurtured
the promise of the crops,
plaited feathered splendor,

24

coaxed the turquoise,
and in textile vines
expressed the world's light.

Mayas, you had felled
the tree of knowledge.
With the fragrance of granary races
structures of inquiry
and death rose up,
and you scrutinized the cenotes,
casting into them golden brides,
the permanence of germs.

Chichén, your whispers grew
in the jungle dawn.
Toil went on shaping
honeycombed symmetry
in your yellow citadel,
and speculation threatened
the blood of the pedestals,
dismantled the sky in the shade,
directed medicine,
wrote upon the stones.

The South was a golden wonder.
The towering retreats
of Macchu Picchu in the gateway to the sky
were filled with oils and songs,
man had defied the dwelling
of the great birds in the heights,
and in the new dominion among the peaks
the tiller of the soil touched the seed
with fingers wounded by the snow.

Cuzco awakened like a throne
of turrets and granaries,
and the pensive flower of the world
was that race of pale shade
in whose opened hands trembled
diadems of imperial amethysts.
Highland corn
germinated on the terraces,
and over the volcanic pathways
traveled vases and gods.
Agriculture perfumed
the kingdom of kitchens

and spread over the roofs
a mantle of husked sun.

(Sweet race, daughter of the sierras,
lineage of tower and turquoise,
close my eyes now
before we return to the sea,
whence our sorrows come.)

That blue jungle was a grotto,
and in the mystery of tree and darkness
the Guaraní sang like
mist that rises in the afternoon,
water upon the foliage,
rain on a day of love,
sadness beside the rivers.

At the bottom of America without name
was Arauco among the vertiginous
waters, separated
by all the planet's cold.
Behold the great solitary South.
No smoke can be seen in the heights.
Nothing but glaciers
and blizzards repelled
by the bristling araucarias.
Do not seek the song of pottery
beneath the dense green.

All is silence of water and wind.

But in the leaves behold the warrior.
Among the cypress trees a cry.
A jaguar's eyes amid
the snowy heights.

Behold the spears at rest.
Listen to the whispering air
pierced by arrows.
Behold the breasts and legs,
the dark hair
shining in the moonlight.

Behold the warriors' absence.

There's no one. The diuca finch trills
like water in the pure night.

The condor cruises its black flight.

There's no one. Do you hear? It's the puma
stepping in the air and the leaves.

There's no one. Listen. Listen to the tree,
listen to the Araucanian tree.

There's no one. Behold the stones.

Behold the stones of Arauco.

There's no one, it's just the trees.

It's just the stones, Arauco.

II

**THE
HEIGHTS
OF MACCHU
PICCHU**

I

From air to air, like an
empty net
I went between the streets and atmosphere,
      arriving and departing,
in the advent of autumn the outstretched coin
of the leaves, and between springtime and the ears
      of corn,
all that the greatest love, as within a falling
glove, hands us like a long moon.

(Days of vivid splendor in the inclemency
of corpses: steel transformed
into acid silence:
nights frayed to the last flour:
beleaguered stamens of the nuptial land.)
Someone awaiting me among the violins
discovered a world like an entombed tower
spiraling down beneath all

the harsh sulphur-colored leaves:
farther down, in the gold of geology,
like a sword enveloped in meteors,
I plunged my turbulent and tender hand
into the genital matrix of the earth.

I put my brow amid the deep waves,
descended like a drop amid the sulphurous peace,
and, like a blind man, returned to the jasmine
of the spent human springtime.

II

If the lofty germ is carried from flower to flower
and the rock preserves its flower disseminated
in its hammered suit of diamond and sand,
man crumples the petal of light which he gathers
in determinate deep-sea springs
and drills the quivering metal in his hands.
And all along, amid clothing and mist, upon the
        sunken table,
like a jumbled quantity, lies the soul:
quartz and vigilance, tears in the ocean
like pools of cold: yet he still
torments it under the habitual rug, rips it
in the hostile vestments of wire.

No: in corridors, air, sea or on roads,
who guards (like red poppies) his blood
without a dagger? Rage has extenuated
the sad trade of the merchant of souls,
and, while at the top of the plum tree, the dew
has left for a thousand years its transparent letter
upon the same branch that awaits it, O heart, O
        brow crushed
between the autumn cavities.

How many times in the wintry streets of a city or
        in
a bus or a boat at dusk, or in the deepest
loneliness, a night of revelry beneath the sound
of shadows and bells, in the very grotto of human
        pleasure

I've tried to stop and seek the eternal
 unfathomable lode
that I touched before on stone or in the lightning
 unleashed by a kiss.

(Whatever in grain like a yellow tale
of swollen little breasts keeps repeating a number
perpetually tender in the germinal layers,
and which, always identical, is stripped to ivory,
and whatever in water is a transparent land, a bell
from the distant snows down to the bloody
 waves.)

I could grasp nothing but a clump of faces or
 precipitous
masks, like rings of empty gold,
like scattered clothes, offspring of an enraged
 autumn
that would have made the miserable tree of the
 frightened races shake.
I had no place to rest my hand,
which, fluid like the water of an impounded
 spring
or firm as a chunk of anthracite or crystal,
would have returned the warmth or cold of my
 outstretched hand.
What was man? In what part of his conversation
 begun
amid shops and whistles, in which of his metallic
 movements
lived the indestructible, the imperishable, life?

III

Like corn man was husked in the bottomless
granary of forgotten deeds, the miserable course
 of
events, from one to seven, to eight,
and not one death but many deaths came to each:
every day a little death, dust, maggot, a lamp
quenched in the mire of the slums, a little thick-
 winged death
entered each man like a short lance,

and man was driven by bread or by knife:
herdsman, child of the seaports, dark captain of
    the plow,
or rodent of the teeming streets:

all were consumed awaiting their death, their daily
    ration of death:
and the ominous adversity of each day was like
a black glass from which they drank trembling.

IV

Mighty death invited me many times:
it was like the invisible salt in the waves,
and what its invisible taste disseminated
was like halves of sinking and rising
or vast structures of wind and glacier.
I came to the cutting edge, to the narrows
of the air, to the shroud of agriculture and stone,
to the stellar void of the final steps
and the vertiginous spiraling road:
but, wide sea, O death! you do not come in
    waves
but in a galloping nocturnal clarity
or like the total numbers of the night.
You never rummaged around in pockets, your
    visit
was not possible without red vestments:
without an auroral carpet of enclosed silence:
without towering entombed patrimonies of tears.

I could not love in each being a tree
with a little autumn on its back (the death of a
    thousand leaves),
all the false deaths and resurrections
without land, without abyss:
I've tried to swim in the most expansive lives,
in the most free-flowing estuaries,
and when man went on denying me
and kept blocking path and door so that
my headspring hands could not touch his
    wounded inexistence,

then I went from street to street and river to
    river,
city to city and bed to bed,
my brackish mask traversed the desert,
and in the last humiliated homes, without light or
    fire,
without bread, without stone, without silence,
    alone,
I rolled on dying of my own death.

V

It was not you, solemn death, iron-plumed bird,
that the poor heir of these rooms
carried, between rushed meals, under his empty
    skin:
rather a poor petal with its cord exterminated:
an atom from the breast that did not come to
    combat
or the harsh dew that did not fall on his brow.
It was what could not be revived, a bit
of the little death without peace or territory:
a bone, a bell that died within him.
I raised the bandages dressed in iodine, sank my
    hands
into the pitiful sorrows killed by death,
and in the wound I found nothing but a chilling
    gust
that entered through the vague interstices of the
    soul.

VI

And so I scaled the ladder of the earth
amid the atrocious maze of lost jungles
up to you, Macchu Picchu.
High citadel of terraced stones,
at long last the dwelling of him whom the earth
did not conceal in its slumbering vestments.
In you, as in two parallel lines,

the cradle of lightning and man
was rocked in a wind of thorns.

Mother of stone, sea spray of the condors.

Towering reef of the human dawn.

Spade lost in the primal sand.

This was the dwelling, this is the site:
here the full kernels of corn rose
and fell again like red hailstones.

Here the golden fiber emerged from the vicuña
to clothe love, tombs, mothers,
the king, prayers, warriors.

Here man's feet rested at night
beside the eagle's feet, in the high gory
retreats, and at dawn
they trod the rarefied mist with feet of thunder
and touched lands and stones
until they recognized them in the night or in
        death.

I behold vestments and hands,
the vestige of water in the sonorous void,
the wall tempered by the touch of a face
that beheld with my eyes the earthen lamps,
that oiled with my hands the vanished
wood: because everything—clothing, skin, vessels,
words, wine, bread—
is gone, fallen to earth.

And the air flowed with orange-blossom
fingers over all the sleeping:
a thousand years of air, months, weeks of air,
of blue wind, of iron cordillera,
like gentle hurricanes of footsteps
polishing the solitary precinct of stone.

VII

O remains of a single abyss, shadows of one
    gorge—
the deep one—the real, most searing death
attained the scale
of your magnitude,
and from the quarried stones,
from the spires,
from the terraced aqueducts
you tumbled as in autumn
to a single death.
Today the empty air no longer weeps,
no longer knows your feet of clay,
has now forgotten your pitchers that filtered the
    sky
when the lightning's knives emptied it,
and the powerful tree was eaten away
by the mist and felled by the wind.
It sustained a hand that fell suddenly
from the heights to the end of time.
You are no more, spider hands, fragile
filaments, spun web:
all that you were has fallen: customs, frayed
syllables, masks of dazzling light.

But a permanence of stone and word:
the citadel was raised like a chalice in the hands
of all, the living, the dead, the silent, sustained
by so much death, a wall, from so much life a
    stroke
of stone petals: the permanent rose, the dwelling:
this Andean reef of glacial colonies.

When the clay-colored hand
turned to clay, when the little eyelids closed,
filled with rough walls, brimming with castles,
and when the entire man was trapped in his hole,
exactitude remained hoisted aloft:
this high site of the human dawn:
the highest vessel that has contained silence:
a life of stone after so many lives.

VIII

Rise up with me, American love.

Kiss the secret stones with me.
The torrential silver of the Urubamba
makes the pollen fly to its yellow cup.
It spans the void of the grapevine,
the petrous plant, the hard wreath
upon the silence of the highland casket.
Come, minuscule life, between the wings
of the earth, while—crystal and cold, pounded air
extracting assailed emeralds—
O, wild water, you run down from the snow.

Love, love, even the abrupt night,
from the sonorous Andean flint
to the dawn's red knees,
contemplates the snow's blind child.

O, sonorous threaded Wilkamayu,
when you beat your lineal thunder
to a white froth, like wounded snow,
when your precipitous storm
sings and batters, awakening the sky,
what language do you bring to the ear recently
wrenched from your Andean froth?

Who seized the cold's lightning
and left it shackled in the heights,
dispersed in its glacial tears,
smitten in its swift swords,
hammering its embattled stamens,
borne on its warrior's bed,
startled in its rocky end?

What are your tormented sparks saying?
Did your secret insurgent lightning
once journey charged with words?
Who keeps on shattering frozen syllables,
black languages, golden banners,
deep mouths, muffled cries,
in your slender arterial waters?

Who keeps on cutting floral eyelids
that come to gaze from the earth?
Who hurls down the dead clusters
that fell in your cascade hands
to strip the night stripped
in the coal of geology?

Who flings the branch down from its bonds?
Who once again entombs farewells?

Love, love, never touch the brink
or worship the sunken head:
let time attain its stature
in its salon of shattered headsprings,
and, between the swift water and the walls,
gather the air from the gorge,
the parallel sheets of the wind,
the cordilleras' blind canal,
the harsh greeting of the dew,
and, rise up, flower by flower, through the dense
    growth,
treading the hurtling serpent.

In the steep zone—forest and stone,
mist of green stars, radiant jungle—
Mantur explodes like a blinding lake
or a new layer of silence.

Come to my very heart, to my dawn,
up to the crowned solitudes.
The dead kingdom is still alive.

And over the Sundial the sanguinary shadow
of the condor crosses like a black ship.

IX

Sidereal eagle, vineyard of mist.
Lost bastion, blind scimitar.
Spangled waistband, solemn bread.
Torrential stairway, immense eyelid.
Triangular tunic, stone pollen.
Granite lamp, stone bread.
Mineral serpent, stone rose.

Entombed ship, stone headspring.
Moonhorse, stone light.
Equinoctial square, stone vapor.
Ultimate geometry, stone book.
Tympanum fashioned amid the squalls.
Madrepore of sunken time.
Rampart tempered by fingers.
Ceiling assailed by feathers.
Mirror bouquets, stormy foundations.
Thrones toppled by the vine.
Regime of the enraged claw.
Hurricane sustained on the slopes.
Immobile cataract of turquoise.
Patriarchal bell of the sleeping.
Hitching ring of the tamed snows.
Iron recumbent upon its statues.
Inaccessible dark tempest.
Puma hands, bloodstained rock.
Towering sombrero, snowy dispute.
Night raised on fingers and roots.
Window of the mists, hardened dove.
Nocturnal plant, statue of thunder.
Essential cordillera, searoof.
Architecture of lost eagles.
Skyrope, heavenly bee.
Bloody level, man-made star.
Mineral bubble, quartz moon.
Andean serpent, brow of amaranth.
Cupola of silence, pure land.
Seabride, tree of cathedrals.
Cluster of salt, black-winged cherry tree.
Snow-capped teeth, cold thunderbolt.
Scored moon, menacing stone.
Headdresses of the cold, action of the air.
Volcano of hands, obscure cataract.
Silver wave, pointer of time.

X

Stone upon stone, and man, where was he?
Air upon air, and man, where was he?
Time upon time, and man, where was he?
Were you too a broken shard

of inconclusive man, of empty raptor,
who on the streets today, on the trails,
on the dead autumn leaves, keeps
tearing away at the heart right up to the grave?
Poor hand, foot, poor life . . .
Did the days of light
unraveled in you, like raindrops
on the banners of a feast day,
give petal by petal of their dark food
to the empty mouth?

                      Hunger, coral of mankind,
hunger, secret plant, woodcutters' stump,
hunger, did the edge of your reef rise up
to these high suspended towers?

I want to know, salt of the roads,
show me the spoon—architecture, let me
scratch at the stamens of stone with a little stick,
ascend the rungs of the air up to the void,
scrape the innards until I touch mankind.

Macchu Picchu, did you put
stone upon stone and, at the base, tatters?
Coal upon coal and, at the bottom, tears?
Fire in gold and, within it, the trembling
drop of red blood?
Bring me back the slave that you buried!
Shake from the earth the hard bread
of the poor wretch, show me
the slave's clothing and his window.
Tell me how he slept when he lived.
Tell me if his sleep was
harsh, gaping, like a black chasm
worn by fatigue upon the wall.
The wall, the wall! If upon his sleep
each layer of stone weighed down, and if he fell
    beneath it
as beneath a moon, with his dream!
Ancient America, sunken bride,
your fingers too,
on leaving the jungle for the high void of the
    gods,
beneath the nuptial standards of light and
    decorum,
mingling with the thunder of drums and spears,
your fingers, your fingers too,

39

which the abstract rose, the cold line, and
the crimson breast of the new grain transferred
to the fabric of radiant substance, to the hard
    cavities—
did you, entombed America, did you too store in
    the depths
of your bitter intestine, like an eagle, hunger?

XI

Through the hazy splendor,
through the stone night, let me plunge my hand,
and let the aged heart of the forsaken beat in me
like a bird captive for a thousand years!
Let me forget, today, this joy, which is greater
    than the sea,
because man is greater than the sea and its islands,
and we must fall into him as into a well to
    emerge from the bottom
with a bouquet of secret water and sunken truths.
Let me forget, great stone, the powerful
    proportion,
the transcendent measure, the honeycombed
    stones,
and from the square let me today run
my hand over the hypotenuse of rough blood and
    sackcloth.
When, like a horseshoe of red elytra, the frenzied
    condor
beats my temples in the order of its flight,
and the hurricane of cruel feathers sweeps the
    somber dust
from the diagonal steps, I do not see the swift
    brute,
I do not see the blind cycle of its claws,
I see the man of old, the servant, asleep in the
    fields,
I see a body, a thousand bodies, a man, a
    thousand women,
black with rain and night, beneath the black
    squall,
with the heavy stone of the statue:
Juan Stonecutter, son of Wiracocha,

Juan Coldeater, son of a green star,
Juan Barefoot, grandson of turquoise,
rise up to be born with me, my brother.

XII

Rise up to be born with me, my brother.

Give me your hand from the deep
zone of your disseminated sorrow.
You'll not return from the bottom of the rocks.
You'll not return from subterranean time.
Your stiff voice will not return.
Your drilled eyes will not return.
Behold me from the depths of the earth,
laborer, weaver, silent herdsman:
tamer of the tutelary guanacos:
mason of the defied scaffold:
bearer of the Andean tears:
jeweler with your fingers crushed:
tiller trembling in the seed:
potter spilt in your clay:
bring to the cup of this new life, brothers,
all your timeless buried sorrows.
Show me your blood and your furrow,
tell me: I was punished here,
because the jewel did not shine or the earth
did not surrender the gemstone or kernel on time:
show me the stone on which you fell
and the wood on which you were crucified,
strike the old flintstones,
the old lamps, the whips sticking
throughout the centuries to your wounds
and the war clubs glistening red.
I've come to speak through your dead mouths.
Throughout the earth join all
the silent scattered lips
and from the depths speak to me all night long,
as if I were anchored with you,
tell me everything, chain by chain,
link by link, and step by step,
sharpen the knives that you've kept,
put them in my breast and in my hand,

like a river of yellow lightning,
like a river of buried jaguars,
and let me weep hours, days, years,
blind ages, stellar centuries.

Give me silence, water, hope.

Give me struggle, iron, volcanoes.

Cling to my body like magnets.

Hasten to my veins and to my mouth.

Speak through my words and my blood.

THE
CONQUISTADORS

*Ccollanan Pachacutec! Ricuy
anceacunac yahuarniy richacaucuta!*

Tupac Amaru I

I

**They Come
Through
the Islands
(1493)**

The butchers razed the islands.
Guanahaní was first
in this story of martyrdom.
The children of clay saw their smile
shattered, beaten
their fragile stature of deer,
and even in death they did not understand.
They were bound and tortured,
burned and branded,
bitten and buried.
And when time finished its waltzing twirl,

dancing in the palms,
the green salon was empty.

Nothing remained but bones
rigidly arranged
in the form of a cross, to the greater
glory of God and mankind.

From the Greater Clays
and the Branches of Sotavento
to the coralline chains,
Narváez's knife kept cutting away.
Here the cross, there the rosary,
here the Virgin of the Cudgel.
The jewel of Columbus, phosphoric Cuba,
received the flag and knees
on its wet sand.

II

**Now It's
Cuba**

Then there was blood and ash.

Soon the palms stood alone.

Cuba, my love, they put you on the rack,
cut your face,
pried open your legs of pale gold,
crushed your pomegranate sex,
stabbed you with knives,
dismembered you, burned you.

Through the valleys of sweetness
the exterminators swooped down.
And on the high hilltops the crests
of your children were lost in the mist,
but there they were overcome,
one by one to the death,
torn in anguish
from their balmy land of flowers
that fled from under the soles of their feet.

Cuba, my love, what shuddering fright
shook you from foam to foam,

until you became purity,
solitude, silence, dense growth,
and the little bones of your children
were fought over by the crabs.

III

**They
Reach the
Gulf of
Mexico
(1519)**

The murderous wind takes wing to Veracruz.
In Veracruz the horses are put ashore.
The ships are packed with claws
and red beards from Castile.
Arias, Reyes, Rojas, Maldonados,
the foundlings of Castilian abandonment,
veterans of hunger in winter
and of lice in the roadside inns.

What do they see leaning over the gunwales?
How much of what is to come and of the
        forsaken
past, of the errant
feudal wind in the scourged homeland?

They did not sail from the seaports of the South
to wield the hands of the people
in plunder and death:
they see green lands, freedom,
broken chains, construction,
and from the ship, the waves that expire
upon the coasts of compact mystery.

Would they die or revive beyond
the palm trees, in the torrid air
that the burning lands send forth
like the total blast from a strange oven?
They were the people, the hirsute heads of
        Montiels,
calloused and cracked hands of Ocañas and
        Piedrahitas,
the arms of blacksmiths, children's eyes
that gazed at the terrible sun and the palm trees.

The ancient hunger of Europe, hunger like the tail
of a dying comet, filled the ship—

hunger was there—stripped,
vagabonding cold hatchet, stepmother
of nations, hunger throws the dice
on the voyage, fills the sails:
"Onward, or I'll eat you, onward,
or it's back
to the homeland, the monk, the Judge and Priest,
the inquisitors, the inferno, the plague.
Onward, onward, far from the louse,
the feudal whip, the dungeon,
the galleys full of excrement."

And in the boundless light
the eyes of Núñez and Bernales
riveted repose,
a life, another life,
the innumerable and chastised
family of the world's poor.

IV

Cortés   Cortés has no country, he's a chilling
thunderbolt, a cold heart clad in armor.
*"Fertile lands, my Liege and Royal Majesty,
temples in which the gold is wrought
by the hands of Indians."*

And he advances driving in daggers,
pounding the lowlands, the prancing
cordilleras of perfumes,
halting his army among orchids
and coronations of pines,
trampling the jasmine,
up to the gates of Tlaxcala.

(Terrified brother, do not
befriend the rosy vulture:
I speak to you from the moss,
from the roots of our kingdom.
Tomorrow it's going to rain blood,
the tears are apt
to form mist, vapor, rivers,
until your eyes dissolve.)

Cortés receives a dove,
he receives a pheasant, a zither
from the monarch's musicians,
but he wants the chamber of gold,
he wants more, and everything
falls into the wolves' treasure chests.
The king looks out from the balcony:
"This is my brother," says he. The stones
of the people fly back in answer,
and Cortés sharpens daggers
on kisses betrayed.

When he returns to Tlaxcala, the wind
brings a quiet murmuring of grief.

V

Cholula

In Cholula the youths wear
their finest cloth, gold, and plumes.
Adorned for the festival,
they question the invader.

Death has answered them.

Thousands of corpses lie there.
Murdered hearts
laid out, pulsing,
opening the moist pit where
they tend the trickle of that day.
(They entered killing on horseback,
they cut off the hand that offered
its tribute of gold and flowers,
they closed off the plaza, exhausted
their arms until they were numbed,
killing the flower of the kingdom,
plunging up to their elbows in the blood
of my startled brethren.)

VI

Alvarado Alvarado fell upon the huts
with claws and knives, he razed
the patrimony of the goldsmith,
ravished the nuptial rose of the tribe,
assaulted races, properties, religions—
he was the copious coffer of the thieves,
the clandestine falcon of death.
Then he went to the great green river,
the Papaloapan, River of Butterflies,
bearing blood on his standard.

The solemn river saw its children
die or survive as slaves,
it saw race and reason, juvenile heads
burning in the bonfires, beside the water.
But grief, inexhaustible,
continued its cruel advance
toward new captaincies.

VII

Guatemala Sweet Guatemala, every gravestone
of your mansion bears a drop
of ancient blood devoured
by the jaguars' snouts.
Alvarado crushed your kin,
smashed the astral stelae,
wallowed in your martyrdom.
And in Yucatán the bishop
followed upon the pale jaguars.
He gathered up the most
profound wisdom apprehended in the air
since the first day of the world,
when the first Maya recorded
in writing the river's tremor,
the science of pollen, the wrath
of the Gods of the Elements,
the migrations through

the first universes,
the beehive's laws,
the green bird's secret,
the language of the stars,
secrets of day and night
reaped on the shores of
earthly development!

VIII

**A
Bishop**

The Bishop raised his arm,
he burned books in the plaza
in the name of his little God,
turning to smoke the old leaves
worn by obscure time.

And the smoke does not return from the sky.

IX

**The
Head
on the
Spear**

Balboa, you brought death and claw
to the corners of the sweet central land,
and among the manhunting dogs,
yours was your soul:
bloody thick-lipped little Leo
brought to bay the fleeing slave,
sank Spanish fangs
into the pulsing throats,
and from the dogs' claws
the flesh went off to martyrdom,
and the treasure fell into the purse.

Accursed be dog and man,
the infamous howl in the primal
jungle, the prowling
step of iron and bandit.

Accursed the thorny
crown of wild brambles
that didn't bristle like a sea urchin
to defend the invaded homeland.

But among the bloodthirsty
captains, the justice of daggers,
the bitter branch of envy
rose out of the shadows.

And when you returned, the name
of Pedrarias stood in the middle
of your road like a noose.

You were tried amid the barks
of Indian-killing dogs.
Now, as you die, do you hear
the pure silence, shattered
by your incited greyhounds?
Now, as you die at the hands
of the fierce captains-general,
do you smell the golden aroma
of the sweet ravaged kingdom?

When they cut off Balboa's
head, it was left impaled
on a spear. His lifeless eyes
released their lightning
and ran down the shaft
in a great drop of filth
that vanished into the earth.

X

**Homage
to Balboa**

Discoverer, centuries later, the vast sea—
my foam, lunar latitude, empire of the water—
speaks to you through my mouth.
Your plenitude came before your death.
You raised fatigue to the sky,
and from the trees' hard night
toil led you to the sum
of the seashore, the great ocean.
In your gaze the marriage of diffused
light and the little heart of man
was consummated, a chalice never
raised before was filled, a seed
of lightning bolts accompanied you,
and a torrential thunder filled the earth.
Balboa, captain—how diminutive

your hand on your visor—mysterious
marionette of the discovering salt,
bridegroom of the oceanic sweetness,
child of the world's new uterus.

The obscure odor of the ravished
marine majesty entered your eyes
like galloping orange blossoms,
an arrogant aurora fell into your blood
until it filled your soul, possessed man!
When you returned to the taciturn lands,
sleepwalker of the sea, green captain,
the earth awaited your corpse,
eager to embrace your bones.

Mortal bridegroom, betrayal was requited.

Not in vain, throughout history
crime has trampled in, the falcon has devoured
its nest, and the serpents have assembled,
striking one another with tongues of gold.

You entered the frenzied twilight
and the lost steps that you took,
still drenched by the depths,
dressed in splendor and wed
by the greatest foam, brought you
to the shores of another sea: death.

XI

**A
Soldier
Sleeps**

Lost in the dense limits,
the soldier arrived. Totally exhausted,
he fell among the vines and leaves,
at the foot of the Great Plumed God
who
was alone with his world recently
emerged from the jungle.

                    He stared at the strange
soldier born of the ocean.
He stared at his eyes, his bloody beard,
his sword, the black sheen
of his armor, fatigue fallen
like mist upon that
savage child's head.

How many zones
of darkness so the Plumed God
could be born and coil its volume
around the forests—on the rosy stone,
how much disorder of riotous waters
and unbridled night, the flooded
channel of unborn light, the rabid ferment
of lives, destruction, the flour
of fertility followed by order,
the order of plant and sect,
the elevation of the sculpted rocks,
the smoke from the ritual lamps,
the firmness of the ground for man,
the establishment of the tribes,
the tribunal of the terrestrial gods.
Each flake of stone trembled,
felt the dread descending
like a plague of insects,
mustered all its power,
made the rain go to the roots,
spoke with the currents of the earth,
dark in its dress
of immobilized cosmic stone,
and it could move neither claws nor teeth,
nor rivers, nor tremors,
nor meteors whistling
in the kingdom's vault,
and there it remained, immobile stone, silence,

while Beltrán de Córdoba slept on.

XII

Ximénez de Quesada (1536)

They're here, they're here, they've come,
dear heart, look at the ships,
the ships in the Magdalena,
Gonzalo Ximénez's ships
have come, the ships are here,
stop them, river, close off
your ravenous banks,
submerge them in your pulse,
tear away their greed,

strike them with your fiery stinger,
your bloodthirsty vertebrates,
your eye-eating eels,
lay the cayman crosswise
with its clay-colored teeth
and its primordial armor,
span it like a bridge
over your sandy waters,
discharge the jaguar's fire
from your trees, born
of your seeds, mother river,
send them your blood-sucking flies,
blind them with your black dung,
plunge them into your hemisphere,
subdue them with your roots
in the darkness of your bed,
and rot all their blood,
devour their lungs
and lips with your crabs.

Now they've entered the forest:
now they're plundering, biting, killing.
O Colombia, defend the veil
of your secret red jungle.

They've put to the sword
the oratory of Iraka:
now they arrest the Zipa,
now they bind him: "Surrender
the jewels of the ancient god,"
the jewels that flourished
and glistened with Colombia's
morning dew.

Now they're torturing the prince.
They've slit his throat, his head
stares at me with eyes that none
can close, beloved eyes
of my green and naked country.
Now they're burning the holy house,
now come the horses,
the torments, the swords,
now only embers remain
and, among the ashes,
the prince's unclosed eyes.

XIII

**Rendezvous
of Ravens**

In Panama the demons convened.
There the ferrets' pact was sealed.
A candle flickered dimly
as the three entered one by one:
first Almagro, ancient and one-eyed,
then Pizarro, the swineherd,
and Friar Luque, a canon versed
in darkness. Each
hid a dagger behind
his partner's back, each
with squalid eyes on the dark
walls divined blood,
and the distant empire's gold drew them
as the moon the accursed stones.
When they made their pact, Luque raised
the host in the Eucharist,
the three thieves kneaded
the wafer with a crude smile.
"Brothers, God has been divided
among us," sustained the canon,
and the three butchers said "Amen"
through purple teeth.
They pounded on the table, spitting.
Because they knew nothing of letters
they cluttered the table, the paper,
the benches, the walls with crosses.

Obscure Peru, submerged,
was singled out, and the crosses,
black, little black crosses,
made sail for the South:
crosses for agonies,
crosses, hairy and sharp,
crosses with a reptile's charm,
crosses spattered with pustules,
crosses with spider legs,
somber manhunting crosses.

XIV

The Agonies

In Cajamarca the agony began.

Young Atahualpa, blue stamen,
noble tree, heard the wind
bring a whisper of steel.
There was a vague
glow and tremor from the coast,
an incredible gallop
—pounding and power—
of iron upon iron over the grass.
The captains-general arrived.
The Inca emerged from his music
surrounded by Señores.

Sweaty and bearded,
the visitors from another planet
went to pay obeisance.
Chaplain
Valverde, treacherous heart, rotten jackal,
offers a strange object, a piece
of basket, a fruit
perhaps from that planet
whence the horses come.
Atahualpa accepts it. He cannot
understand: it doesn't shine, it makes
no sound, and he drops it, smiling.

"Death,
vengeance, kill, for I absolve you all,"
shouts the jackal with the murderous cross.
The thunder takes sides with the brigands.
Our blood is spilt in its cradle.
In the hour of agony, the princes
surround the Inca like a chorus.

Ten thousand Peruvians fall
to the cross and the sword, blood
soaks the vestments of Atahualpa.
Pizarro, the swine from Extremadura,
has the Inca's delicate arms
bound. Night falls
over Peru like a black ember.

XV

**The
Red Line**

Later the monarch raised
his weary hand, and above
the bandits' brows
he touched the walls.
There they drew
the red line.
Three chambers
were ordered filled with gold and silver,
up to that line of his blood.
The wheel of gold turned, night after night.
The wheel of martyrdom day and night.

They scored the earth, dismantled
treasures made with love and foam,
tore away the bride's jewels,
disarmed their gods.
The tiller surrendered his medal,
the fisherman his droplet of gold,
and the ingots trembled in response,
while message and voice throughout the
highlands, the wheel of gold kept turning.
Then the jaguars assembled
and divided up the blood and tears.

Atahualpa waited with sad resignation
on the precipitous Andean day.
The doors were not opened. Down to
the last jewel the vultures divided—
ritual turquoise, spattered
by carnage, silver-plated
garments—the plundering claws
kept measuring, and the king
listened sadly to the laughter
of the friar amid the executioners.

His heart was an urn filled
with an anguish bitter
as the bitter essence of quinine.
He thought about his limits, about lofty Cuzco,

the princesses, his age,
the shuddering chill of his kingdom.
He was pensive within, his desperate
tranquility was sorrow. He thought about
    Huáscar.
Could he have sent the foreigners?
All was enigma, all was knife,
all solitude, only the vivid red line
kept pulsing on,
swallowing the yellow innards
of the muted moribund kingdom.

Then Valverde entered with Death.
"Your name will be Juan," he told him
as he prepared the bonfire.
Solemnly he replied: "Juan,
my name for death is Juan,"
without understanding even his death.

They put a rope to his neck, and a gaff
plunged into the soul of Peru.

XVI

Elegy

Alone, in the wilderness,
I want to weep like the rivers, I want
to grow dark, to sleep
like an ancient mineral night.
Why did the radiant keys
reach the bandit's hands? Rise up,
maternal Oello, rest your secret
upon this night's long fatigue
and infuse my veins with your advice.
I don't ask you yet for the Yupanquis' sun.
I speak to you from my sleep, calling
from land to land, Peruvian
mother, cordilleran matrix.
How did the avalanche of daggers
penetrate your sandy precinct?

Immobile in your hands,
I feel the metals stretching away
in the subterranean channels.

I'm made of your roots
but I don't understand, the earth
doesn't grant me your wisdom,
I see nothing but night upon night
beneath the starry lands.
What senseless serpent's dream
slithered up to the red line?
Bereaved eyes, sinister plant.
How did you come to this vinegar wind,
how did Capac not raise
his tiara of blinding clay
amid the pinnacles of wrath?

Beneath the pavilions, let
me suffer and sink like the lifeless
root that will never beam forth.
Beneath the harsh hard night
I'll descend through the earth until
I reach the jaws of gold.

I want to stretch out on the nocturnal stone.

I want to reach calamity.

XVII

**The
Wars**
Later an incendiary flame
reached the granite Clock.
Almagros and Pizarros and Valverdes,
Castillos and Uriases and Beltranes
stabbed one another in the back, sowing
among themselves the betrayals acquired,
stealing one another's women and gold,
disputing the dynasty.
They lynched one another in the corrals,
stripped one another in the plaza,
hanged one another in the Councils.
The tree of plunder fell
among stabbings and gangrene.

From that gallop of Pizarros
in the flaxen territories
a stupefied silence was born.

Everything abounded with death
and over the bottomless agony
of their ill-starred children,
in the territory (gnawed
to the bone by the rats),
they clutched their entrails
before killing and being killed.

Assassins of fury and gallows,
centaurs fallen in the mire
of greed, idols
shattered by the gold's light,
you exterminated your own
bloody-nailed kin
and beside the stone walls
of high crowned Cuzco,
before the sun of the highest spikes,
you performed in the Inca's
golden dust the theater
of imperial infernos:
Plunder with a green snout,
Lust lubricated in blood,
Greed with golden fingernails,
Betrayal, with crooked teeth,
the Cross like a ravenous reptile,
the Gallows set against the snow,

and Death fine as the air,

immobile in its armor.

XVIII

**Discoverers
of Chile**

From the north Almagro brought his wrinkled
 lightning.
And over the territory, between explosion and
 twilight,
he leaned day and night as over a letter.
Shade of thorns, shade of thistle and wax,
the Spaniard united with his parched semblance,
appraising the land's somber strategies.
Night, snow, and sand compose the shape
of my slender homeland.

All the silence is in its long line,
all the foam flows from its seabeard,
all the coal fills it with mysterious kisses.
Like an ember gold burns in its fingers
and silver illuminates its rugged form
of a brooding plane like a green moon.
The Spaniard seated beside the rose one day,
beside the oil, beside the wine, the ancient sky,
never imagined this speck of wrathful stone
born beneath the dung of the sea eagle.

XIX

**The
Combatant
Land**

First the land resisted.

The Araucanian snow burned
the invaders' advance
like a white bonfire.
Fingers succumbed to the cold,
the hands, the feet of Almagro,
and the claws that devoured
and buried monarchies
were, in the snow, a speck
of frozen flesh, silence.
In the sea of the cordilleras.

The Chilean air lashed out,
scoring stars, toppling
greed and cavalries.

Then hunger followed behind
Almagro like invisible
chattering jaws.
The horses were eaten
in the glacial feast.

And death from the South stripped
the Almagroses' gallop,
until his horse turned
toward Peru, where the repulsed
discoverer found
death from the North, waiting
in the road, with a hatchet.

XX

Araucania, cluster of torrential southland beech,
O merciless Homeland, my dark love,
solitary in your rainy kingdom:
You were only mineral gullets,
hands of cold, fists
accustomed to splitting rocks:
Homeland, you were the peace of hardness
and your men were whisper,
harsh apparition, fierce wind.

My Araucanian ancestors had no
crests of luminous plumes,
they didn't rest on nuptial flowers,
they spun no gold for the priest:
they were stone and tree, roots
of the intractable brambles,
lance-shaped leaves,
heads of militant metal.
Ancestors, you had just raised
your ear to the gallop, just over
the hilltops, when Araucania's
lightning struck.
The forefathers of stone became shadows,
they were bound to the forest, the natural
darkness, they became icy light,
asperities of land and thorns,
and so they waited in the depths
of the indomitable wilds:
one was a red tree that watched,
another a fragment of metal that listened,
another a blasting wind and drill,
another blended in with the trail.
Homeland, ship of snow,
harsh foliage:
you were born there, when your man
asked the earth for his standard
and when land and air and stone and rain,
leaf, root, perfume, howl,
covered the child like a mantle,
they loved him and defended him.
That's how the country was born unanimous:
unity before combat.

XXI

But they returned.
                        (His name was Pedro.)
Valdivia, the intrusive captain,
cut up my land among thieves
with his sword: "This is yours,
this is yours, Valdés, Montero,
this is yours, Inés, this is the site
of the Council."
They divided up my homeland
like a lifeless ass.
"Take
this piece of moon and woodland,
devour this river with twilight,"
while the great cordillera
raised bronze and whiteness.

Arauco loomed. Adobes, towers,
streets, the silent
master of the house awakened smiling.
He worked with his hands soaked
by his water and his mud, he brought
clay and poured the Andean water:
but he refused to become a slave.
Then the hangman Valdivia
attacked with fire and death.
And so the blood began, the blood
of three centuries, the blood ocean,
the blood atmosphere that shrouded my land
and immense time, like no other war.
The wrathful vulture emerged
from his funereal armor
and bit the chief, broke
the pact written in the silence
of Huelén, in the Andean air.
Arauco began to boil its dish
of blood and stones.
                        Seven princes
went to parley.
                        They were imprisoned.

Before the eyes of Araucania,
they beheaded the chiefs.
The executioners took heart. All
steeped in entrails, howling,
Inés de Suárez, soldier of fortune,
held the imperial necks
between her infernal harpy's knees.
And she impaled them upon the palisade,
bathing herself in noble blood,
covering herself with scarlet clay.
That's how they hoped to subdue Arauco.
But here the somber unity
of tree and stone, spear and face,
transmitted the crime in the wind.
The borderland tree heard it,
the fisherman, the king, the medicine man,
the antarctic tribesman heard it,
the maternal waters
of the Bío-Bío.

      And so the people's war began.
Valdivia drove his dripping spear
into Arauco's stony bowels,
he plunged his hand
into the pulse, squeezed his fingers
around the Araucanian heart,
emptied the tribe's
wild veins,

      exterminated
the pastoral dawn,

      sent martyrdom
to the kingdom of the forest, burned
the master of the forest's house,
chopped off the chieftain's hands,
returned the prisoners
with their noses and ears cut off,
impaled the Chief, murdered
the woman warrior,
and with his bloody glove
soiled the country's stones,
leaving it full of corpses,
and solitude and scars.

XXII

Ercilla
Stones of Arauco and unleashed fluvial
roses, territories of roots
engage the man arrived from Spain.
They attack his armor with gigantic lichens.
The fern's shadows invade his sword.
Primal ivy puts blue hands
on the planet's newly arrived silence.
Worthy man, sonorous Ercilla, I hear the pulsing
water of your first dawn, a frenzy of birds
and a thunderclap in the foliage.
Leave, oh, leave your blond
eagle's imprint, crush
your cheek against the wild corn,
everything will be devoured in the dust.
Sonorous, you alone will not drink the chalice
of blood, sonorous, only to the sudden
glow radiating from you
will time's secret mouth arrive in vain
to tell you: in vain.
In vain, in vain
blood in the branches of spattered crystal,
in vain through the puma's nights
the soldier's defiant advance,
the orders,
the footsteps
of the wounded.
All returns to the feather-crowned silence
where a distant king devours vines.

XXIII

The Spears
Are
Buried
And so the patrimony was partitioned.
Blood divided the entire country.
(I'll speak in other lines about
the struggle of my people.)
But the land was cut into pieces
by the invading knives.
Loyola's grandchildren, the usurers
from Euzkadi, came to colonize

the legacy. From the cordillera
to the ocean they divided up,
along with trees and bodies,
the planet's recumbent shade.
The encomiendas upon the battered,
scarred, and burned earth,
the distribution of forest and water
in their pockets, the Errázuriz
who arrive with their coat of arms:
a whip and a rope-soled sandal.

XXIV

**The
Magellanic
Heart
(1519)**

Where am I from, I sometimes ask myself, where
    in the devil
do I come from, what day's today, what's
    happening,
a roar, amid the dream, the tree, the night,
and a wave, rising like an eyelid, begets
a day, a flash with a jaguar's snout.

**I Awaken
Suddenly
in the Night
Thinking
about the
Far South**

The day breaks and asks me: "Do you hear
the lingering water,
the water,
over Patagonia?"
And I reply: "Yes, I hear it."
The day breaks and tells me: "A wild sheep,
faraway, in the region, licks the frozen color
of a stone. Don't you hear the bleating, don't you
    discern
the blue squall, in whose hands
the moon is a wineglass, don't you see the flock,
    the bitter
finger of the wind
touching wave and life with its emtpy ring?"

**I Remember
the Solitude
of the Strait**

I'm going to the home of the long night and the
    pine tree.
And the silent acid, fatigue, the top of the barrel,

all that I have in life, turns upside down.
A snowflake weeps on and on at my door,
showing its transparent and tattered dress
of a minute comet that seeks me and sobs.
No one sees the gust of wind, the extension, the
    air
howling in the meadowlands.
I draw near and say: onward. I touch the South,
    rush
into the sand, see the dry black plant, all root and
    rock,
the islands scarred by water and sky,
the River of Hunger, the Heart of Ash,
the lugubrious Patio of the Sea, and where the
    solitary
serpent hisses, where the last
wounded fox buries its bloody treasure,
I encounter the tempest and its ruptured voice,
its voice of an old book, its mouth of a hundred
    lips
tells me something, something that the air devours
    each day.

**The
Discoverers
Appear
and Nothing
Is Left
of Them**

The water remembers everything that happened to
    the ship.
The strange harsh land guards over its skulls
that echo like bugles in the austral panic,
and the eyes of man and ox give the day its
    hollowness,
its ring, its sound of an implacable wake.
The old sky seeks the sail,
                    no one
now survives: the wrecked ship
lives on with the bitter sailor's ash,
and of the stores of gold, the rawhide skins
of pestilent wheat, and
the cold flame of the voyages
(what a pounding at night [rock and hulk] in the
    deeps)
nothing remains in the burned and bodiless
    dominion but
the incessant inclemency broken only
by a black fragment
of quenched fire.

**Only
Destruction
Prevails**

Sphere that slowly destroys the night, water, ice,
extension assailed by weather and time,
with their violent mark, with the blue end
of the wild rainbow,
my country's feet sink in your shadow
and the crushed rose shrieks its dying breath.

**Memorial
to the Old
Discoverer**

Navigating the channel again,
the frozen grain, the beard of combat,
the glacial Autumn, the transitory casualty.
With him, with the ancient man, with his corpse
stripped by the rabid water,
with him, in his storm, with his brow.
The albatross and the rotted leather rope
still follow him, with his bulging eyes,
and the devoured mouse, amid the broken masts,
stares blindly at the angry splendor,
while ring and bone fall into the void,
sliding over the sea cow.

Magellan

Which is the passing god? Behold his beard
    crawling with maggots
and his breeches in which the dense atmosphere
clings and snaps like a shipwrecked dog:
his stature lies heavy like a doomed anchor,
the brine hisses and the norther drives down
to his wet feet.
                    Seashell of the obscure
shadow of time,
                moldy spur,
old master of coastal mourning, baton
of bastardy, tainted fountainhead, the dung
of the Strait sends you
and your breast has nothing of the cross but a cry
from the sea, a white cry, with sealight, and with
the bite, from boom to boom, of a demolished
    stinger.

**He Reaches
the Pacific**

For the sinister day of the sea ends one day,
and the nocturnal hand severs its fingers one by
      one
until it is no more, until man is born
and the captain discovers the steel within
and America sends up its bubble
and the coast raises its pale reef
murky with dawn, turbid with birth,
until a cry calls out from the ship and is drowned,
and another cry and the dawn that is born of the
      foam.

**All Have
Perished**

Brethren from water and lice, from a carnivorous
      planet:
did you see, at last, the mainmast toppled
by the storm? Did you see the stone crushed
beneath the wild brusque snow of the squall?
At last, you have your paradise lost,
at last, you have your cursing garrison,
at last, your phantoms pierced by the air
kiss the seal's tracks on the sand.
At last, to your ringless fingers
comes the spare sun of the wastelands, the day
      consumed,
trembling, in its hospital of waves and stones.

XXV

**Despite
the Fury**

Corroded helmets, lifeless horseshoes!

But through fire and horseshoe,
as from a fountain illuminated
by the somber blood,
with the metal engulfed by the tempest,
a light was cast over the earth:
number, name, line and structure.

Pages of water, transparent power
of murmuring languages, sweet drops
shaped like clusters,
platinum syllables in the tenderness

of some pure breasts bathed in dew,
and a classical mouth of diamonds
gave the territory its snow-clad splendor.

Far and away the statue deposited
its lifeless marble,
                        and in the world's
springtime, machinery dawned.

Technology exalted its dominion
and time was velocity and flurry
on the merchants' banners.

Moon of geography
that discovered plant and planet
unfolding geometrical beauty
in its developing movement.
Asia yielded its virginal aroma.
Intelligence followed the blood
with an icy thread, spinning the day.
Paper disseminated the raw honey
stored in the darkness.

A flock
of doves burst from the painting
with a flush of red and ultramarine blue.
And the languages of man coupled
in the primal fury, before song.

So with the cruel
titan of stone,
the death-dealing falcon,
not only blood but wheat arrived.

The light came despite the daggers.

THE
LIBERATORS

**The
Liberators**

*Here comes the tree, the tree
of the storm, the tree of the people.
Its heroes rise up from the earth
as leaves from the sap,
and the wind spangles the whispering
multitude's foliage,
until the seed falls
again from the bread to the earth.*

*Here comes the tree, the tree
nourished by naked corpses,
corpses scourged and wounded,
corpses with impossible faces,
impaled on spears,
reduced to dust in the bonfire,
decapitated by ax,
quartered by horse,
crucified in church.*

*Here comes the tree, the tree
whose roots are alive,
it fed on martyrdom's nitrate,*

its roots consumed blood,
and it extracted tears from the soil:
raised them through its branches,
dispersed them in its architecture.
They were invisible flowers—
sometimes, buried flowers,
other times they illuminated
its petals, like planets.

And in the branches mankind harvested
the hard corollas,
passed them from hand to hand
like magnolias or pomegranates,
and suddenly, they opened the earth,
grew up to the stars.

This is the tree of the emancipated.
The earth tree, the cloud tree.
The bread tree, the arrow tree,
the fist tree, the fire tree.
The stormy water of our nocturnal
epoch floods it,
but its mast balances
the arena of its might.

At times, the branches broken
by wrath fall again,
and a foreboding ash
covers its ancient majesty:
just as it survived times past,
so too it rose from agony
until a secret hand,
countless arms, the people,
preserved the fragments,
hid invariable trunks,
and their lips were the leaves
of the immense divided tree,
disseminated everywhere,
walking with its roots.
This is the tree, the tree
of the people, of all the peoples
struggling for freedom.

Look at its hair:
touch its renewed rays:
plunge your hands into the factories

where its pulsing fruit
propagates its light each day.
Raise this earth in your hands,
partake of this splendor,
take your bread and your apple,
your heart and your horse
and mount guard on the frontier,
at the limits of its leaves.

Defend the destiny of its corollas,
share the hostile nights,
guard the cycle of the dawn,
breathe in the starry heights,
sustaining the tree, the tree
that grows in the middle of the earth.

I

Cuauhtemoc
(1520)

Young brother, never at rest,
unconsoled for time on endless time,
youth shaken in Mexico's
metallic darkness, I read your
naked country's gift on your hand.

On it your smile is born and grows
like a line between the light and the gold.

Your lips sealed by death are
the purest entombed silence.

The fountain submerged
beneath all the earth's mouths.

Did you hear, did you hear, by chance,
from distant Anáhuac,
a waterway, a wind
of shattered springtime?
It was perhaps the cedar's voice.
It was a white wave from Acapulco.

But in the night your heart
fled to the borderlands
like a bewildered deer,

amid the bloody monuments,
beneath the foundering moon.

All the shade prepared shade.
The land was a dark kitchen,
stone and caldron, black steam,
nameless wall, a nightmare
calling you from the nocturnal
metals of your country.

But there is no shade on your standard.

The fateful hour has arrived,
and among your people
you're bread and root, spear and star.
The invader has stopped his advance.
Moctezuma is not extinct
like a fallen chalice,
he's armored lightning,
Quetzal plume, flower of the people,
a flaming crest amid the ships.

But a hand hard as centuries of stone
gripped your throat. They didn't choke
your smile, they didn't make
the secret corn's kernels
fall, but they dragged you,
captive conqueror,
through the far reaches of your kingdom,
amid cascades and chains,
over sandbanks and thorns,
like an incessant column,
like a sorrowful witness,
until a noose snared
the column of purity
and hanged the dangling body
over the hapless land.

II

Brother
Bartolomé
de Las Casas

On the way home from the union,
at night, exhausted in the cold
May fog (in the grinding

daily struggle, winter
rain dripping from the eaves, the dull
throb of constant suffering), one thinks
about this masked resurrection,
astute, corrupt,
of the enslaver, of enslavement,
and when grief climbs up
to the lock to enter with you,
an ancient light shines forth, smooth
and hard as metal, like a buried star.
Father Bartolomé, thank you for this
gift from a bleak midnight,

thank you, for your thread was invincible:

It could have been crushed to death, devoured
by the dog's angry jaws,
it could have remained in the ashes
of the burned house,
it could have been cut by the countless
assassins' cold blades
or hatred administered with smiles
(the betrayal of the following crusade),
the lie heaved at the window.
The crystalline thread could have died,
the irreducible transparency
transformed into action, into the combatant
and plunging cascade's steel.
Mankind's given few lives like yours,
few shades in the tree like your shade—
all the continent's live coals repair to it,
all the razed conditions, the wound
of the mutilated, the exterminated
villages, everything's reborn
under your shade, from the limits
of agony you engender hope.
Father, it was fortunate for mankind
that you arrived on the plantation,
that you bit into crime's
black grains, drank
the daily cup of wrath.
Naked mortal, who put you
between the fury's teeth?
How did the eyes of another metal
see the light, when you were born?

How are ferments crossed
in the hidden human flour
to knead your immutable kernel
into the world's bread?

You were reality amid bloodthirsty
phantoms, you were
the eternity of tenderness
over the tempest of punishment.
From combat to combat your hope
was transformed into precise tools:
solitary struggle branched,
fruitless tears formed a party.

Piety was useless. When you showed
your columns, your protective nave,
your blessing hand, your mantle,
the enemy trampled the tears
and crushed the lily's color.
Piety, lofty and empty
as an abandoned cathedral, was useless.
It was your invincible decision, active
resistance, an armed heart.

Reason was your titanic material.

Organic flower your structure.

The conquistadors wanted to contemplate you
from above (from their heights),
leaning on their broadswords
like stone shadows, swamping
the lands of your initiative
with their sarcastic spit,
saying: "There goes the agitator";
lying: "The foreigners
paid him,"
"He has no homeland," "He's a traitor";
but your prayer was no
fragile minute, transient
guideline, travel clock.
Your wood was an assailed forest,
iron in its natural stock, hidden
from all light by the flowery land,
and furthermore, it was deeper:

in the unity of time, in the course
of your lifetime, your outstretched hand was
a zodiacal star, a sign of the people.
Today, Father, enter this house with me.
I'll show you the letters, the torment
of my people, of persecuted mankind.
I'll show you the ancient sorrows.

And to keep me from falling, to help me plant
     my
feet firmly on the ground, to continue fighting,
bequeath to my heart the errant wine
and the implacable bread of your sweetness.

III

**Advancing
in the
Lands of
Chile**

Spain drove into the South of the World.
Overwhelmed, the tall Spaniards explored the
    snow.
The Bío-Bío, solemn river,
told Spain: "Halt."
The forest of maytens whose green
threads weep like a tremor of rain
told Spain: "Stop here." The southland cypress,
titan of the silent borderlands,
spoke in a thundering voice.
But the invader kept coming, fist and dagger,
down to the bottom of my country.
Near the banks of the Imperial River, where
my heart awakened in the clover,
the hurricane struck in the morning.
The wide riverbed of the egrets stretched
from the islands to the furious sea,
filled like a bottomless wineglass,
between the banks of dark crystal.
On its shores the pollen raised
a carpet of turbulent stamens,
and from the sea the air stirred
all the syllables of springtime.
Araucania's hazel tree
raised bonfires and clusters
where the rain trickled

over the gathering of purity.
Everything was laced with fragrance,
steeped in green and rainy light,
and every pungent thicket
was a deep winter bouquet
or a lost marine formation
still full of oceanic dew.

Towers of birds and feathers
and a gale of sonorous solitude
rose up from the ravines,
while in the moist intimacy
amid the giant fern's
curly down, the flowery topa-topa
was a rosary of yellow kisses.

IV

**The Men
Rise Up**

That is where the chiefs germinated.
From that black moisture,
from that rain fermented
in the volcanoes' cones
majestic breasts emerged,
bright vegetal arrows,
teeth of savage stone,
inexorable crops of stakes,
the water's glacial unity.

Arauco was a cold uterus
made of wounds, mauled,
raped, conceived
amid sharp thorns,
scraped in the glaciers,
defended by serpents.

That's how the earth extracted man.

He grew like a fortress.
He was born of ravished blood.
He bristled his hair
like a little red puma,
and his hard stone eyes

shone from within
like the implacable glare
of a hunted beast.

V

Caupolicán grew, torso and tempest,
from the southland beech's secret stock,
and when he aimed his people
at the invading firearms,
the tree walked,
the homeland's hard tree walked.
The invaders saw foliage
moving amid the green mist,
heavy branches clothed
in countless leaves and threats,
the terrestrial trunk becoming people,
the territory's roots emerging.
They knew the hour had advanced
to the clock of life or death.

Other trees came with him.

The entire tribe of red branches,
all the braids of wild sorrow,
the entire knot of hatred in the wood.
Caupolicán raises his mask of lianas
in front of the lost invader:
it's not the regal painted plume,
not the throne of fragrant plants,
not the priest's glittering necklace,
not the glove or the golden prince:
it's a woodland face,
a giant mask of hewn acacias,
a countenance cracked by rain,
a head with vines.

Chief Caupolicán has the deep-set
look of a mountainous universe,
the implacable eyes of the earth,
and the titan's cheeks are walls
scaled by thunderbolts and roots.

VI

The Civil War

Araucania strangled the song
of the rose in the earthen vase, cut
the threads
on the silver bride's loom.
The illustrious shamaness descended
her ladder, and in the dispersed rivers, in the clay,
beneath the militant araucarias'
hirsute crowns,
a clamor of buried bells
rang forth. The mother of war
jumped over the brook's sweet stones,
sheltered the fisherman's family,
and the newlywed farmer kissed the stones
before they flew off to the wound.

Behind the Chief's woodland face
Arauco mounted its defense:
eyes and spears, dense multitudes
of foreboding silence,
indelible waists, proud,
dark hands, united fists.

Behind the tall Chief, the mountain,
and on the mountain, innumerable Arauco.

Arauco was the whisper of meandering water.

Arauco the shadowy silence.

In his severed hand the messenger
kept gathering Arauco's drops.

Arauco was the wave of war.
Arauco the night fires.

Everything seethed behind the august Chief,
and when he advanced there were shadows,
sands, forests, lands,
unanimous bonfires, hurricanes,
phosphoric appearance of pumas.

VII

Impaled   But Caupolicán met with torture.

Impaled on the sacrificial spear,
he entered the trees' lingering death.

Arauco withdrew its green attack,
quivered in the shadows,
buried its head in the ground,
retreated to nurse its wounds.
The Chief slumbered in death.
An iron clang reached
the encampment, a crown
of foreign cackles,
and in the veiled forests
the night alone throbbed.

It wasn't the pain, the volcano's
bite opened in the viscera,
it was just a forest dream,
the bleeding tree.

The murderous blade plunged
into my country's intestines,
wounding the sacred lands.
The burning blood fell
from silence to silence,
down under, where the seed
is waiting for springtime.

This blood ran deeper.

It ran to the roots.

It ran to the dead.

To those yet to be born.

VIII

**Lautaro
(1550)**

The blood touches a gallery of quartz.
The stone grows where the drop falls.
That's how Lautaro is born of the earth.

IX

**The Chief's
Training**

Lautaro was a slender arrow.
Our father was elastic and blue.
His tender years were nothing but silence.
His adolescence was dominion.
His youth a driving wind.
He prepared himself like a long spear.
He accustomed his feet to the cascades.
He trained his head in the thorns.
He executed the guanaco's trials.
He lived in snowy dens.
He stalked the eagles' food.
He clawed at the crags' secrets.
He tended the fire's petals.
He nursed on cold springtime.
He was burned in the infernal gorges.
He was hunter among the cruel birds.
His hands were tinged with victories.
He read the night's aggressions.
He sustained sulphur landslides.

He became velocity, sudden light.

He acquired Autumn's slowness.
He labored in invisible lairs.
He slept on the glaciers' sheets.
He followed the arrows' path.
He drank wild blood on the trails.
He wrested treasure from the waves.
He loomed like a menacing god.
He ate in every kitchen of his people.
He learned the lightning's alphabet.
He scented out the scattered ashes.
He cloaked his heart with black furs.

He deciphered the smoke's spiraling plume.
He was made of taciturn fibers.
He was oiled like the olive's pith.
He became crystal of hard transparency.
He studied to become a cyclone.
He struggled to temper his blood.

Only then was he worthy of his people.

X

**Lautaro
Among the
Invaders**

He entered Valdivia's house.
He followed him like the light.
He slept covered with daggers.
He saw his own blood spilt,
his own eyes crushed,
and he slept in the stables,
accumulated his power.
Not a hair stirred
as he examined the torments:
he looked beyond the air
toward his stripped race.

He stood guard at Valdivia's feet.

He heard his bloody dream
growing in the somber night
like an implacable column.
He divined those dreams.
He could have raised the sleeping
captain's golden beard,
severed the dream in his throat,
but he learned—tending shadows—
the nocturnal law of the timetable.

He marched by day, caressing
the wet-skinned horses that
kept plunging into his homeland.
He divined those horses.
He marched with the inscrutable gods.
He divined their armor.
He witnessed their battles,
as he entered step by step
the fire of Araucania.

XI

**Lautaro
Against the
Centaur
(1554)**

Then Lautaro attacked in waves.
He disciplined the Araucanian shadows:
before, the Castilian knife plunged
into the red mass' heart.
Today guerrilla warfare was sown
beneath all the forest eaves,
from stone to stone and ford to ford,
watching from behind the copihues,
lying in wait beneath the rocks.
Valdivia tried to retreat.
It was too late.
Lautaro arrived in a suit of lightning.
He followed the anguished Conquistador.
They made their way through the wet
thickets of the austral twilight.
                              Lautaro arrived
in a black gallop of horses.

Fatigue and death led
Valdivia's troops through the foliage.

Lautaro's spears drew near.

Amid corpses and leaves Pedro de Valdivia
advanced, as in a tunnel.

Lautaro came in the dark.

He thought about stony Extremadura,
about golden olive oil in the kitchen,
the jasmine left beyond the seas.

He recognized Lautaro's war cry.

The sheep, the harsh homesteads,
whitewashed walls, the Extremaduran afternoon.

Lautaro's night fell.

Intoxicated with blood, his captains
staggered homeward, through night and rain.

Lautaro's arrows quivered.

From tumble to tumble, the bleeding
captaincy kept retreating.

Now they touched Lautaro's bosom.

Valdivia saw the light coming, the dawn,
perhaps life, the sea.
                                    It was Lautaro.

XII

Pedro de Valdivia's Heart

We laid Valdivia beneath the tree.

It was a rainy blue morning with cold
filaments of frayed sun.
All the glory, the thunder,
chaotically heaped
in piles of mangled steel.
The cinnamon laurel raised its language
and the glow of a wet firefly
in all its pompous monarchy.

We brought cloth and earthen vessels,
fabric thick as conjugal braids,
gemstones like moon almonds,
and drums that filled Araucania
with their leathery light.
We heaped bowls with sweets
and danced, pounding the earth
made of our own dark stock.

Then we pounded the enemy face.

Then we cut the brave throat.

How beautiful the hangman's blood,
divided like a pomegranate
while it still burned brightly.
Then we drove a spear into his chest

85

and offered the heart, winged
like a bird, to the Araucanian tree.
A whisper of blood ran up to its crown.

And so, from the earth
made of our bodies, the war song,
song of the sun and the crops,
rose up to the volcanoes' magnitude.
Then we shared the bleeding heart.
I sank my teeth into that corolla,
fulfilling the rites of the earth:

"Give me your coldness, evil foreigner.
Give me your great jaguar's bravery.
Give me your fury in your blood.
Let your death join me
and strike your kind with terror.
Give me the war you brought.
Give me your horse and your eyes.
Give me your twisted darkness.
Give me the mother of maize.
Give me the horse's tongue.
Give me the homeland without thorns.
Give me victorious peace.
Give me the air where the cinnamon laurel,
the blossoming eminence, breathes."

XIII

**The
Protracted
War**

Then, land and oceans, cities,
ships and books, you know the history
of the territory that, intractable
as a shaken stone,
filled the depths of time
with blue petals.
For three centuries the warrior
race of the southland beech fought on,
for three centuries Arauco's lightning
filled the imperial cavities
with ashes.
For three centuries the captain's
shirts fell mortally wounded,
for three hundred years they devastated

farmlands and beehives,
for three hundred years they scourged
every invader's name,
for three centuries they ripped
the plundering eagles' skin,
for three centuries they swallowed,
like the ocean's mouth,
roofs and bones, armor,
towers and gilded titles.
A gallop of horses
and a tempest of ashes
fell on the wrathful spurs
and the engraved guitars.
The ships returned to the harsh
territory, spikes of grain were born,
Spanish eyes grew
in the kingdom of rain,
but Arauco razed the tiles,
ground the stones, destroyed
fortress walls and grapevines,
willpower and gowns.
See how the bitter children
of hatred fall to the earth.
Villagras, Mendozas, Reinosos,
Reyes, Morales, Alderetes
tumbled down to the white depths
of the glacial Americas.
And in the night of the majestic time
Imperial fell, Santiago fell,
Villarica fell in the snow,
Valdivia tumbled downriver
until the Bío-Bío's
fluvial kingdom stopped
over the centuries of blood
and established freedom
in the bled sands.

XIV

(INTERLUDE)

**The Colony
Covers
Our Lands
(1)**

When the sword was put to rest,
and from kingdoms and jungles
hard Spain's spectral children
sent mountains of paper with outcries
to the brooding monarch's throne:
when the entire story had passed from hand to hand
in the side streets of Toledo
and the bend of the River Guadalquivir,
after the tattered ends
of the spectral conquistadors
wandered through the heart of the seaports
and the last corpses were laid
in coffins, with processions,
in churches built by the sword,
law came to the world of rivers
and the merchant arrived with his little purse.

The morning expanses grew dark,
gowns and spiderwebs sowed
obscurity, temptation, the devil's
eternal fire in every dwelling.
A candle lit vast America,
full of glaciers and honeycombs,
and for centuries it whispered to man,
trotted through the narrow streets coughing,
pursued pennies with the sign of the cross.
The Creole arrived in the world's streets,
emaciated, cleaning the gutters,
longing for love amid the crosses,
seeking life's
hidden path
in the closet of the sacristy.
The city fermented in the sperm
of shoemaker's wax, beneath the black
vestments, and fashioned infernal apples
out of the wax shavings.

America, the crown of mahogany,
was then an ulcerous twilight,
a leprosarium engulfed in shadows,

and reverence for the worm grew
in the ancient expanse of freshness.
Over the pustules gold raised
massive flowers, silent ivy,
structures of submerged shadow.

A woman collected pus,
and drank the glassful of substance
to the honor of each day's heaven,
while hunger danced in the mines
of golden Mexico,
and Peru's Andean heart
wept softly
from the cold beneath the tatters.

In the sinister day's shadows
the merchant built his empire,
dimly lit by the bonfire
in which the writhing heretic,
reduced to ash, received
his little spoon of Christ.
The following day, the ladies,
adjusting their petticoats,
recalled the agonizing body,
beaten and consumed by the flames,
while the bailiff examined
the minuscule spot left by
the burned man—grease, ash, blood—
licked up by the dogs.

XV

The
Haciendas
(2)

The land passed between the entailed estates,
doubloon to doubloon, dispossessed,
paste of apparitions and convents,
until the entire blue geography was
divided into haciendas and encomiendas.
The mestizo's ulcer, the overseer's
and slaver's whip
moved through the lifeless space.
The Creole was an impoverished specter
who picked up the crumbs,
until he saved enough
to acquire a little title
painted with gilt letters.

And in the dark carnival
he masqueraded as a count,
a proud man among beggars,
with his little silver cane.

XVI

The New
Proprietors
(3)

So time stagnated in the cistern.

Man dominated in the empty
crossroads—a pebble in the castle,
ink in the court of inquiry—filled
the closed American city with mouths.

When all was peace and harmony,
hospital and viceroy, when Arrellano,
Rojas, Tapia, Castillo, Núñez, Pérez,
Rosales, López, Jorquera, Bermúdez,
the last of the soldiers from Castile
aged behind the Royal Tribunal,
they were buried under the bundles of paper,
they went off with their lice to the tomb
where they spun the dream
of the imperial storerooms—when
the rat was the last plague
of the bloody lands,
the Biscayans appeared with their sacks:
Errázuriz with his rope-soled sandals,
Fernández Larraín and his candles,
Aldunate with his floor cloths,
Eyzaguirre, king of socks.

They all entered like the hungry masses
that fled misfortune, the police.

Soon, undershirt by undershirt,
they expelled the conquistador
and established the conquest
of the grocery store.
Then they acquired pride
bought on the black market.
They were adjudged
haciendas, whips, slaves,
catechisms, commissaries,

alms boxes, tenements, brothels,
and all this they called
holy western culture.

XVII

It was Manuela Beltrán (when she broke the
    oppressor's
banns and cried, "Down with the despots")
who scattered the new grain
over our land.
It was in New Granada, town
of Socorro. The commoners
shook the viceroyalty
in a precursory eclipse.

They united against the state commissaries,
against stained privilege,
they raised petitions
of the people's rights,
united with firearms and stones,
minutemen and women, the people,
order and fury, marching
on Bogotá and its highborn.

Then the Archbishop stepped down.
"You'll have all your rights,
I promise you in the name of God."

The people assembled in the plaza.

And the Archbishop celebrated
a mass and swore an oath.

He was righteous justice.
"Put down your firearms, repair
to your homes," he pronounced.

The commoners surrendered
their arms. In Bogotá
they feted the Archbishop,
celebrated his betrayal,
his perjury, in the perfidious mass,
and they denied bread and rights.

They executed the leaders,
distributed the recently decapitated
heads among the towns,
with the Prelate's blessings
and dances in the Viceroyalty.

O first, heavy seeds
cast to the regions,
you'll remain, blind statues,
incubating the insurrection
of spikes in the hostile night.

XVIII

**Tupac
Amaru
(1781)**

Condorcanqui Tupac Amaru,
wise man, just forefather,
you saw the desolate springtime
of the Andean scaffolds
climb up to Tungasuca
with salt and calamity,
iniquities and torments.

Noble Inca, great Chief,
everything was stored in your eyes
as in a coffer burned to dust
by love and sadness.

The Indian showed you his back
on which the new bites
shone over the healed scars
of former punishments,
and it was back after back,
all the highlands shaken
by cascading sobs.

It was sob after sob.
Until you prepared the clay—
colored people's march,
gathered the tears in your cup,
and hardened the trails.
The father of the mountains came,
the gunpowder opened roads,
and the father of combat
came to the humiliated peoples.

They threw their ponchos into the dust,
the old knives united,
and the conch shell
called the scattered bonds.
Against the cruel stone,
against calamitous inertia,
against the metal of the chains.
But they divided your people
and sent brother against
brother, until the stones
of your fortress fell.
They bound your weary members
to four raging horses
and quartered the light
of the implacable dawn.

Tupac Amaru, vanquished sun,
a vanished light rises
from your sundered glory
like the sun over the sea.
The deep tribes of clay,
the sacrificed looms,
the wet sand houses
say in silence: "Tupac,"
and Tupac is a seed,
they say in silence: "Tupac,"
and Tupac is preserved in the furrow,
they say in silence: "Tupac,"
and Tupac germinates in the ground.

XIX

**Insurgent
America
(1800)**

Our land—wide land, wilderness—
was filled with murmurs, arms, mouths.
A mute syllable kept burning,
congregating the clandestine rose,
until the meadows shook,
trampled by metals and gallops.

Truth was hard as a ploughshare.

It broke the earth, established desire,
sank in its germinal propaganda,
and was born in the secret springtime.

Its flower was silent, its gathering of light
repulsed—the collective yeast,
the hidden banners' kiss
was beaten back,
but it rose up breaking the walls,
uprooting the jails from the soil.

The dark race, its cup,
received the repulsed substance,
dispersed it in the marine limits,
crushed it in indomitable mortars.
And it emerged with its pages hammered
and springtime on the road.
Yesterday's hour, noontime,
today's hour again, hour awaited
between the minute expired and the newborn,
in the bristling age of the lie.

O homeland born of woodcutters,
of unbaptized children, carpenters,
those who gave, like a rare bird,
a drop of winged blood,
today you'll be born harshly,
whence the traitor and the jailer
believe you're submerged forever.

Today, as then, you'll be born of the people.

Today you'll emerge from the coal and the dew.
Today you'll come to shake the doors
with bruised hands, with bits
of surviving soul, with clusters
of expressions that death did not extinguish,
with intractable tools
hidden beneath your tatters.

XX

Bernardo O'Higgins Riquelme (1810)

O'Higgins, to celebrate you
in the twilight we must light up the room.
In the South's autumn twilight
with an infinite tremor of poplars.

You're Chile, between patriarch and cowboy,
a poncho from the provinces, a child
who doesn't know his name yet,
iron-willed and shy in school,
a sad little country boy.
In Santiago you're ill at ease, they
stare at your baggy black clothes,
and when they placed the ribbon across
your rustic statue's breast, the flag
of the country you gave us, it smelled
of wild mustard in the early morning.

Youth, Professor Winter
accustomed you to the rain,
you received your degrees from
the University of the Streets of London,
and an impoverished wanderer,
wildfire of our freedom,
gave you a prudent eagle's counsel
and embarked you in History.

"What's your name?" laughed
the "gentlemen" from Santiago:
child of love, on a winter's night,
your forsaken condition
shaped you with rough mortar,
with the seriousness of a home or
of wood, definitive, worked in the South.
Time changes all, all but your face.
O'Higgins, you're an invariable clock
with a single hour on your candid sphere:
Chile's hour, the last minute
left on the red timetable
of combatant dignity.

So you're one and the same amid the rosewood
furniture and the daughters of Santiago,
as surrounded in Rancagua by gunpowder and
        death.

You're the same solid portrait
of him who has no father but fatherland,
of him who has no bride but that
land with orange blossoms
conquered by your artillery.

I picture you in Peru writing letters.
No exile your equal, no greater outcast.
The entire province is exiled.

Chile was lit up like a salon
when you were away. A wasteful
rigadoon of the rich substituted
your ascetic soldier's discipline,
and without you, the country you won
was governed like a dance watched
from without by the hungry masses.

You could no longer enter the fiesta
with the blood, sweat, and dust from Rancagua.
The capital gentlemen
would have judged it improper.
The road would have entered with you,
a smell of sweat and horses,
the smell of the homeland in Springtime.

You couldn't make this dance.
Your fiesta was a castle of explosions.
Struggle your disorderly dance.
The end of your fiesta the shock
of defeat, the ill-fated future near
Mendoza, the country cradled in your arms.

Now look toward the bottom of the map,
Chile's narrow belt,
and put little soldiers in the snow,
pensive youths in the sand,
sappers that shine and fade away.

Shut your eyes, sleep, dream a while,
your only dream, the only one that returns
to your heart: a tricolored
flag in the South, the rain
falling, the rural sun on the soil,
the gunshots of the people in revolt,
and two or three of your words
when strictly necessary.
If you're dreaming, today your dream's fulfilled.
Dream it, at least, in the tomb.

May you know nothing else because, as before,
after the victorious battles

the dandies are dancing at Court,
and the same hungry face
looks on from the shadows in the streets.

But we've inherited your firmness,
your unalterable composed heart,
your indestructible paternal position,
and today, amid the blinding avalanche
of hussars from the past, amid the agile
blue and gold uniforms,
today you're with us, you're ours,
father of the people, immutable soldier.

XXI

**San
Martín
(1810)** San Martín, from so much walking place to place
I discarded your uniform, your spurs,
knowing that someday, walking the roads
made for returning, in the limits
of the cordillera, in the purity
of the elements we inherited from you,
we'd see one another sooner or later.

It's hard to differentiate amid the mahogany's
knots, amid roots,
to see your face amid the footpaths,
to distinguish your gaze amid the birds,
to find your existence in the air.

You're the land you gave us, a branch
of cedrón with an aroma that stuns—we cannot
place it, we don't know where the smell
of the meadows in the homeland comes from.
We gallop you, San Martín, early in the
morning we rise to traverse your body,
to inhale acres of your shade,
to build campfires upon your stature.

You're vast among all the heroes.

Others traveled from table to table,
a cloud of dust on the crossroads—
you were made of remote parts,

and we've begun to see your geography,
your wide open spaces, your territory.

The more time disperses
like eternal water the clumps
of bitterness, the bonfire's
keen disclosures, the more terrain
you'll comprise, the more the seeds
of your tranquility will cover the hills,
the more you'll extend the springtime.

The man who builds then becomes the
        smoke of all he built, no one's reborn
of his own consumed fire: he turned
his dying flame to vital spark,
he died away and turned to dust.

You embraced more space in your death.

Your death was like a silent granary.
Your life and other lives passed on,
doors were opened, walls were raised,
the spike of grain was sown again.

San Martín, other captains
shine brighter than you, with their
embroidered tendrils of phosphorescent salt,
others still speak like waterfalls,
but there's none like you, clothed
in earth and solitude, in snow and clover.
We meet you returning from the river,
we greet you in the agrarian manner
of flowery Tucumán,
and on the roads we cross you
on horseback, galloping and raising
your vestments, dusty forefather.

Today the sun and the moon, the great wind,
mature your stock, your simple
composition: your truth was
an earthen truth, a gritty mixture,
stable as bread, a fresh sheet
of clay and grain, pure pampa.

To this day you've remained moon and gallop,
a soldier's season, inclemency,
where we're waging war again,
traveling the towns and prairies,
establishing your earthy truth,
disseminating your spacious germ,
winnowing the pages of wheat.

So be it, and let there be
no peace until we've entered
your spirit, after combat,
and you can sleep the measure we've found
in your expanse of germinating peace.

XXII

**Mina
(1817)**

Mina, from mountain headsprings
you came like a thread of hard water.
Clear Spain, transparent Spain
bore you in pain, indomitable,
and you possess the luminous hardness
of torrential mountain water.

For a long time, in centuries and lands,
shadow and splendor fought in your cradle,
rampant claws slaughtered
the people's clarity,
and the ancient falconers
in their ecclesiastic battlements
stalked the bread, denied
entry to the river of the poor.

But in your merciless tower, Spain,
you always made room
for the insurgent diamond and its stock
of dying and renascent light.

Not in vain Castile's banner
bears the color of the commoner's wind,
not in vain Garcilaso's blue light
flows through your granite basins,
not in vain in Córdoba, amid priestly
spiders, Góngora leaves

his trays of jewels
bedewed by ice.

Spain, in your talons
of cruel antiquity, your pure people
shook the roots of torment,
backed the feudal beasts of burden
with invincible spilt blood,
and in you the light, old as the shadow,
is consumed in devouring scars.
Beside the stonemason's peace,
crossed by the oaks' breath,
beside the spangled headsprings
where ribbons and syllables shine,
the gyrfalcon dwells on its stairway
like an ominous shiver over your age.

Hunger and pain were the silica
of your ancestral sands
and a muted tumult, entwined
to your peoples' roots,
gave the world's freedom
an eternity of lightning,
of songs and warriors.

Navarre's ravines
tended the recent ray.
Mina withdrew his chain
of soldiers from the precipice:
from the invaded villages,
from the nocturnal towns
he extracted the fire, nourished
the scorching resistance,
traversed snow-clad springs,
attacked in sudden bends,
surged from the gorges,
rose up from the bakeries.

They buried him in prisons,
and he returned in the high
sierra wind, angry and sonorous,
his fountainhead intransigent.

The wind of Spanish freedom
carries him to America,
he traverses forests again

and his inexhaustible heart
fertilizes the meadowlands.

In our struggle, in our land
his crystal was bled,
fighting for freedom
indivisible and banished.

In Mexico they impounded the water
of the Spanish headsprings.
And his abundant transparency
remained motionless and mute.

XXIII

**Miranda
Dies in
the Fog
(1816)**

If you enter Europe late dressed in top hat
in the garden decorated
by more than one Autumn beside
the marble fountain while leaves
of tattered gold fall on the Empire
if the figure in the gateway is framed
against the Saint Petersburg night
sleighbells jingling
if someone in the white solitude someone
same step same question
if you leave Europe through the flowery
gateway a uniformed gentleman shadow
intelligence insignia gold braid
Liberty Equality behold his brow
amid the thundering artillery
if he's acknowledged by the Islands' carpet
the one that receives oceans Come in By all means
How many boats And the fog
accompanying his journey step by step
if in the cavities of lodges bookstores
there's someone glove sword map
pullulating portfolio filled
with towns ships air
if in Trinidad near the coast the smoke
of combat after combat the sea again
and again the Bay Street stairway the atmosphere
that receives him impenetrable
as the compact core of an apple

and this patrician hand again this blue
guerrilla glove in the antechamber
long roads wars and gardens
defeat on his lips another salt
another salt another burning vinegar
if in Cádiz bound to the wall
by the heavy chain his thoughts the cold
piercing horror time captivity
if you go underground amid rats
leprous masonry another bolt
in a hanged man's coffin the old face
on which death has choked a word
a word our name the land
where his footsteps wanted to go
freedom for his wandering fire
they lower him with ropes to the wet
enemy earth no one salutes it's cold
cold as a tomb in Europe

XXIV

EPISODE

**José Miguel
Carrera
(1810)**

You were the first to say Freedom,
when the whisper passed from stone to stone,
hidden in the patios, humiliated.

You were the first to say Freedom.
You freed the slave's child.
The merchants moved like shadows
selling blood from foreign seas.
You freed the slave's child.

You founded the first press.
Letters reached the obscured people,
the secret news opened lips.
You founded the first press.
You implanted school in the convent.
The fat spiderweb, the niche
of suffocating tithes, retreated.
You implanted school in the convent.

CHORUS

Let your proud condition be known.
Scintillating and seasoned warrior.
Let your swiftness that fell shining
over the country be known.
Fierce flight, purple heart.

Let your fugitive keys unlocking
the night's bolts be known.
Green horseman, tempestuous lightning.
Let your generous love be known,
your lamp of vertiginous light.
Bursting grapevine's cluster.
Let your instantaneous splendor be known,
your roving heart, your diurnal fire.

Angry iron, patrician petal.
Let your imminent thunderbolt destroying
the cowardly cupolas be known.
Stormy tower, cluster of acacia.
Let your vigilant sword be known.
Your foundation of strength and meteor.
Let your swift grandeur be known.
Your indomitable gallantry.

EPISODE

He sails the seas, amid languages,
gowns, foreign birds,
brings freedom ships,
writes fire, marshals clouds,
deciphers sun and soldiers,
walks in the Baltimore fog,
from door to door, fatigued,
swamped by credits and men,
accompanied by all the waves.
By the Montevideo seaside,
in his exiled room,
he opens a press, prints bullets.
His insurgent arrow

wings its way to Chile,
the crystalline fury that
guides him burns, and he leads
the cavalcade of rescue
mounted on the cyclonic mane
of his hurtling agony.
His annihilated brothers
shout to him from the firing wall
of revenge. His blood
stains his tragic empty throne
like a firestorm
in the adobes of Mendoza.
He shakes the pampa's
planetary peace like a circuit
of infernal fireflies.
He scourges the citadels
with tribal war cries.
He impales captive heads
on the hurricane of lances.
His unleashed poncho
flashes in the cloud of smoke
and in the horses' death.

Young Pueyrredón, don't report
the desolate chill
of his end, don't torment me
with his night of abandonment,
when they take him to Mendoza
displaying his ivory mask,
the solitude of his agony.

CHORUS

Homeland, preserve him in your mantle,
reap this itinerant love:
don't let it roll to the bottom
of his dark despair:
raise this splendor, this unforgettable
lamp, to your brow,
fold this frenzied rein,
call this starry eyelid,
save this ball of blood

for your proud fabrics.
Homeland, reap his race,
the light, the mortally wounded drop,
this dying crystal,
this volcanic ring.
Homeland, gallop and defend him,
gallop, run, run like the wind.

EXODUS

They take him to the walls of Mendoza,
to the cruel tree, to the stream
of inaugurated blood, the solitary
torment, the cold end of the star.
He passes inconclusive roads,
brambles and toothless adobe walls,
poplars that throw him dead gold,
encircled by his pride, useless
as a tattered tunic
on which the dust of death collects.
He thinks about his bled dynasty,
about the new moon upon the heartrending
southland beech of his infancy,
the Castilian school and the Hispanic
militia's red and virile scutcheon,
his murdered tribe, the sweetness
of marriage, amid the orange blossoms,
exile, struggles throughout the world,
O'Higgins, the enigmatic standard bearer,
Javiera, unaware in the remote
gardens of Santiago.
Mendoza insults his black lineage,
strikes his vanquished investiture,
and amid the flying stones he climbs
toward death.

Never did a man have
a more exact death. From the harsh
assaults, amid wind and beasts,
to this blind alley where they bled
all those of his blood.
Each step
of the scaffold adjusts him to his fate.

Now the wrath can continue no more.
Revenge, love, shut their doors.
The roads bound the wanderer.
And when they shoot him, and blood
appears on the prince of the people's
clothing, it's blood that knows
the infamous earth, blood that has gone
where it had to go, to the soil
of the thirsty wine presses awaiting
the crushed grapes of his death.

He questioned the homeland's snow.
All was mist in the bristling heights.

He saw the rifles whose iron
brought his collapsing love to birth,
he felt uprooted, a passenger
of the smoke, in the solitary battle,
and he fell enveloped in dust and blood,
as in two bannered arms.

CHORUS

Ill-starred Hussar, blazing jewel,
briar aflame in the snow-clad country.

Weep for him, women, weep until
your tears soak the earth,
the earth he loved, his idolatry.
Weep, hard warriors from Chile,
accustomed to mountain and wave,
this glacial void,
this death, the sea that pounds us.
Don't ask why, no one could tell
the truth destroyed by the gunpowder.
Don't ask who, no one can uproot
the growth of springtime,
no one killed our brother's rose.
Let's preserve our anger, sorrow, and tears,
let's fill the desolate void,
and let the night bonfire evoke
the light of the fallen stars.

Sister, preserve your sacred rage.
The people's victory needs the voice
of your triturated tenderness.
Spread mantles over his absence
that he may, cold and buried,
sustain the homeland with his silence.

His life was more than one life.

He pursued his integrity like a flame.
Death went with him until it left him
forever complete and consumed.

ANTISTROPHE

O disconsolate laurel, preserve his extreme winter
    substance.
Let's take radiant sand to his crown of thorns.
O filaments of Araucanian stock, protect the
    mortuary moon.
O boldu tree leaves, resolve the peace of his
    tomb,
the snow nourished in Chile's immense and dark
    waters,
plants that he loved, lemon balm in cups of wild
    clay,
harsh plants loved by the yellow centaur,
black clusters brimming with electric autumn in
    the earth,
dark eyes that burned beneath his earthy kisses.
O homeland, flush your birds, your unjust wings,
    your red eyelids,
let the watery lapwing's voice fly to the wounded
    hussar,
let the red-breasted meadowlark bleed its scarlet-
    stained aroma, paying tribute
to him whose flight extended the nuptial night of
    the land
and let the condor suspended in the immutable
    heights crown with bloody feathers
the sleeping breast, the bonfire that lies on the
    steps of the cordillera,

let the soldier break the wrathful rose crushed on
    the stormed wall,
let the compatriot mount the black-saddled horse
    with muzzle afoam,
return to the rural slave his rooted peace, his
    mourning scutcheon,
let the mechanic erect his pale tower woven of
    nocturnal tin:
the people born in the cradle wickered by the
    hero's hands,
the people who emerge from black adobe mines
    and sulphuric shafts,
let the people raise martyrdom and the urn and
    envelop the naked memory
with its railroader's greatness and its eternal
    balance of stones and wounds
until the fragrant earth decrees wet copihues and
    open books
to the invincible child, to the eminent storm, to
    the tender terrifying and bitter soldier.
And preserve his name in the hard dominion of
    the people in their struggle
like the ship's name resists marine combat:
let the country on its prow inscribe it and the
    lightning kiss it
for that was the essence of his free and slender
    and fiery matter.

XXV

CUECA

Manuel   Oh missus they're saying where,
Rodríguez   my mother they're saying they said,
              the water and wind are saying
              they saw the soldier ahead.

Life   It could be a bishop,
              it could or could not,
              it could be only the wind
              over the snow:

Passion

over the snow, *sí*,
mother, don't look,
he's galloping toward us
Manuel Rodríguez.
The soldier's coming hither.
Crossing the river.

CUECA

Passion Departing from Melipilla,
galloping through Talagante,
passing through San Fernando,
awakening in Pomaire.

Passing through Rancagua,
through San Rosendo,
through Cauquenes, through Chena,
through Nacimiento:
through Nacimiento, *sí*,
from distant Chiñigüe,
everywhere he's coming
Manuel Rodríguez.
Hand him this carnation. We're going with him.

CUECA

Let the guitar be muted,
for the country is dressed in mourning.
Our country is growing darker.
Now they have murdered our soldier.

And In Til-Til
Death he was murdered by the assassins.
His back is bleeding
upon the highway:
upon the highway, *sí*.

Who'd have believed it,
he who was our brother,
our own happiness.

The whole country is weeping.
In silence we're marching.

XXVI

1

Artigas

Artigas grew amid the brush and his march was
tempestuous for in the meadows the booming
    gallop of stone or bell
jolted the wasteland's inclemency like a repeated
    spark,
amassed the celestial color extending the
    resounding hooves
until a flag drenched in Uruguayan dew was born.

2

Uruguay, Uruguay, chime the songs of the River
    Uruguay,
the troupials the plaintive call of the turtledoves,
    the tower of Uruguayan thunder
proclaiming the celestial cry that rings Uruguay in
    the wind
and if the cascade resounds and repeats the bitter
    horsemen's gallop
harvesting in the borderlands the last grains of
    their victorious defeat,
extending a pure bird's unisonous name,
the violin light that baptizes the violent homeland.

3

O Artigas, soldier of the crescent countryside,
    when all the troops needed nothing but
your poncho spangled by constellations you knew,
until the blood corrupts and redeems the dawn
    and your marching men
overcome by the day's dusty trails awaken.
O constant father of the itinerary, trailblazer,
    centaur of the dust!

4

The days of a century passed and the hours lagged
    behind your exile:
behind the jungle tangled by a thousand iron
    spiderwebs:
behind the silence in which only the rotten fruits
    fell upon the swamps,
the leaves, the pounding rain, the barn owl's
    music,
the Paraguayans' barefoot steps entering and
    leaving the shade's sun,
the whip's braid, the stocks, the bodies eaten
    away by beetles:
a solemn bolt asserted itself, removing the jungle's
    color
and with its belts the livid dusk closed
Artigas' wistful eyes that seek the Uruguayan
    light.

5

"The bitter toil of exile," wrote that soul brother,
and so America's curtain dropped like a dark
    eyelid
over the gaze of Artigas, bloodcurdling horseman,
overcome by a despot's motionless glassy gaze, in
    an empty kingdom.

6

Your America trembled in penitential pain:
Oribes, Alveares, Carreras rushed naked to
    sacrifice:
they died, they were born, they fell: the blind
    man's eyes killed: the voice of the mute
spoke. The dead, at last they found their party,
they met at last their patrician sect in death.
And all those bloodstained men discovered their
rank was the same: the earth has no adversaries.

7

Uruguay is a bird song, the language of water,
a cascading syllable, a tempest of crystalware—
Uruguay, the voice of fruits in fragrant
    springtime,
a fluvial kiss of the forests and the blue mask of
    the Atlantic.
Uruguay is wash put out to dry in the gold of a
    windy day,
bread on America's table, and the purity of bread
    on the table.

8

And if Pablo Neruda, chronicler of everything,
    owed you, Uruguay, this song,
this story, this mite of a spike of grain, this
    Artigas,
I did not neglect my duty or accept the scruples
    of the intransigent:
I waited for a restful hour, stalked a restless hour,
    harvested the river's herbs,
immersed my head in your sand and in the
    mackerels' silver,
in your children's bright friendship, in your
    tumbledown markets I purged myself
until I felt myself a debtor to your odor and your
    love.
And perhaps the murmur that your love and odor
    granted me
is written in these dark words, which I leave in
    memory of your luminous captain.

XXVII

**Guavaquil
(1822)**

When San Martín entered, something nocturnal
of an impalpable road—shade, leather—
entered the room.
                 Bolívar was waiting.
He sensed what was coming.
He was aerial, swift, metallic,

all anticipation, science of flight,
his contained being trembled
there, in the room arrested
in the darkness of history.

He came from the indescribable heights,
from the starry atmosphere,
his army advanced
overcoming night and distance,
captain of an invisible body,
of the snow that trailed behind him.
The lamp flickered, the door
behind San Martín sustained
the night, its baying, the tepid
murmur of a river outlet.
The words blazed a trail
that went between them.
Those two bodies spoke,
repelled each other, hid from one another,
cut one another off, fled from each other.

San Martín brought from the South
a sack of gray numbers,
the solitude of the indefatigable
saddles, galloping horses
pounding ahead, joining
his gritty fortitude.
Chile's tough muleteers
entered with him, a slow
iron army,
the preparatory space,
flags with names
aged in the pampa.

Whatever they said fell body to body
in the silence, in the gaping interstice.
It wasn't words, it was a deep
emanation of adverse lands,
of human stone touching
another inaccessible metal.
The words returned to their source.

Each saw his flags
before his eyes.
One, the time with dazzling flowers,
the other, the corroded past,
the troops in tatters.

Beside Bolívar a white hand
awaited him, dismissed him,
amassed its burning spur,
spread linen on the marriage bed.
San Martín was faithful to his meadow.
His dream was a gallop,
a mesh of leather straps and danger.
His freedom a unanimous pampa.
A cereal order his victory.

Bolívar forged a dream,
an ignored dimension, a fire
of enduring velocity,
so confined that it made him
prisoner, surrendered to its substance.

Words and silence fell.

The door was opened again, again
the entire American night, the wide
many-lipped river pulsed a second.

San Martín returned that night
to the open spaces, to the wheat.
Bolívar continued alone.

XXVIII

Sucre   Sucre in the highlands, overrunning
the mountains' yellow profile,
Hidalgo falls, Morelos reaps
the resonance, the tremor of a bell
broadcast in the earth and the blood.
Páez travels the roads
dispersing conquered air,
in Cundinamarca the dew falls
on the fraternity of wounds,
all the restless people rise up
from latitude to secret
cell, a world of good-byes
and gallops emerges,
every minute a flag is born
like an anticipated flower:

flags made of bloody
handkerchiefs and free books,
flags dragged over the dusty
roads, tattered
by the cavalry, torn
by explosions and lightning.

The Flags

Our flags of that fragrant
time, freshly embroidered,
newborn, secret
as deep love, suddenly
aflame in the precious
gunpowder's blue wind.

America, vast cradle, starry
space, ripe pomegranate,
your geography was suddenly
filled with bees, a buzzing
conducted by adobes
and stones, from hand to hand,
the street was filled with clothes,
like a dazed beehive.

In the night of the gunfire
the dance shone in their eyes,
orange blossoms climbed
their shirts, like an orange,
good-bye kisses, kisses of wheat,
love-bound kisses,
and war singing along
the roads with its guitar.

XXIX

**Castro Alves
from Brazil**

Castro Alves from Brazil, for whom did you sing?
Did you sing for the flower? For the water
whose beauty sings words to the stones?
Did you sing for those eyes, for the truncated
profile of the one you then loved? For springtime?

Yes, but those petals had no dew,
those black waters had no words,

those were the eyes that saw death,
martyrdom burned on behind love,
springtime was spattered with blood.

"I sang for the slaves who sailed aboard the ships
like a dark cluster from the tree of wrath,
and the ship was bled in the seaport,
leaving us the burden of stolen blood.

"I sang in those days against the inferno,
against the sharp tongues of greed,
against the gold drenched in the tempest,
against the hand that brandished the whip,
against the directors of darkness.

"Every rose held a corpse in its roots.
The light, the night, the sky rained tears,
eyes shunned the wounded hands
and my voice alone filled the silence.

"I wanted man's deliverance from man,
I thought the road passed through man himself,
that our destiny issued from him.
I sang for those who had no voice.
My voice knocked on doors closed until then
so that, fighting, Freedom might enter."

Castro Alves from Brazil, since your pure book
is born again today for the free land,
allow me, poet of our poor America,
to crown your head with laurel from the people.
Your voice merged with the eternal lofty voice of
       mankind.
You sang well. You sang as one should sing.

XXX

Toussaint
L'Ouverture

Haiti, from its entwined sweetness,
extracts pathetic petals,
rectitude of gardens, grandiose
structures, the sea
lulls its ancient dignity of skin
and space like a dark grandfather.

Toussaint L'Ouverture binds
the vegetable sovereignty,
the shackled majesty,
the mute voice of the drums,
and he attacks, blocks the way, rises,
commands, repels, defies
like a natural monarch,
until he falls in the sinister net
and is taken overseas,
dragged and trampled
like the return of his race,
cast to the secret death
of sewers and cellars.

But on the Island the cliffs burn,
hidden branches speak,
hopes are transmitted,
the bastion's walls rise up.
Freedom is your forest,
dark brother, preserve
your memory of suffering,
and let heroes of the past
safekeep your magic foam.

XXXI

**Morazán
(1842)**

It's high night and Morazán keeps the watch.
Is it today, yesterday, tomorrow? You'll know.

Central waistband, American strait
made by the blue pounding
of the two seas, raising aloft
cordilleras and emerald plumes:
territory, unity, slender goddess
born in the combat of foam.

Children and maggots consume you,
you're crawling with vermin
and pincers tear away your dream
and a dagger spatters you with your blood
while your standard is torn to shreds.

It's high night and Morazán keeps the watch.

Now the jaguar comes brandishing an ax.
They've come to devour intestines.
They've come to divide the star.
                              They're coming,
fragrant little America,
to nail you to the cross, to flay you,
to strike the metal of your flag.

It's high night and Morazán keeps the watch.

Invaders occupied your dwelling.
They split you like fallen fruit,
and others clamped over your back
the teeth of a bloodthirsty pedigree,
and others sacked you in the seaports,
loading blood upon your sorrows.

Is it today, yesterday, tomorrow? You'll know.

Brothers, the day is dawning. (And Morazán
        keeps
the watch.)

XXXII

**Journey
Through
the Night
of Juárez**

Juárez, if we mined
the intimate stratum, the matter
from the depths, if digging we could strike
the deep metal of your republics,
this unity would be your structure,
your impassive kindness, your callous hand.
Whoever sees your frock coat,
your frugal ceremony, your silence,
your face made of American earth,
if they're not from here, if they weren't born
in these prairies, in the mountain clay
of our wilds, they'll not understand.
When they talk to you they'll see a quarry.
They'll cross you like they cross a river.
They'll shake hands with a tree, a vine,
a dark earthen road.

For us you're bread and stone,
oven and product of the dark race.
Your face was born of our clay.
Your majesty is my snow-clad region,
your eyes buried earthenware.

Others may possess the atom and the drop
of electric radiance, of restless ember:
you're the wall made of our blood,
your impenetrable rectitude
issues from our hard geology.

You've nothing to say to the air,
to the golden wind that comes from afar,
let the introspective earth say it,
the quicklime, minerals, the yeast.

I visited the walls of Querétaro,
touched every pinnacle of rock,
the remoteness, scar and crater,
the spiny-stemmed cacti:
no one remains there, the phantom went away,
no one still sleeps in the harshness:
there's only light, thorns
from the chaparral, a pure presence:
Juárez, your just night's peace,
definitive, ferrous, starry.

XXXIII

**The
Wind
over
Lincoln**

Sometimes the wind from the South glides
over Lincoln's grave bringing
voices and wisps of cities and trees
nothing stirs in his tomb the letters don't move
the marble grows smooth with the slowness of
    centuries
the old gentleman no longer lives
the hole in his ancient shirt is gone
fibers of time and human dust have fused
what a life of commitment says a tremulous
lady from Virginia a school that sings
more than one school sings thinking about other
    things

but the wind from the South emanation of lands
roads sometimes lingers in his tomb
its transparency a modern newspaper
silent rage laments like those in the wind
the motionless victorious dream lay
beneath the muddy feet that have passed
singing and tracking so much fatigue and blood
and so this morning hatred returns to the marble
the white South's hatred toward the dormant old
     man
in church the Blacks alone with God
with God or so they believe in towns
in trains the world has certain signs
that segregate heaven water air
what a perfect life says the dainty
girl and in Georgia they beat
a Black to death weekly
while Paul Robeson sings like the earth
like the beginning of sea and life
sings about cruelty and coca-cola
advertisements sings for brothers and sisters
world to world amid punishments
sings for the newborn so that mankind
will listen and hold its whip in check
hand the cruel hand that Lincoln toppled
hand that strikes again like a white viper
wind the wind glides over the grave bringing
conversations scraps of oaths something
that weeps on the marble like a misty rain
of ancient forgotten unburied grief
the Klan murdered a savage hunting
lynching the poor screaming Black burning him
alive and riddled with bullets
beneath their hoods the prosperous rotarians
know nothing think it's just hangmen
cowards butchers detritus of the dollar
with the cross of Cain returning
to wash their hands praying on Sunday
phoning the Senate to divulge their deeds
the dead man from Illinois knows nothing of this
for today's wind speaks a language
of slavery rage chains
and the man in the grave is gone
he's the fine dust of victory
victory razed after the hollow triumph
not only the man's shirt has worn away

not only the hole of death consumes us
but recurrent springtime the flux
that devours the victor with its cowardly song
yesterday's valor dies and evil's
furious flags are flying again
somebody's singing beside the monument
a chorus of schoolgirls' acid voices
that rise without touching the external dust
that fade away without reaching the sleeping
    woodcutter
victory dead beneath the reverences
while the South's mocking and roving wind
    smiles on.

XXXIV

**Martí
(1890)**

Cuba, foamy flower, effervescent
scarlet lily, jasmine,
it's hard to find your dark
martyred coal beneath the flowery net,
the ancient wrinkle left by death,
the scar concealed by the foam.

But within you, as in a clear
geometry of germinated snow,
where your ultimate cortices unfold,
Martí lies like a pure almond.

He's in the circular depths of the air,
in the blue center of the territory,
and his dormant seed's purity
sparkles like a raindrop.

Crystal the night that covers him.
Suddenly, tears and sorrow, cruel drops
penetrate the earth down to the precinct
of infinite slumbering clarity.
The people sometimes sink their roots
through the night until they reach
his hidden mantle's still water.
At times perverse rage
tramples seeded surfaces
and a corpse falls into the people's cup.

At times the buried whip cracks again
in the air of the cupola
and a drop of blood falls to earth
like a petal and descends to the silence.
Everything reaches the immaculate splendor.
The minuscule tremors pound
on the hidden man's crystal doors.

Every tear reaches his current.

Every fire shakes his structure.
And so from the dormant fortitude,
from the teeming germ,
the island's combatants emerge.

They rise from a determined headspring.

They're born of a crystalline fountain.

XXXV

**Balmaceda
from Chile
(1891)**

Mr. North arrived from London.

He's a nitrate magnate.
He worked in the pampa before,
as a day laborer, for a time,
but he saw the light and left.
Now he's back, wrapped in sterling.
He bears two small Arabian horses
and a little locomotive,
pure gold. They are gifts
for the President, Mr.
José Manuel Balmaceda.

"You are very clever, Mr. North."

Rubén Darío enters this house,
this Presidency, at will.
A bottle of cognac awaits him.
The young Minotaur enveloped
in river mist, transfixed by sound,
scales the great ladder, doubtlessly

too difficult for Mr. North to scale.
Recently the President returned
from the desolate saltpetrous North,
where he pronounced: "This land, this wealth
will belong to Chile, I'll transform this
white substance into schools, roads,
bread for my people."
Surrounded now by papers, in the palace,
his refined form, his intense gaze
are fixed on the nitrate deserts.

His noble face does not smile.

His stately pallid head
bears the ancient mien of the dead,
of the fatherland's venerable forebears.

His entire being is solemn examination.

Something disturbs his peace, his
pensive movements, like a chilling gust.

He refused Mr. North's horses, the little
gold engine, sent them back to their owner,
the powerful gringo, without looking at them.
He gestured slightly with his disdainful hand.
"Now, Mr. North, I cannot
grant you these concessions,
I cannot bind my country
to the mysteries of the City."

Mr. North becomes established in the Club.
One hundred whiskies for his table,
one hundred dinners for lawyers,
for Parliament, champagne
for the traditionalists.
Agents scurry Northward,
the threads spin back and forth.
The smooth sterling pounds
weave like golden spiders
an English cloth, legitimate,
for my people, a suit tailored
with blood, gunpowder and misery.

"You are very clever, Mr. North."

The shadows besiege Balmaceda.

When the day comes they insult him,
the aristocrats ridicule him,
they bark at him in Parliament,
they berate and slander him.
They wage war, and they win.
But that's not enough: they must twist
history. The good vineyards
are "sacrificed" and alcohol
fills the miserable night.
The elegant dandies
mark the doors and a horde
assaults the houses, throws
pianos from the balconies.
Aristocratic picnic
with corpses in the canal
and French champagne in the Club.

"You are very clever, Mr. North."

The Argentine Embassy opened
its doors to the President.

That afternoon he writes with the same
refined self-assurance,
the shadow enters his large eyes
like a dark butterfly,
profoundly fatigued.

And the magnitude of his brow
departs the solitary world
of the small room,
illuminates the dark night.
He writes the letters of his clear name
with the bold stroke
of his betrayed doctrine.

He holds the revolver in his hand.

He stares out the window at
the last fragment of the homeland,
thinking about Chile's
long body, dark
as a nocturnal page.
He looks far away, as through

a train window, without seeing
the passing fields, towns,
water towers, brimming riverbanks,
poverty, grief, tatters.
He dreamed a precise dream,
tried to change the razed
landscape, dared to defend
the people's consumed body.

Too late now—he hears scattered
gunfire, the savage raiders'
victorious cries, the howls
of the "aristocracy," he hears the final
sound, the great silence, and he slumps
forward, enters death with it.

XXXVI

To Emiliano Zapata with Music by Tata Nacho

When sorrows multiplied
on the land, and desolate thorns
were the peasants' estate
and, like yesteryear, rapacious
ceremonial beards and whips,
then flower and fire on the gallop . . .

> *Borrachita me voy*
> *hacia la capital*

the land rent by knives
reared up in the transitory dawn,
from his bitter den the peon
fell like husked corn
upon the vertiginous solitude.

> *a pedirle el patrón*
> *que me mandó llamar*

Then Zapata was land and dawn.
On the entire horizon the multitude
of his armed seed appeared.
In an attack of waters and frontiers
Coahuila's ferrous fountainhead,
Sonora's stellar stones:

everything joined his forward march,
his agrarian tempest of horseshoes.

> *que si se va del rancho*
> *muy pronto volverá*

Distribute bread, land:
                            I'll follow you.
I renounce my celestial eyelids.
I, Zapata, depart with
the cavalries' morning dew,
a gunshot from the prickly pears
to the pink-walled houses.

> *. . . cintitas pa tu pelo*
> *no llores por tu Pancho . . .*

The moon's asleep on the saddles.
Death, stacked and distributed,
lies with Zapata's soldiers.
Beneath the heavy night's bastions
the dream hides his destiny,
his somber incubating sheet.
The bonfire draws the vigilant air:
grease, sweat, and nocturnal gunpowder.

> *. . . Borrachita me voy*
> *para olvidarte . . .*

We asked for a homeland for the humiliated.
Your knife divides the patrimony
and gunfire and chargers put punishments
and hangman's beard to flight.
Land is distributed with a rifle.
Dusty peasant, don't wait,
after your sweat, for the true light
and heaven parceled on your knees.
Rise up and gallop with Zapata.

> *. . . Yo la quise traer*
> *dijo que no . . .*

Mexico, obstinate agriculture, beloved
land distributed among the dark:
your sweaty centurians rose up
from the swords of maize to the sun.

From the snowy South I've come to sing to you.

Let me gallop in your destiny and take
my fill of gunpowder and ploughshares.

> . . . *Que si habrá de llorar*
> *pa qué volver* . . .

XXXVII

Sandino
(1926)

It was when the crosses
were buried
in our land—they were spent,
invalid, professional.
The dollar came with aggressive teeth
to bite territory,
in America's pastoral throat.
It seized Panama with powerful jaws,
sank its fangs into the fresh earth,
wallowed in mud, whisky, blood,
and swore in a President with a frock coat:
"Give us this day our
daily bribe."
            Later, steel came,
and the canal segregated residences,
the masters here, the servants there.

They rushed to Nicaragua.

They disembarked, dressed in white,
firing dollars and bullets.
But there a captain rose forth,
saying: "No, here you're not putting
your concessions, your bottle."
They promised him a portrait
of the President, with gloves,
ribbons, and patent leather
shoes, recently acquired.
Sandino took off his boots,
plunged into the quivering swamps,
wore the wet ribbon
of freedom in the jungle,

and, bullet by bullet, he answered
the "civilizers."

North American fury
was indescribable: documented
ambassadors convinced
the world that their love was
Nicaragua, sooner or later
order must reach
its sleepy intestines.

Sandino hanged the intruders.

The Wall Street heroes
were devoured by the swamp,
a thunderbolt struck them down,
more than one machete followed them,
a noose awakened them
like a serpent in the night,
and hanging from a tree they were
carried off slowly
by blue beetles
and devouring vines.

Sandino was in the silence,
in the Plaza of the People,
everywhere Sandino,
killing North Americans,
executing invaders.
And when the air corps came,
the offensive of the armed
forces, the incision of
pulverizing powers,
Sandino, with his guerrillas,
was a jungle specter,
a coiled tree
or a sleeping tortoise
or a gliding river.
But tree, tortoise, current
were avenging death,
jungle systems,
the spider's mortal symptoms.

(In 1948
a guerrilla
from Greece, Sparta column,

was the urn of light attacked
by the dollar's mercenaries.
From the mountains he fired
on the octupi from Chicago
and, like Sandino, the stalwart man
from Nicaragua, he was named
"the mountain bandit.")

But when fire, blood,
and dollar didn't destroy
Sandino's proud tower,
the Wall Street guerrillas
made peace, invited
the guerrilla to celebrate,

and a newly hired traitor

shot him with his rifle.

His name is Somoza. To this day
he's ruling in Nicaragua:
the thirty dollars grew
and multiplied in his belly.

This is the story of Sandino,
captain from Nicaragua,
heartbreaking incarnation
of our sand betrayed,
divided and assailed,
martyred and sacked.

XXXVIII

1

**Toward
Recabarren**

The land, the land's metal, the compact
beauty, the iron peacefulness
transformed into spear, lamp or ring,
pure matter, action
of time, welfare
of the naked land.

The mineral was like a star,
fallen and buried.

With the planet's blows, gram
by gram, its light was concealed.
Harsh stratum, clay, sand
covered your hemisphere.

But I loved your salt, your surface.
Your teardrop, your eyelid, your statue.

On the carat of hard purity
my hand sang: I was summoned
in the emerald's nuptial eclogue,
and in the iron pit I put my face one day
until I emanated abyss, resistance, and expansion.

But I knew nothing,

Iron, copper, the salt knew.

Every petal of gold was torn out with blood.
Every metal contains a soldier.

2

Copper   I went to the copper, to Chuquicamata.

It was late in the cordilleras.
The air was a chilled wineglass
of dry transparency.
I lived before on many ships,
but in the desert night
the immense mine glittered
like a blinding ship
with the dazzling dew
of those nocturnal heights.

I closed my eyes: sleep and shadow
spread their massive wings
over me like gigantic birds.
Creeping along, from bump to bump,
while the car danced,
the oblique star, the penetrating
planet, hurled at me, like a spear,
an icy thunderbolt
of cold fire, fraught with doom.

3

It was now midnight, deep night,
like the empty hollow of a bell.
And before my eyes I saw the implacable walls,
the devastated copper in the pyramid.
The blood of those lands was green.

The nocturnal green magnitude
towered to the drenched planets.
Drop by drop a turquoise milk,
a stone dawn,
was built by man
and burned in the immensity,
in the starry open land
of the entire sandy night.

Step by step, then, the shadow
                                led me
by the hand to the Union.
                        It was the month of
    July
in Chile, the cold season.
Other steps and feet, known by
the copper alone, went beside my
steps for many days (or centuries)
(or simply copper months,
stone and stone and stone,
which is to say, of hell in time:
of infinity sustained
by a sulphurous hand).

It was a grimy multitude,
hunger and shreds, solitude,
that excavated the gallery.
That night I didn't see
the countless wounds file by
along the mine's cruel rim.

But I was part of those torments.

The copper vertebrae were wet,
laid bare by sweaty strokes
in the Andean air's infinite light.
To excavate those mineral bones

of the statue buried by centuries,
man constituted the galleries
of an empty theater.
But the hard essence,
the stone in its stature, the copper's
victory fled leaving a crater
disposed like a volcano, as if
that statue, green star, had been torn
from the breast of an iron god
leaving a wan pit hollowed out of the heights.

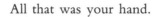

4

**The
Chileans**

All that was your hand.

Your hand was the fingernail
of the mineral compatriot, the beleaguered
     underdog,
the downtrodden human matter,
the tattered little man.
Your hand was like your geography:
it excavated this crater of green darkness,
founded a planet of oceanic stone.

He worked around the arsenals
wielding broken shovels
and setting gunpowder
everywhere, like the eggs
of a deafening hen.

It's an essentially remote crater:
even from the full moon
you could see its depth
made hand by hand by
a certain Rodríguez, a certain Carrasco,
a certain Díaz Iturrieta,
a certain Abarca, a certain Gumersindo,
a certain Chilean named Thousand.

This immensity, fingernail by fingernail,
the broken Chilean, one day and another
day, another winter, sweating blood,
at full speed, in the torpid

atmosphere of the heights,
took it from the mortar,
established it in the regions.

5

**The
Hero**

It wasn't only the tumultuous firmness
of many fingers, not only the shovel,
not only the arm, the hip, the burden
of the entire man and his energy:
it was grief, the uncertainty and rage
of those who excavated the centimeter
of calcareous heights, seeking
the star's green veins,
the phosphorescent recesses
of the buried comets.

Bloody salts were born
of the man consumed in his abyss.
Because it's aggressive Reinaldo
searching for stones, the infinite
Sepúlveda, your son, nephew
of your aunt Eduviges Rojas,
the blazing hero, who dismantles
the mineral cordillera.

And it was, so to speak, by knowing,
by entering the uterine originality
of the womb, in earth and in life,
that I began to die away:
until I immersed into man, into water
teary like stalactites,
like poor gushing blood,
like sweat fallen in the dust.

6

Trades

Other times, with Laferte,
we went farther, to Tarapacá,
by way of blue and ascetic Iquique,
through the limits of the sand.

Elías showed me
the miners' shovels,
every finger of man

worked into the wood,
worn by the friction of every fingertip.
The pressure of those hands melted
the shovels' flint,
and that's how they opened galleries
of earth and stone, metal and acid,
these bitter fingernails, these
blackened belts
of hands that break planets,
and raise the salts to heaven,
saying as the story says,
in the celestial history: "This
is the first day upon the earth."

So that man whom no one saw before
(before that original day),
the prototype of the pickax,
stood over the crusts
of hell: he subdued them
with his rough burning hands,
opened the earth's leaves,
and the captain with white teeth,
the conqueror of nitrate,
appeared in a blue shirt.

7

The   The harsh noon of the great sands
Desert has arrived:
the world is naked,
broad, sterile, and clean to the farthest
sandy frontiers:
listen to the brittle sound
of the live salt, alone in the salt marshes:
the sun shatters its crystals in the empty
expanse and the earth rattles with the
moaning salt's dry and muffled sound.

8

(NOCTURNE)

They see the desert circuit,
the high ethereal pampa night,

the nocturnal circle, space and star,
where the zone of Tamarugal gathers
all the silence lost in time.

A thousand years of silence in a wineglass
of calcareous blue, of distance and moon,
shape the night's naked geography.

I love you, pure land, like so many
contrary things I've loved:
flowers, streets, abundance, rites.

I love you, pure sister of the ocean.
So hard for me, this empty school
in which there was no man, or wall,
or plant—nothing to lean on.

I was alone.
Life was space and solitude.

This was the world's virile bosom.

And I loved the system of your unswerving form,

the extensive precision of your emptiness.

9

**The
Wasteland**

In the wasteland man lived
biting the dust, annihilated.
I went straight to his lair,
thrust my hand amid the lice,
walked the rails to
the desolate dawn,
slept on hard planks,
came off the afternoon shift,
was burned by fumes and iodine,
shook man's hand,
talked with the lady of the house,
indoors among the chickens,
among tatters, in the stench
of scorching poverty.

And when I'd assembled so much
sorrow, when I'd collected so much

blood in the hollow of my heart,
I saw a man made of the same sand
coming from the pure space
of the boundless pampas,
his face calm and expansive,
a full-bodied suit,
his squinting eyes
like indomitable lamps.

Recabarren was his name.

XXXIX

Recabarren
(1921)

His name was Recabarren.

Good-natured, stout, deliberate,
open face, firm forehead,
his broad bearing covered
the deposits of strength
like the numerous sand.
On America's pampa, look
(branch rivers, bright snow,
iron chasms)
at Chile's fractured
biology, like a broken
limb, like an arm
whose phalanges were dispersed
by the traffic of tempests.

On the muscular areas
of metal and nitrate,
on the athletic grandeur
of recently excavated copper,
the little inhabitant lives,
heaped in disorder,
with a forced contract,
teeming with tattered children,
scattered over the desert's
salty surface.

It's the Chilean interrupted
by unemployment or death.

It's the rugged Chilean,

survivor of toil
or shrouded by salt.

The captain of the people
arrived there with his pamphlets.
He took the solitary affronted man
who wrapped his hungry
children in tattered shawls,
who accepted those cruel
injustices, and told him:
"Join your voice to another voice.
Join your hand to another hand."
He frequented the nitrate's
ominous retreats, filled the pampa
with his paternal investiture,
and in the invisible den
all the miners saw him.

Every clobbered "stiff" arrived,
each and every grievance came:
they entered like phantoms
with pale pulverized voices
and left his hands with a new dignity.
The word was spread throughout the pampa.
And he traveled the entire country
founding *pueblo*, raising
broken spirits.
His freshly printed newspapers
entered the galleries
of coal, rose up to the copper,
and the people kissed the columns
that for the first time carried
the voice of the downtrodden.

He organized the wilderness.
He took books and songs
to the walls of terror,
united grievance after grievance,
and the slave without voice or mouth,
the widespread suffering,
assumed a name—it was called People,
Proletariat, Union—
it had person and presence.

And this transformed inhabitant
formed in combat,

this valiant organism,
this implacable spirit,
this unalterable metal,
this unity of sorrows,
this fortress of mankind,
this road toward tomorrow,
this infinite cordillera,
this germinal springtime,
this armament of the poor
issued from that suffering,
from the country's bowels,
from everything harsh and hammered,
from the loftiest and most eternal,
and it was called Party.

                              Communist
Party.

                    That was its name.
The struggle was fierce. The gold's
owners fell like vultures.
They countered with calumny.
"This Communist Party
is financed by Peru,
by Bolivia, by foreigners."
They fell on the presses
acquired drop by drop
with the combatants' sweat,
and they attacked, breaking them,
burning them, scattering
the people's typography.
They persecuted Recabarren,
denied him entry and movement.
But he congregated his seed
in the abandoned tunnels
and the bastion was defended.

Then North American
and English entrepreneurs,
their lawyers, senators,
representatives, presidents,
spilt blood in the arena—
they corralled, bound,
and assassinated our kin,
the deep strength of Chile,
left crosses of executed workers

beside the pathways of the
immense yellow pampa,
bodies heaped
in the sandy hollows.

Once they made the men
who asked for school and bread
come to Iquique, on the coast.
There, corralled together in a patio,
they were disposed
for death.
      They fired
with a hissing machine gun,
with rifles tacitly
disposed, upon the heaping
pile of sleeping workers.
The blood soaked Iquique's
pale sand like a river,
and there lies the fallen blood,
still burning over the years
like an implacable corolla.

But the resistance survived.
The light organized by Recabarren's
hands, the red flags,
traveled from mines to towns,
from cities to seedbeds,
they rolled with the train wheels,
assumed cement foundations,
conquered streets, plazas, farms,
factories choked with dust,
wounds opened by springtime:
everything sang and struggled to overcome
in the unity of the dawning time.

How much has happened since then,
how much blood upon blood,
how many struggles upon the earth.
Hours of splendid conquest,
triumphs won drop by drop,
bitter streets, defeated,
zones dark as tunnels,
razor-edged betrayals
that seemed to sever life,
repressions armed with hatred,
militarily crowned.

The earth seemed to give way.

But the struggle goes on.

**Envoi
(1949)**

Recabarren, in these days
of persecution, in the anguish
of my exiled brothers,
assailed by a traitor, and with
the homeland enveloped in hatred,
struck by tyranny,
I remember the terrible struggle
of your imprisonment, your first
steps, your solitude
of an unyielding turret,
and when, leaving the wasteland,
one man and another joined you
to collect the dough
of the humble bread defended
by the unity of the august people.

**Father
of Chile**

Recabarren, Chile's offspring,
father of Chile, our father,
in your construction, in your line
forged in lands and tempests,
the strength of the victorious
days to come is born.

You're homeland, pampa and people,
sand, clay, school, home,
resurrection, fist, offensive,
order, march, attack, wheat,
struggle, greatness, resistance.

Recabarren, beneath your gaze
we swear we'll cleanse the country's
festering mutilations.

We swear that freedom
will raise its naked flower
over the dishonored sand.

We swear we'll follow in your footsteps
to the victory of the people.

XL

August Brazil, how much love I'd need
to stretch out in your lap,
to wrap myself in your giant leaves,
in vegetable growth, in the living
detritus of emeralds: to stalk you,
Brazil, from the sacred
rivers that nourish you,
to dance on the terraces in the light
of the fluvial moon, to disperse myself
among your uninhabited territories,
seeing massive beasts being
born in the clay, surrounded
by metallic white birds.

How many meanders you'd give me.
To enter the old seaport again,
to stroll through the barrios, to smell
your strange rite, to descend
to your circulatory centers,
to your generous heart.

But I cannot.

Once, in Bahía, women
from the martyred district,
from the ancient slave market
(where today the new slavery—hunger,
tatters, the sorrowful state—
lives on as before in the same land),
gave me flowers and a letter,
some tender words and some flowers.

I cannot separate my voice from whatever suffers.
I know how much
invisible truth your spacious
natural shores would give me.
I know that the secret flower, the fluttering
multitude of butterflies,
all the fertile ferments

of lives and forests
await me with their theory
of inexhaustible moisture,

but I cannot, I cannot

but wrench from your silence
the people's voice again,
hold it aloft like the jungle's
most splendorous feather,
set it beside me and love it
until it sings through my lips.

That's why I see Prestes marching
toward freedom, toward the doors
that in you, Brazil, seem closed,
nailed shut to sorrow, impenetrable.
I see Prestes, his hunger-conquering
column, crossing the jungle
toward Bolivia, pursued
by the pale-eyed tyrant.
When he returns to his people
and rings his combatant bells,
they imprison him, and deliver
his consort to Germany's
brown-shirted executioner.

          (Poet, in your book you seek
ancient Greek sorrows,
the orbs oppressed
by ancient maledictions,
your twisted eyelids
pursue invented torments,
and you don't see at your own doorstep
the oceans that pound
the people's dark breast.)
His daughter is born in martyrdom.
But she disappears
beneath the ax, in the gas, swallowed
by the Gestapo's
murderous swamps.
                    O, prisoner's
torment! O, unspeakable
confined suffering
of our aggrieved captain!

Prestes from Brazil (1949)

(Poet, strike from your book
Prometheus and his chain.
The ancient fable does not possess
such calcined grandeur,
such terrifying tragedy.)

For eleven years they keep Prestes
behind iron bars,
in the deathly silence,
not daring to assassinate him.

There's no news for his people.
Tyranny expunges the name
of Prestes in its dark world.

And his name was mute for eleven years.
His name lived like a tree,
revered and awaited
among all his people.

Until freedom fetched him
from his penitentiary
and he rose to the light again,
beloved, victorious, and kindly,
free of all the hatred
they heaped on his head.
I remember that in 1945
I was with him in São Paulo.
(His frame fragile and firm,
pale as marble
unearthed in the cistern,
fine as the purity
of air in the wilds,
pure as grandeur
safekept by sorrow.)
For the first time he spoke
to his people, in Pacaembú.
The great stadium throbbed with
one hundred thousand red hearts
that waited to see him and touch him.
He arrived in an indescribable
surge of song and tenderness,
one hundred thousand handkerchiefs
waved at him like a forest.
He looked on beside me with
his deep eyes while I spoke.

XLI

Pronounced
in Pacaembú
(Brazil, 1945)

How many things I'd like to tell you today,
    Brazilians,
how many stories, struggles, disappointments,
    victories
harbored in my heart for many years, unexpressed
    thoughts
and greetings. Greetings from the Andean snows,
greetings from the Pacific Ocean, words spoken to
    me
by passing workers, by miners and stonemasons,
    all
the founders of my faraway country.
What did the snow, cloud, and fog tell me?
What secret did the sailor tell me?
The little girl who gave me some spikes of grain?

Their message was one. It was: Greetings to
    Prestes.
Go look for him, they told me, in the jungles and
    rivers.
Remove his shackles, look for his cell, call him.
And if they don't let you talk to him, look at him
    until
your eyes are tired, and tell us tomorrow what
    you've seen.

Today I'm proud to see him surrounded
by a sea of victorious hearts.
I'm going to tell Chile: I greeted him in the air
of his people's free flags.

I remember in Paris, years ago, one night
I spoke to the multitude, I went to seek help
for Republican Spain, for the struggling nation.
Spain was full of ruins and glory.
The French quietly heeded my summons.
I sought help in the name of all that exists
and told them: The new heroes, those who in
    Spain are fighting and dying,
Modesto, Líster, Pasionaria, Lorca,
are the offspring of America's heroes, the brethren
of Bolívar, O'Higgins, San Martín, Prestes.

Pronounced in Pacaembú (Brazil, 1945)

And when I mentioned the name of Prestes there
    was an immense swelling sound
in France's air: Paris was hailing him.
Old workers with teary eyes
looked to the depths of Brazil and Spain.

I'm going to tell you a little story.

Beside the great coal mines, which advance
    beneath the sea
in Chile, in the cold seaport of Talcahuano,
long ago, a Soviet freighter made port.
(Chile had not yet established relations
with the Union of Soviet Socialist Republics.
That's why the stupid police
prohibited the Russian sailors from going ashore,
the Chileans from going aboard.)
When night fell
miners arrived by the thousands from the great
    mines,
men, women, children, and from the hills,
with their little miners' lamps,
throughout the night they flashed signals
to the ship that came from Soviet seaports.

That dark night had stars:
human stars, the lamps of the people.

Today, too, from the far corners
of our America, from free Mexico, from thirsty
    Peru,
from Cuba, from populous Argentina,
from Uruguay, asylum of exiled brothers,
the people greet you, Prestes, with their little
    lamps
in which the high hopes of mankind shine on.
That's why they sent me through America's air,
so I could see you and tell them then
how you were, what their captain silent for
so many years of
solitude and shadow was saying.

I'm going to tell them that you bear no hatred.
That you only want your country to live.

And that freedom may grow in the depths
of Brazil like an eternal tree.

I would like to tell you, Brazil, many unspoken
    things
carried all these years between skin and soul—
    blood,
sorrows, triumphs, everything that poets and
    people
should say to one another: sometime, someday,
    perhaps.

Today I ask for a great silence of volcanoes and
    rivers.

I ask for a great silence of lands and worthy men.

I ask America for silence from the snow to the
    pampa.

Silence: The Word to the Captain of the People.

Silence: Let Brazil speak through his mouth.

XLII

**The
Tyrants
Again**

Today the hunt spreads
over Brazil again,
the slave traders' cold greed
runs in hot pursuit:
on Wall Street they ordered
their porcine satellites
to bury their fangs
in the people's wounds,
and the hunt began
in Chile, in Brazil, in all
our Americas ravaged
by merchants and executioners.

My people concealed my path,
hid my verses with their hands,
preserved me from death,
and in Brazil the people's

infinite door closes the roads
where Prestes again
resists the oppressor.

Brazil, may your sorrowing
captain be safekept for you,
Brazil, may you not have
to reconstruct his effigy
from memory, tomorrow,
piece by piece,
to erect it in austere stone,
not having allowed your heart
to savor the freedom that he can
still, still conquer for you, Brazil.

XLIII

**The Day
Will Come**

Liberators, in this twilight
of America, in the morning's
forsaken darkness,
I give you my people's
infinite leaf, the exultation
of every hour of struggle.

Blue hussars, fallen
in the depths of time,
soldiers in whose newly
embroidered flags awaken
today's soldiers, communists,
combatant heirs
of the metallurgic torrents,
heed my voice born
of the glaciers, raised
aloft in the daily bonfire
through sheer love of duty.
We're from the same land, the same
persecuted people,
the same struggle encircles the waist
of our America:
                    Have you seen
in the night your brother's
somber cave?

      Have you fathomed
his sinister life?
            The scattered heart
of the people, abandoned and submerged!
Someone who received the hero's peace
stored it away in his wine cellar, someone
stole the fruits of the bloody harvest
and divided the geography,
establishing hostile shores,
zones of desolate blind shadow.

Glean from the lands the shrouded
throb of sorrow, the solitude,
the wheat of the threshed fields:
something germinates beneath the flags:
the ancient voice calls us again.
Descend to the mineral roots,
and in the desolate metal's veins
reach mankind's struggle on earth,
beyond the martyrdom that mauls
the hands destined for the light.
Don't renounce the day bestowed on you
by those who died struggling. Every spike
is born of a grain seeded in the earth,
and like the wheat, the innumerable people
join roots, accumulate spikes,
and in the tempest unleashed
they rise up to the light of the universe.

THE
SAND
BETRAYED

Perhaps, perhaps oblivion on earth, like a mantle
can develop growth and nourish life
(maybe), like dark humus in the forest.

Perhaps, perhaps man, like a blacksmith, seeks
live coals, the hammering of iron on iron,
without entering the coal's blind cities,
without closing his eyes, not sounding
the depths, waters, minerals, catastrophes.
Perhaps, but my plate's another, my food's distinct:
my eyes didn't come to bite oblivion:
my lips open over all time, and all time,
not just part of time has consumed my hands.

That's why I'll tell you these sorrows I'd like to put
     aside,
I'll oblige you to live among their burns again,
not to mark time as in a terminal, before departing,
or to beat the earth with our brows,
or to fill our hearts with salt water,
but to set forth knowing, to touch rectitude
with decisions infinitely charged with meaning,

that severity may be a condition of happiness, that
we may thus become invincible.

I

The Hangmen

Saurian, scaly America coiled
around vegetable growth, around the flagpole
erected in the swamp:
you nursed terrible children
with poisonous serpent's milk,
torrid cradles incubated
and covered a bloodthirsty
progeny with yellow clay.
The cat and the scorpion fornicated
in the savage land.

The light fled from branch to branch,
but slumbering man did not awaken.

The blanket smelled of sugarcane,
machetes had rolled into
the surliest siesta site,
and in the cantinas' rarefied crest
the shoeless day laborer
spat out his boastful independence.

Doctor Francia

The Paraná in the tangled wet
zones, palpitating with other rivers
where the water network—Yabebiri,
Acaray, Igurey, twin jewels
tinged with quebracho, enveloped
by dense crowns of copal—
runs toward the Atlantic sheets
dredging the delirium of the purple
nazarene tree, the roots
of the curupay in its sandy sleep.

From the hot ooze, from the devouring
alligator's thrones, amid
the wild pestilence
Dr. Francia cruised

toward Paraguay's easy chair.
And he lived amid rose windows
of rose-colored masonry
like a sordid Caesarian statue
shrouded by the dark spider's veils.

Solitary grandeur in the parlor
filled with mirrors, black
bugbear on red felt
and frightened rats in the night.
False column, perverse
academy, agnosticism
of a leprous king surrounded
by extensive maté fields,
drinking platonic numbers
on the gallows of the executed,
counting triangles of stars,
measuring stellar keys,
stalking Paraguay's
orange-colored dusk,
timing the agony
of the man executed at his window,
with his hand on the bolt
of the shackled twilight.

Studies on the table,
eyes on the firmament's
spur, on geometry's
inverted crystalware,
while the intestinal blood
of the man murdered by rifle butts
ran down the steps,
sucked up by green swarms
of glistening flies.

He sealed Paraguay like
his majesty's nest, bound
torture and mud to its borders.
When his silhouette glides
through the streets, the Indians
turn their eyes toward the walls:
his shadow slithers along leaving
two shivering walls.

When death visits
Dr. Francia, he's mute,

motionless, tied up within,
alone in his cave, arrested
by ropes of paralysis,
and he dies alone, without anyone
entering his chamber: no one dares
touch the master's door.

And bound by his serpents,
tongue-tied, stewing in his juice,
he rattles and dies, lost
in the palace's solitude,
while the night, established
like a chair of learning, devours
the miserable capitals
spattered by martyrdom.

Rosas
(1829–1849)

It is so hard to see through the earth
(not through time, which raises its transparent
    glass,
illuminating the lofty dew's résumé),
but the dense earth of flour and rancor,
storeroom hardened with corpses and metals,
doesn't let me peer into the depths
where the interwoven solitude rejects me.

But I'll speak to them, to mine, those who one
    day
fled to my flag, when purity was
a crystal star in its fabric.

Sarmiento, Alberdi, Oro, del Carril:
my pure land, later soiled,
preserved for you
the light of its metallic slenderness,
and among poor agricultural adobes
exiled thoughts
were being spun with hard minerals
and spurs of vineyard sugar.

Chile disseminated them in her fortitude,
gave them salt from her seaboard,
and sowed the exiled seeds.

Meanwhile, the gallop on the prairies.
The hitching ring was split over strands

of celestial hair,
and the pampa bit the horseshoes
of the wet frenzied beasts.

Daggers, government thugs' guffaws
atop martyrdom. From river to river,
the moon crowned atop the whiteness
with a crest of indescribable darkness!

Argentina plundered by rifle butt
in the misty dawn, beaten
and bled to madness, deserted,
ridden roughshod by savage overseers!

You became a procession of red vineyards,
you were a mask, a sealed tremor,
substituted in the air
by a tragic wax hand.
It emerged from you one night—
passageways, slabs of blackened stone,
steps where sound was submerged, carnival
crossroads, with corpses and buffoons,
and an eyelid's silence closing
over all the night's eyes.

Your foamy wheat, where did it flee?
Your fruit-bearing elegance, your wide mouth,
everything that moves your strings
to sing, your vibrant leather
of a great drum, a boundless star,
were silenced beneath the enclosed
cupola's implacable solitude.

Planet, latitude, powerful clarity,
the nocturnal silence that came mounted
on a vertiginous sea was gathered
on your rim, on the ribbon of shared snow,
and wave after wave the naked water reported,
the trembling gray wind unleashed its sand,
the night stirred us with its steppe-land lament.

But people and wheat were kneaded: then
the earthly head was groomed, the buried
light's filaments were combed, agony
tested the free doors, destroyed by the wind,
and from the clouds of dust on the road, one

by one, submerged dignities, schools,
intelligence, faces, ascended in the dust
until they became starry unities,
statues of light, pure meadowlands.

Ecuador

Tunguragua gushes red oil,
Sangay pours burning
honey on the snow,
from your loftiest snow-crowned
churches Imbabura spews
fish and plants, hard branches
from the inaccessible infinity,
and toward the wastelands—coppery
moon, crackling edifice—
lets your scars fall
like veins on Antisana,
in Pumachaca's wrinkled
solitude, in Pambamarca's
sulphuric solemnity,
volcano and moon, cold and quartz,
glacial flames, catastrophic
movement, vaporous
and tempestuous patrimony.

Ecuador, Ecuador, violet tail
of an absent comet, in the iridescent
multitudes that cover you
with a fruit shop's infinite skin,
death makes the rounds with its funnel,
fever burns in the poor barrios,
hunger's a plowshare
with barbed tines in the earth,
and pity pounds on your breast
with coarse cloth and convents,
like a disease soaked
in fermentations of tears.

**García
Moreno**

That's where the tyrant emerged.
García Moreno's his name.
The gloved jackal, a patient
sacristy bat,
gathers ash and torment

in his silk hat
and plunges his fingernails
into the equatorial rivers' blood.

With his little feet sheathed
in patent leather slippers,
waxing and crossing himself
on the altar carpets,
his cassock submerged
in processional waters,
he dances in crime, dragging
freshly executed cadavers,
ripping the breasts of the dead,
parading their bones, flying
over the coffins, dressed
in plumes of ominous cloth.

In the Indian villages, blood
falls aimlessly, there's fear
in all the streets and shadows
(beneath the bells there's fear
that rings and rises to the night),
and the monasteries' thick walls,
upright, immobile, sealed,
weigh heavily on Quito.

Everything sleeps with the oxidized
gold fleurons in the cornices,
the angels sleep hanging
from their sacramental coatracks,
everything sleeps like a priestly
tissue, everything suffers
beneath the membranous night.

But cruelty doesn't sleep.
Cruelty with white mustachios
struts with gloves and claws,
nails obscure hearts
to the dominion's iron gate.
Until the day when light penetrates
the palace like a dagger
and pierces the vest, plunging a thunderbolt
into the immaculate shirt.

So García Moreno left
the palace once more, flying off

to inspect the graves,
determinedly mortuary,
but this time he tumbled to the bottom
of the massacres, confined,
amid the nameless victims,
to the dampness of the dump heap.

America's Witches

Central America—trampled by owls,
lubricated by acid sweat—
before entering your burned jasmine,
consider me your ship's fiber,
a wing of your wood assailed
by the twin foam,
and fill me with intoxicating aroma,
pollen and plumes from your cup,
your waters' germinal shores,
the curly lines of your nest.
But the witches murder the metals
of resurrection, shut the doors
and darken the dwelling
of the dazzling birds.

Estrada

Perhaps Estrada's coming, diminutive,
in his ancient dwarf's frock,
and between coughs
Guatemala's walls ferment,
incessantly irrigated
by urine and tears.

Ubico

Or Ubico takes to the trails,
passing through prisons
on motorcycle, cold
as stone, figurehead
of the hierarchy of fear.

Gómez

Gómez, Venezuela's quagmire,
slowly submerges faces,

intellects, in his crater.
Man falls in at night,
flailing his arms, protecting
his face from the cruel blows,
and swallowed up by the quaking bogs,
he sinks into subterranean chambers,
appears on roads
digging, shackled in irons,
until he dies, mangled,
missing, lost.

Machado

In Cuba Machado harnessed his Island
with machines, imported torments
manufactured in the United States,
machine guns spat,
mowing down phosphorescence,
the marine nectar of Cuba,
and the student with a flesh wound
was cast into the water where
the sharks finished
His Excellency's job.
The assassin's hand reached
Mexico, and Mella spun into the street
like a bloodied discus thrower
while Cuba burned, blue,
papered in lottery,
mortgaged with sugar.

Melgarejo

Bolivia dies within its walls
like a rare flower:
defeated generals
ride high in their saddles
and blast the skies with pistol shots.
Mask of Melgarejo,
besotted beast, filthy scum
of betrayed minerals,
beard of infamy, horrendous beard
above the embittered mountains,
beard dragged in delirium,
beard filled with bloodclots,
beard discovered in gangrenous
nightmares, roving beard

galloping in the pastures,
cohabiting in the parlors,
while the Indian and his burden traverse
the last sheet of oxygen,
trotting through the bled
corridors of poverty.

Bolivia
(22 March
1865)

Belzu has triumphed. Night. La Paz blazes
with the last gunshots. Dry dust
and sad dance rise to the heights
entwined with lunar alcohol
and horrendous purple, freshly spilt.
Melgarejo has fallen, his head
strikes against the bloody summit's
mineral ridge, his gold
braid, his gold-embroidered
dress coat, his torn
shirt drenched in malignant sweat,
lie beside the horse's detritus
and the recently executed man's brains.
Belzu at Court, amid gloves
and frock coats, receives smiles,
the dominion of the dark people
in the alcoholic heights is divided up,
new favorites glide
through waxed drawing rooms,
and lights from tears and lanterns
fall on the velvet, bedraggled
by a number of flash fires.

Melgarejo, tempestuous specter
barely sustained by his fury,
circulates among the multitudes.
He hears the constituency that was once his,
the deafened masses, the piercing
cry, the fire blazing
above the hills, the new
conqueror's window.

His life (fragment
of blind force and opera unleashed
above the craters and mesetas,
regiment dream, in which clothes
are spilt upon the defenseless land

with cardboard sabers, but there are wounds
that stain, with real death
and decapitations, rural plazas left,
in the wake of His Excellency's
masked chorus and speeches,
with horse manure, silk, blood,
and shifts of the dead, battered, stiff,
pierced by the rapid riflemens'
thunderous volleys)
has fallen to the depths of the dust,
of everything despicable and empty,
of a presumed death swamped
in ignominy, but he snatches his jaws
from defeat like an imperial bull,
paws the metallic sands,
and the Bolivian minotaur
staggers headlong
toward the strident gold drawing rooms.
He enters the crowd, cuts through
nameless masses, clumsily scales
the estranged throne,
and attacks the conquering caudillo. Belzu
tumbles down, his starch soiled, broken his glass
that falls scattering its liquid light,
his breast riddled forever,
while the conflagration's solitary
assailant bloody buffalo
leans his bulk against the balcony,
shouting: "Belzu died. Who's alive?
Answer." And from the plaza,
a hoarse earthly voice, a black roar
of panic and horror, replies: "Viva,
sí, Malgarejo, viva Melgarejo,"
the dead man's same followers,
who celebrated the cadaver bleeding
on the Palace steps: "Viva,"
shouts the colossal puppet that covers
the entire balcony with tattered clothes,
slum mud and filthy blood.

Martínez　Martínez, the quack
(1932)　from El Salvador, distributes flasks
of multicolored remedies
which the ministers accept

with deep bows and scraping.
The little vegetarian witch doctor
passes his time prescribing in the palace
while torturous hunger
howls in the cane fields.
Martínez then decrees:
and in a few days twenty thousand
assassinated peasants
decompose in the villages
that Martínez orders burned
with ordinances of hygiene.
Back in the Palace he returns
to his syrups, and receives
the American ambassador's
swift congratulations.
"Western culture
is safe," says he—
"western Christianity,
and besides, good business,
banana concessions
and control of customs."

And together they drink a long
glass of champagne, while hot
rain falls on the putrid
gatherings of the charnel house.

The Satrapies

Trujillo, Somoza, Carías,
until today, until this bitter
month of September
of the year 1948,
with Moriñigo (or Natalicio)
in Paraguay: our history's
voracious hyenas, rodents
of our flags conquered
with so much blood and so much fire,
wallowing in their haciendas,
infernal plunderers,
satraps a thousand times sellouts
and sellers, egged on
by New York's wolves.
Dollar-hungry machines,
soiled in the martyred
peoples' sacrifice,

pandering merchants
of American bread and air,
slimy executioners, herd
of whoremongering caciques
with no law other than torture
and the people's gnawing hunger.

Doctors "honoris causa"
from Columbia University,
their gowns concealing tusks
and knives, ferocious
nomads of the Waldorf Astoria
and the accursed chambers
where the prisoner's eternal
ages decompose.
Little vultures received
by Mr. Truman, deluged
with watches, decorated
for "Loyalty," bloodsuckers
of nations, there's just one
worse than you, just one,
and my country spawned him one day
for the sorrow of my people.

II

**The
Oligarchies**

No, the flags had not yet dried,
the soldiers had not yet slept
when freedom changed clothes,
and was turned into a hacienda:
a caste emerged from
the newly sown lands, a quadrille
of nouveaux riches with coats of arms,
with police and with prisons.

They drew a black line:
"Here on our side, Mexico's
Porfiristas, Chile's
'gentlemen,' gentry from
the Jockey Club of Buenos Aires,
Uruguay's slicked
freebooters, the Ecuadorian
upper crust, clerical
dandies everywhere."

"There on your side, rabble, half-breeds,
Mexico's down-and-outers, gauchos
heaped together in pigsties,
defenseless, tattered bums,
vermin, trash, riffraff,
derelicts, miserable scum,
filthy, shiftless, masses."

Everything was built upon the line.
The Archbishop baptized this wall
and pronounced incendiary anathemas
against the rebel who disregarded
the caste wall.
Bilbao's books were ordered
burned by the hangman.
                          The police
guarded this wall, and the hungry person
who approached the sacred marbles
was clubbed on the head
or locked in agricultural stocks
or booted into the army.

They felt safe and carefree.
The people turned to the streets and countryside
to live crammed together, without windows,
without floors, without shirts,
without schools, without bread.

A phantom wanders, throughout our America,
nourished on detritus, illiterate,
homeless—in our latitudes, as well,
an impoverished fugitive emerges
from the filthy jails, branded
by the fearsome compatriot armed
with suits, warrants and bow ties.

In Mexico they produced pulque
for him, in Chile
violet-colored rotgut wine:
they poisoned him, scraped
his soul, bit by bit,
denied him books and light,
until he gradually bit the dust,
submerged in the tubercular garret,
and then he had no church

burial: his ceremony consisted of
casting him naked amid the rest
of the nameless carrion.

Promulgation of the Funnel Law

They declared themselves patriots.
In the clubs they decorated one another
and set about writing history.
Parliaments were filled with pomp.
Then they divided up
the land, the law,
the best streets, air,
the University, shoes.

Their extraordinary initiative
was the State erected in this
form, the rigid imposture.
It was debated, as usual,
with solemnity and banquets,
first in agricultural circles,
with the military and lawyers.
And the supreme Law was finally
taken to Congress—the famous,
respected, untouchable
Funnel Law.
                    It was passed.

For the rich, square meals.

Garbage for the poor.

Money for the rich.

For the poor, work.

For the rich, mansions.

Hovels for the poor.

Exemptions for the robber baron.

Jail for the man who steals a loaf.

Paris, Paris for the dandies.

The poor to the mines, the desert.

Mr. Rodríguez de la Crota
spoke in the Senate with a mellifluous
elegant voice.
                    "This law, at long last, establishes
the obligatory hierarchy
and above all the principles
of Christianity.
                    It was
necessary as water.
Only the communists, conceived
in hell, as you're well aware,
could object to the Funnel
code, sagacious and severe.
But this Asiatic opposition,
proceeding from subman,
is easy to suppress: to jail with
them all, to the concentration camp,
and that way the distinguished
gentlemen and the obliging
Radical Party lackeys
will stand alone."

There was a round of applause
from the aristocratic benches:
what eloquence, how spiritual,
what a philosopher, what a luminary!
And everyone ran off to fill
his pockets in his business,
one monopolizing milk,
another racketeering in wire,
another stealing in sugar,
and all boisterously proclaiming
themselves patriots, with a monopoly
of patriotism, also accounted for
in the Funnel Law.

**Election in
Chimborongo
(1947)**

In Chimborongo, Chile, long ago
I went to a senatorial election.
I saw how the pillars
of society were elected.
At eleven in the morning
ox carts crammed with sharecroppers

arrived from the country.
It was winter. Wet,
dirty, hungry, barefoot,
the serfs from Chimborongo
climb down from the ox carts.
Grim, sunburnt, tattered,
they're packed together, led
ballots in hand,
marshaled in a bunch
to draw their pay and,
herded like horses,
they're led back
to the ox carts again.

                    Then
they're thrown meat and wine
until they're left brutally
debauched and forgotten.

Later I heard the speech
of the senator thus elected:
"We, Christian patriots,
we, defenders of the order,
we, children of the spirit."
And his belly trembled,
his voice of a besotted cow
that seemed to sway
like a mammoth's trunk
in the sinister caverns
of howling prehistory.

**The
Cream**

Grotesque, false aristocrats
of our America, recently
stuccoed mammals, sterile
youths, judicious asses,
malignant landed gentry, heroes
of the binge at the Club,
bank and bourse robbers,
fops, dandies, swells,
dapper Embassy tigers,
pallid principal daughters,
carnivorous flowers, harvests
of the perfumed caverns,
blood, manure-and-sweat-

sucking vines,
strangling lianas,
chains of feudal boas.

While the meadows trembled
with the gallop of Bolívar
or O'Higgins (poor soldiers,
scourged masses, barefoot heroes),
you formed the ranks
of the king, the clerical cesspool,
the betrayal of the flags,
but when the defiant wind
of the people, waving their lances,
left us the country in our arms,
you rose up wiring lands,
measuring fences, hoarding
areas and beings, distributing
police and monopolies.

The people returned from the wars,
plunged into the mines, into the dark
depths of the slums—they
fell into stony furrows,
powered greasy factories,
procreating in tenements,
in rooms filled
with other wretched beings.

They foundered in wine until they
were lost, abandoned, invaded
by an army of lice
and vampires, surrounded
by walls and police stations,
without bread, without music,
falling into the dementing solitude
where Orpheus leaves nothing but
a guitar for their soul,
a guitar adorned
with ribbons and laments,
and he sings above peoples
like the bird of poverty.

Celestial
Poets

What did you do, Gidists,
intellectualists, Rilkists,

mistificators, false existentialist
sorcerers, surrealist
butterflies burning
in a tomb, Europeanized
cadavers of fashion,
pale worms of capitalist
cheese, what did you do
in the presence of the reign of anguish,
in the face of this obscure human being,
this trampled composure,
this head submerged
in manure, this essence
of harsh downtrodden lives?

You did nothing but flee:
you sold heaped detritus,
pursued celestial hair,
cowardly plants, broken fingernails,
"pure Beauty," "sortilege,"
works of the fainthearted
designed to avert the eyes,
to entangle delicate
pupils, to subsist
on a plate of filthy leftovers
thrown to you by the gentlemen,
without seeing the stone in agony,
without defending, without conquering,
blinder than wreaths
in the graveyard, when rain
falls on the tombs'
motionless decomposed flowers.

Exploiters   That's how your life was
denied, subdued, scratched,
stolen, young America.

From the precipices of rage,
where the caudillo trampled
freshly buried ashes and smiles,
to the patriarchal masks
of the mustachioed gentlemen
who presided at the table
blessing those present
and concealing their real

faces of dark satiety,
of somber concupiscence
and covetous cavities:
fauna of the city's cold
carnivores, terrible tigers,
man–eaters,
experts in hunting
the people submerged in darkness,
defenseless in the corners,
in the cellars of the earth.

Fops   The blue product, the petal of arrogant
putrefaction, lived among
the cattle-raising, paper-pushing,
or cocktail-tippling miasma.

There was Chile's fop, little
Raúl Aldunate (conqueror
of magazines with others' hands,
hands that murdered Indians),
Lieutenant Peacock, Major
Business, he who buys letters
and esteems himself lettered, buys
a saber and believes he's a soldier,
but can't buy purity,
so spits like a snake.

Poor America resold
in the blood markets
by buried suckers
that resurface
"grandstanding" in the salons
of Santiago and Minas Gerais,
little canine lady-killers,
useless stuffed shirts,
graveyard golf clubs.
Poor America masked
by elegant transients,
falsifiers of faces,
while below, black wind
pierces the battered heart
and the coal's hero rolls
into the bone pit of the poor,
swept away by pestilence,

blanketed by darkness,
leaving seven hungry children
to be turned out to the roads.

**The
Favorites**

In tyranny's dense
purple cheese another worm
awakens: the favorite.

He's the skulking coward hired
to praise dirty hands.
He's an orator or journalist.
Suddenly he surfaces in the palace,
enthusiastically masticating
the sovereign's dejections,
lucubrating at length
on his gestures, muddying
the water and casting for his fish
in the purulent lagoon.
Let's just call him Darío Poblete,
or Jorge Delano "Coke."
(It's all the same, call him
as you like, he existed when
Machado slandered Mella,
after assassinating him.)

There Poblete would have written
about the "Vile enemies"
of the "Pericles from Havana."
Later Poblete kissed
Trujillo's horseshoes,
Moriñigo's saddle,
Gabriel González's anus.

He was the same yesterday
(working as a soldier of fortune,
hired to lie, to hide
executions and plundering)
as today, raising his cowardly
pen over Pisagua's
torments, over the grief
of thousands of men and women.

The tyrants in our black
martyred geography

always found a slimy clerk
to spread the lie
and say, *the Supreme Commander,*
the Founding Father, the Great Statesman
who governs us, sliding his
thieving black claws
through the prostituted ink.
When the cheese is consumed
and the tyrant tumbles to hell,
Poblete disappears,
Delano "Coke" vanishes,
the worm returns to the manure
to wait for the turn of the infamous wheel
that brings tyrannies to and fro,
to emerge smiling
with a new speech written
for the despot that rises forth.

Therefore, people, pursue
the worm above all, crush its soul
and let its squished liquid,
its dark viscous matter,
be the final script,
the farewell to an ink
we'll expunge from the earth.

**The
Dollar's
Lawyers**

American inferno, our bread
soaked in poison, there's another
tongue in your perfidious fire:
the native lawyer
of the foreign company.

It's he who shackles the irons
of slavery in your country,
and disdainfully parades
with the managerial caste
beholding our tattered flags
with a superior air.

When New York's imperial
advance guards (engineers,
calculators, surveyors,
experts) come
to measure conquered land,
tin, petroleum, bananas,

nitrate, copper, manganese,
sugar, iron, rubber, soil,
an obscure midget steps forth,
with a yellow smile,
and suavely advises
the new invaders:

You don't have to pay
these natives so much,
it's imprudent to raise
their salaries. It's ill-advised.
These wastrels, these half-breeds
would only get drunk
with so much money. God forbid.
They're primitives, little more
than beasts, I know them well.
Don't pay them so much.

He's adopted. They clothe him
in livery. He dresses like a gringo,
spits like a gringo. He dances
like a gringo, and climbs.

He has a car, whisky, a printing press,
they elect him judge and representative,
decorate him, he becomes Minister,
and has the Government's ear.
He knows who's bribable.
He knows who's bribed.
He licks, lubricates, decorates,
cajoles, smiles, threatens.
And so the bled republics
are drained through the seaports.

Where, you'll ask, does this virus
live—this lawyer,
this ferment of detritus,
this hard bloodthirsty louse,
fattened on our blood?
He inhabits the low equatorial
regions, Brazil,
but his dwelling is also
America's central sash.

You'll find him in the craggy
heights of Chuquicamata.

Wherever he smells riches he climbs
mountains, crosses abysses,
with his code's prescriptions
for stealing our land.
You'll find him in Puerto Limón,
in Ciudad Trujillo, in Iquique,
in Caracas, in Maracaibo,
in Antofagasta, in Honduras,
jailing our brother,
accusing his compatriot,
dispossessing peons, opening
landowners' and judges' doors,
buying newspapers, directing
the police, the club, the rifle,
against his forsaken family.

Strutting about, dressed
in tuxedo, at receptions,
inaugurating monuments
with this phrase: *Ladies and gentlemen,*
our Country before our lives,
she's our mother, she's our soil,
let's defend the order, let's make
new prisons, more jails.

And he dies in glory, this eminent,
patrician, "patriotic" senator—
decorated by the Pope,
illustrious, prosperous, feared—
while the tragic dispossessed
among our dead, those who plunged
their hands into the copper, scraped
the deep and severe earth,
die beaten and forgotten,
hurriedly placed
in their burial boxes:
a name, a number on the cross
buffeted by the wind,
obliterating even the heroes' cipher.

Diplomats
(1948)

If you're born a fool in Rumania
you pursue the fool's profession,
if you're a fool in Avignon
your quality is known

by France's venerable stones,
by the schools and disrespectful
farm boys.
But if you're born a fool in Chile
you'll soon be appointed Ambassador.
Whether your name is fool John Doe
or fool Joaquín Fernández or fool
So-and-So, keep a well-trimmed
beard if at all possible.
It's all that's required
to "enter into negotiations."

Then you'll send an expert report
on your spectacular
presentation of credentials,
saying: *Etc., the carriage,*
etc., His Excellency, etc.,
clichés, etc., benevolent.

Assume a solemn voice and a
protective cow's tone,
be decorated jointly
with Trujillo's envoy,
discreetly maintain
a "garçonière" ("You know
the convenience of these things
for Border Treaties"),
remit in slightly disguised form
the doctoral newspaper's
editorial that you read over breakfast
the day before yesterday: it's a "report."

Mingle with the "cream"
of "society," with that country's
fools, acquire all
the silver you can buy,
speak at anniversaries
beside bronze horses,
saying: *Ahem, the ties,*
etc., ahem, etc.,
ahem, the descendants,
etc., the race, ahem, the pure,
the sacrosanct, ahem, etc.

And keep a stiff upper lip:
You're a good Chilean

diplomat, you're a decorated
and prodigious fool.

The Bordellos

The bordello, born of prosperity,
accompanied the banner
of stacked bills:
respected bilge
of capital, ship's hold
of my times.
                They were mechanized
brothels in the hair
of Buenos Aires, fresh meat
exported, owing to adversity
in remote cities and fields,
where money stalked
the earthen pitchers' movements
and imprisoned the vine.
Rural brothels, of a winter
night, with horses
at the village outskirts
and bewildered girls
falling from sale to sale
in the magnates' hands.
Langorous provincial call houses
in which the town's gentry
—dictators of the wine harvest—
startle the venereal night
with chilling death rattles.
Hidden in the corners,
a flock of whores, inconstant
phantoms, passengers
of the mortal train—now they've taken you,
now you're in the sullied net,
now you can't return to the sea,
now they stalked you and hunted you down,
now you're dead in the void
of the rawest part of life,
now your shadow slinks
along the walls: throughout
the earth these walls
lead to death alone.

**Procession
in Lima
(1947)**

There were many carrying
the idol on their shoulders,
the crowd's tail
was a dense sea swell
with purple phosphorescence.
Dancing, they jumped, raising
solemn masticated murmurs
that merged with frying food
and doleful drums.

Purple vests, purple
shoes, hats,
filled the avenues with
violet stains, like a river
of pustulent diseases
emptying into the cathedral's
useless stained glass.
Something infinitely lugubrious
like incense, the copious
agglomeration of sores
merged with the compact human
river's aphrodisiac flames,
wounding the eyes.

I saw the obese landowner,
sweating in his surplices,
scratch the large drops of holy
wax on the nape of his neck.

I saw the sterile mountains'
downtrodden serf,
the Indian, face lost
in his earthen vessels, the herder
of sweet llamas, austere girls
of the sacristy,
village teachers
with blue, hungry faces.

Narcotized dancers
with purple gowns,
the blacks stomped along
on invisible drums.

And all Peru pounded
its breast, gazing at the statue
of a prudish lady,

sky blue and primrose,
navigating those heads
in her candied fruit boat
swollen with sweaty air.

**Standard
Oil Co.**

When the drill bored down
toward the stony fissures
and plunged its implacable intestine
into the subterranean estates,
and dead years, eyes
of the ages, imprisoned
plants' roots
and scaly systems
became strata of water,
fire shot up through the tubes
transformed into cold liquid,
in the customs house of the heights,
issuing from its world
of sinister depth,
it encountered a pale engineer
and a title deed.

However entangled the petroleum's
arteries may be, however the layers
may change their silent site
and move their sovereignty
amid the earth's bowels,
when the fountain gushes
its paraffin foliage,
Standard Oil arrived beforehand
with its checks and its guns,
with its governments and its prisoners.

Their obese emperors
from New York are suave
smiling assassins
who buy silk, nylon, cigars,
petty tyrants and dictators.

They buy countries, people, seas,
police, county councils,
distant regions where
the poor hoard their corn
like misers their gold:

Standard Oil awakens them,
clothes them in uniforms, designates
which brother is the enemy.
The Paraguayan fights its war,
and the Bolivian wastes away
in the jungle with its machine gun.

A President assassinated
for a drop of petroleum,
a million-acre
mortgage, a swift
execution on a morning
mortal with light, petrified,
a new prison camp for
subversives, in Patagonia,
a betrayal, scattered shots
beneath a petroliferous moon,
a subtle change of ministers
in the capital, a whisper
like an oil tide,
and zap, you'll see
how Standard Oil's letters
shine above the clouds,
above the seas, in your home,
illuminating their dominions.

**Anaconda
Copper
Mining Co.**

Name of a coiled snake,
insatiable gullet, green monster,
in the clustered heights,
in my country's rarefied
saddle, beneath the moon
of hardness—excavator—
you open the mineral's
lunar craters, the galleries
of virgin copper, sheathed
in its granite sands.

In Chuquicamata's eternal
night, in the heights,
I've seen the sacrificial fire burn,
the profuse crackling
of the Cyclops that devoured
the Chileans' hands, weight
and waist, coiling them

beneath its copper vertebrae,
draining their warm blood,
crushing their skeletons
and spitting them out in the
desolate desert wastelands.

Air resounds in the heights
of starry Chuquicamata.
The galleries annihilate
the planet's resistance
with man's little hands,
the gorges' sulphuric bird
trembles, the metal's
iron cold mutinies
with its sullen scars,
and when the horns blast
the earth swallows a procession
of minuscule men who descend
to the crater's mandibles.

They're tiny captains,
my nephews, my children,
and when they pour the ingots
toward the seas, wipe
their brows and return shuddering
to the uttermost chill,
the great serpent eats them up,
reduces them, crushes them,
covers them with malignant spittle,
casts them out to the roads,
murders them with police,
sets them to rot in Pisagua,
imprisons them, spits on them,
buys a treacherous president
who insults and persecutes them,
kills them with hunger on the plains
of the sandy immensity.

And on the infernal slopes
there's cross after twisted cross,
the only kindling scattered
by the tree of mining.

**United
Fruit Co.**

When the trumpet blared everything
on earth was prepared
and Jehovah distributed the world
to Coca-Cola Inc., Anaconda,
Ford Motors and other entities:
United Fruit Inc.
reserved for itself the juiciest,
the central seaboard of my land,
America's sweet waist.
It rebaptized its lands
the "Banana Republics,"
and upon the slumbering corpses,
upon the restless heroes
who conquered renown,
freedom and flags,
it established the comic opera:
it alienated self-destiny,
regaled Caesar's crowns,
unsheathed envy, drew
the dictatorship of flies:
Trujillo flies, Tacho flies,
Carías flies, Martínez flies,
Ubico flies, flies soaked
in humble blood and jam,
drunk flies that drone
over the common graves,
circus flies, clever flies
versed in tyranny.

Among the bloodthirsty flies
the Fruit Co. disembarks,
ravaging coffee and fruits
for its ships that spirit away
our submerged lands' treasures
like serving trays.

Meanwhile, in the seaports'
sugary abysses,
Indians collapsed, buried
in the morning mist:
a body rolls down, a nameless
thing, a fallen number,
a bunch of lifeless fruit
dumped in the rubbish heap.

**Lands
and Men**

Aged landowners incrusted
in the earth like the bones
of bloodthirsty animals,
superstitious heirs
of the encomienda, emperors
of a dark land, closed
with hatred and barbed wire fences.

The human being's stamen
was smothered between the fences,
the child was buried alive,
denied bread and letters,
branded a sharecropper,
condemned to the corrals.
Poor wretched peon
amid the brambles, bound
to the nonexistence, in the shadows
of the wild grasslands.

Without books you were helpless flesh,
and then a senseless skeleton,
bought from life to life,
rejected at the white door
with no more love than a guitar,
heartrending in its sadness,
and a dance, dimly lit
like a line squall.

But man's wound was not
in the fields alone. They
penetrated further, closer, deeper:
in the city, beside the palace,
the leprous tenement grew,
its accusing gangrene
pullulating with putrefaction.

In Talcahuano's harsh bends,
in the ashen sludge of the hills,
I've seen poverty's
foul petals seethe, the batch
of degraded hearts,
the pustule opened
in the shadow
of the submarine twilight,
the scar of tatters,

and the aged substance
of man, hirsute and subdued.

I entered homes, deep
rat holes drenched
in nitrate and putrid salt:
I saw hungry beings shuffle along,
toothless obscurities
who tried to smile at me
through the accursed air.

My people's suffering
pierced me, entangled
my soul like barbed wire:
gripped my heart:
I went to cry out at the crossroads,
I went out to weep, enveloped in mist,
I touched the doors and they wounded me
like sharp-pointed knives,
I called out to the impassive faces
that I adored before like stars,
and they showed me their void.

Then I became a soldier:
obscure number, regiment,
order of combatant fists,
systematic intelligence,
fiber of innumerable time,
armed tree, man's
indestructible road on earth.

And I saw how many we were,
how many there were beside me—they
were nobody, they were all mankind,
they were faceless, they were the people,
they were metal, they were roads.
And I walked with the same steps
of springtime in the world.

**The
Beggars**   Beside the cathedral, knotted
to the wall, they dragged their feet,
their nondescript shapes, their black stares,
their livid gargoyle growths,
their tattered tins of food,

and from there, from the hard
sanctity of stone,
they became street flora, vagrant
flowers of legal pestilences.

The park has its beggars,
like its trees of tortured
branches and roots:
the slave lives at the foot of the garden,
like the extremity of mankind, reduced to rubbish,
his impure symmetry accepted,
ready for the broom of death.

Charity buries him
in its hole of leprous earth:
he's an object lesson for the man of my times,
who should learn to trample and plunge
the species into the swamps of contempt,
place his foot on the brow of the being
with the uniform of the defeated,
or at least understand him
as the product of nature.
American beggar, child of the year
1948, grandchild
of cathedrals, I don't venerate you,
I'm not going to put ancient ivory
or a regal beard in your written image,
as you're justified in books,
I'm going to expunge you with hope:
you'll not enter my organized love,
you'll not enter my breast with your kind,
with those who created you
spitting on your degraded form:
I'll remove your clay from the earth
until they build you with metals
and you emerge to shine like a sword.

The Indians

The Indian fled from his skin to
the depths of ancient immensity from which
he rose one day like the islands: defeated,
he turned into invisible atmosphere,
kept expanding in the earth, pouring
his secret sign over the sand.

The Indians

He who spent the moon and combed
the world's mysterious solitude,
he who didn't transpire without rising up
in lofty air-crowned stones,
he who endured like celestial light
beneath his forest's magnitude,
was suddenly worn threadbare,
transformed into wrinkles,
his torrential towers demolished,
and he received his packet of rags.

I saw him in Amatitlán's
magnetized heights, gnawing the shores
of impenetrable water: one day I walked
the Bolivian altiplano's
stunning majesty, with its remains
of bird and root.
                                I saw Alberti,
my brother of possessed poetry,
weep in the Araucanian precincts
when they surrounded him like Ercilla,
and instead of those red gods, they
were a purple chain of corpses.

Further beyond, in Tierra del Fuego's
network of wild waters,
I saw them clambering, O, squalid
sea dogs, into their battered canoes,
to beg for bread on the Ocean.

They systematically murdered
every fiber of those deserted domains,
and the hunter of Indians received
filthy bounty for bringing back the heads
of those masters of the air, kings
of the snowy antarctic solitude.

Those who paid for crimes sit
today in Parliament, licensing
their marriages in Presidencies,
living with Cardinals and Managers,
and flowers grow above the severed
throats of the masters of the South.

Then Araucania's crests
were dissipated by wine,

ravaged in taverns,
blackened by lawyers
at the service of that kingdom's theft,
and those who shot them down,
those who entered firing and negotiating
on the roads defended
by the dazzling gladiator
of our own seashores,
were called "Pacifiers,"
and their epaulettes were multiplied.

The collapse of the Indian's heritage
was so invisible that he lost without
seeing: he didn't see the banners,
he didn't send his bloody arrow flying,
so he was gnawed, bit by bit:
judges, pickpockets, landowners,
all took his imperial sweetness,
all entangled him in his blanket,
until they threw him bleeding into
America's uttermost swamps.

From the green sheets, from the foliage's
pure and innumerable sky,
from the immortal dwelling made
of heavy granite petals,
he was led to the dilapidated shack,
to the arid dung heap of misery.
From his gleaming nakedness,
his golden breast and pale waist,
or from the mineral ornaments
that joined his skin to all the dew,
they led him by the thread of his rags,
gave him lifeless pants, and that's how
his patched majesty came to parade through
the air of the world that was once his.

That's how this torment was committed.

The deed was invisible like a traitor's
entry, like impalpable cancer,
until our father was overwhelmed,
until they taught him to be a phantom,
and he entered the only door open to him,
the door of the other poor, that
of the entire earth's downtrodden.

The
Judges

In high Peru, in Nicaragua,
throughout Patagonia, in the cities,
you've had no rights, you've nothing:
cup of misery, America's
abandoned child, there's no
law, no judge to protect your land,
your little house with corn.

When your chiefs came,
your masters, by now forgotten
the ancient dream of talons and knives,
the law came to depopulate your sky,
to seize your revered fields,
to debate the rivers' water,
to steal the kingdom of trees.

They testified against you, stamped
your shirts, stuffed your heart
with leaves and papers,
buried you in cold edicts,
and when you awakened on the edge
of the most precipitous calamity,
dispossessed, solitary, vagrant,
they gave you jail, bound you,
shackled you so that swimming
you couldn't escape the water of the poor,
so that you'd drown kicking.

The benign judge reads you clause
number Four Thousand, Third Paragraph,
the same used in the entire
blue geography liberated
by others like you who fell,
and you're instituted by his codicil
without appeal, mangy cur.

Your blood asks, how were the wealthy
and the law interwoven? With what
sulphurous iron fabric? How did the
poor keep falling into the tribunals?

How did the land become so bitter
for poor children, harshly
nourished on stone and grief?
So it was, and so I leave it written.
Their lives wrote it on my brow.

III

**The Corpses
in the Plaza
(28 January 1946,
Santiago de Chile)**

I don't come to weep here where they fell:
I come to you, I repair to the living.
I appeal to you and me and I beat on your breast.
Others fell before. Do you remember? Of course
        you do.
Others who had the same names:
in San Gregorio, in rainy Lonquimay,
in Ranquil, scattered by the wind,
in Iquique, buried by sand,
all along the sea and desert,
all along the mist and rain,
from the pampas to the archipelagoes,
other men were assassinated,
others like you named Antonio,
who were fishermen or blacksmiths like you:
Chile's flesh, faces
scarred by the wind,
martyred by the pampa,
marked by suffering.

Along the country's walls,
beside the snow and its crystalwork,
behind the river of green foliage,
beneath the nitrate and thorns,
I found a drop of my people's blood,
and each drop burned like fire.

**The
Massacres**

But then the blood was hidden
                    behind the roots, it was
        washed
and denied
(it was so far), the South's rain expunged it from
        the earth
(far, far away), the nitrate devoured it in the
        pampa:
the people's death was as it has always been:
as if nobody had died, nothing,
as if those were stones falling
on the earth, or water on water.

186

The Nitrate Men

From North to South, where the dead
were ground or burned,
they were buried in darkness
or burned at night in silence,
heaped in mine shafts,
or their bones spit into the sea:
nobody knows where they are now,
they have no grave, their martyred fingers
are dispersed in the country's roots:
their executed hearts:
the Chileans' smile:
the pampa's valiant:
the captains of silence.

Nobody knows where the assassins
buried these bodies,
but they'll rise from the earth
to redeem the fallen blood
in the resurrection of the people.

In the middle of the Plaza this crime was
        committed.

The thornscrub didn't hide the people's
pure blood, nor was it swallowed by the pampa's
        sand.

Nobody hid this crime.

This crime was committed in the middle of the
        Plaza.

**The
Nitrate
Men**

I was in the saltpeter, with the obscure heroes,
with those who dig the fine fertilizing snow
in the planet's hard crust,
and I proudly shook their earthy hands.

They told me: "Look,
brother, how we live,
here in 'Humberstone,' here in 'Mapocho,'
in 'Ricaventura,' in 'Paloma,'
in 'Pan de Azúcar,' in 'Piojillo.' "

And they showed me their rations
of miserable food,
the dirt floors in their homes,
the sun, the dust, the bedbugs,
and the immense solitude.

And I saw the work of the pick-and-shovel
men, who leave their hands'
entire imprint hollowed out
in the shovel's wood handle.

I heard a voice rise up
from the mineshaft's narrow bowels,
as from an infernal uterus,
and then a faceless creature
loomed forth,
a powdery mask
of sweat, blood and dust.

And he told me: "Wherever you go,
speak of these torments,
speak, brother, about your brother
who lives below, in hell."

Death   My people, here you decided to lend your hand
to the pampa's persecuted worker, and you called,
a year ago you called
man, woman and child to this Plaza.
                                        And your
    blood fell here.
In the middle of the country it was spilt,
in front of the palace, in the middle of the street,
so that everyone would see it
and no one could expunge it,
and its red stains remained
like implacable planets.

It was when hand after Chilean hand
reached its fingers out to the pampa,
and with a resolute heart
the unity of their words would go forth:
my people, it was when you were going

to sing an old song with tears,
with hope and with sorrows:
the hangman's hand came
and bathed the plaza with blood!

**How
Flags
Are Born**

That's how our flags are to this day.
The people embroidered them with their
     tenderness,
sewed the rags with their suffering.

They fastened the star with their burning hands.
And cut, from shirt or firmament,
blue for the country's star.

The red, drop by drop, was being born.

**I Invoke
Them**

One by one I'll speak with them this afternoon.
One by one, you return in memory,
this afternoon, to this plaza.

Manuel Antonio López,
comrade.

Lisboa Calderón,
others betrayed you, we'll take over your shift.

Alejandro Gutiérrez,
the banner that fell with you
rises above the entire earth.

César Tapia,
your heart's in these flags,
it flutters today in the wind of the plaza.

Filomeno Chávez,
I never shook your hand, but your hand's here:
it's a pure hand that death cannot still.

Ramona Parra,
shining starlet,
Ramona Parra, fragile heroine,
Ramona Parra, bloodstained flower,

our friend, valiant heart,
exemplary child, golden warrior:
we swear in your name to continue this struggle
that your spilt blood may thus flower.

**The
Enemies**

Here they brought rifles loaded
with gunpowder, they ordered bitter
        extermination:
here they found the people singing,
a people united by duty and love,
and the slender child fell with her flag,
and the smiling young man rolled wounded beside
        her,
and the people's stupor saw the dead fall
with fury and with grief.
Then, on the site
where the assassinated fell,
they lowered the flags to bathe them in blood,
to raise them again in the assassins' presence.

For these dead, our dead,
I demand punishment.

For those who spattered the country with blood,
I demand punishment.

For the executioner who ordered this death,
I demand punishment.

For the traitor who rose above the crime,
I demand punishment.

For him who gave the order of agony,
I demand punishment.

For those who defended this crime,
I demand punishment,

I don't want them to give me their hand
bathed in our blood.
I demand punishment.
I don't want them to be Ambassadors,
or at home, in peace:

I want to see them tried here,
in this plaza, in this place.

I want punishment.

**They Are
Here**

I must summon them here as if they were here.
Brothers and Sisters: rest assured that our
struggle on earth will continue.

It will continue in the factories and fields,
in the streets and nitrate works.

In the crater of green and red copper,
in the coal and its terrible cave.
Our struggle will be everywhere,
and in our hearts, these flags
that witnessed your death,
that were bathed in your blood,
will be multiplied like the leaves
of the infinite springtime.

Forever

Though feet may walk on this site for a thousand
    years,
they'll never expunge the blood of those who fell
    here.

And the hour on which you fell will not expire,
though thousands of voices may cross this silence.
The rain will soak the plaza's stones,
but it won't extinguish your blazing names.

A thousand dark-winged nights will fall,
without destroying the day these dead await.

The day so many of us await throughout
the world, the final day of suffering.

A just day conquered in struggle,
and you, fallen brothers, in silence,
will be with us on that vast day,
the final day of our struggle.

IV

**Chronicle
of 1948
(America)**

A bleak year, *year of rats, impure year.*

Your line is lofty and metallic
on the shores of ocean
and air, like a wire
of tempests and tension.
But, America, you're also
nocturnal, blue and boggy:
swamp and sky, an agony
of hearts broken
like black oranges crushed
in your storeroom silence.

Paraguay

Unbridled Paraguay!
What was the purpose of the pure moon
illuminating golden
geometry's papers?
To what avail was the knowledge
inherited from the columns
and the solemn numbers?

For this hole swamped
with rotten blood, for
this equinoctial liver
seized by death.
For monarchic Moriñigo,
enthroned upon prisons
in his pool of kerosene,
while the electric hummingbirds'
scarlet plumes
hover and glow above
the humble corpses in the jungle.

Bleak year, year of blighted roses,
year of carbines—look down
with your eyes, don't be blinded
by the airplane's aluminum, the music
of its dry sonorous speed—look at

your bread, your land, your torn masses,
your battered lineage!
                           Do you see that green
and ashen valley from the lofty sky?
Pale agriculture, tattered
mining, silence and weeping
like wheat, falling
and rising
                      in a malevolent eternity.

Brazil   Brazil, Dutra, bloodcurdling
turkey of the tropics,
fattened on the poisonous
air's bitter branches:
toad from the black swamps
of our American moon:
gilt buttons, livid rat's
beady eyes:
O, Lord of our poor starving
mother's intestines,
of so many dreams and resplendent
liberators, of so much
sweat in the mine
shafts, of so, so much
solitude on the plantations,
America, you suddenly raise
to your planetary clarity
a Dutra extracted from the bottom
of your snake pit, from your
mute depths and prehistory.

And so it was!
                O, Brazilian
stonemasons, hammer the frontier,
O, fishermen, weep at night
upon the coastal waters,
while Dutra, with his little
wild pig eyes,
breaks printing presses with an ax,
burns books in the plaza,
jails, persecutes and plunders
until our sinister night
grows silent.

Cuba　　In Cuba they're assassinating!

Now they've put Jesús Menéndez
in a newly purchased coffin.
He emerged from the people like a king,
and went forth to examine roots,
stopping passersby,
beating on the breasts of the sleeping,
establishing the ages,
mending broken hearts,
and raising from the sugar
the bloody cane fields,
sweat that rots the stones,
asking in humble kitchens:
"Who are you? How much do you eat?"
touching this arm, this wound,
and accumulating these silences
in a single voice, the hoarse
choked voice of Cuba.

A little captain, a little general
assassinated him: in a train
he told him: "Come," and the little
general shot him in the back
so that the cane fields'
coarse voice would be silent.

Central　　*A bleak year—do you see our geography's*
America　　*waist beyond the dense shadow*
　　　　　　of the forests?
　　　　　　　　　　Like a honeycomb,
　　　　a wave dashes its blue bees
　　　　against the seacoast and the double
　　　　sea's sparks fly over the narrow land . . .

Land slender as a whip,
brewing like a storm,
your passage in Honduras, your blood
in Santo Domingo, at night,
your eyes from Nicaragua
touch me, call me, entreat me,
and throughout the American land
I touch doors to speak,

I touch bound tongues,
raise curtains, plunge
my hand into the blood:

                O, my suffering
land, O, death gasp
of the great silence established,
O, nations of long agony,
O, weeping waistline.

**Puerto
Rico**

Mr. Truman arrives in the Island
of Puerto Rico,

                the blue water
of our pure seas washes
his bloody fingers.
He has just ordered the death
of two hundred Greek youths,
his machine guns function
strictly:

        daily,
by his orders, Doric
heads—grape and olive—
the ancient sea's eyes,
the Corinthian corolla's petals,
fall to the Greek dust.

                The assassins
raise Cyprus's sweet wineglass
with North American experts,
their moustaches trickling,
amid great guffaws,
cold olive oil and Greek blood.

Truman comes to our waters
to wash his red hands of
the distant blood. As
he decrees, preaches and smiles
in the University, in his language,
he shuts the Castilian mouth,
covers the light of words
that circulate there like a
river of crystalline stock
and ordains: "Death to your language,
Puerto Rico."

Greece

(Greek blood
flows down this very hour. It's born
in the hills.

It's a simple
stream amid dust and stones:
Herders tread the blood
of other herders:

it's a simple
slender trickle that runs
from the hills to the sea,
down to the sea that knows and sings.)

. . . Turn your eyes toward your land, your sea,
behold the clarity in the austral
waters and snows—the sun builds grapes,
the desert shines, Chile's sea surges
with its battered line . . .

The deep coal mines are
in Lota: it's a cold seaport,
of the solemn austral winter, rain
keeps falling on the roofs,
mist-colored gull wings,
and beneath the somber sea, man
keeps digging the black enclosure.
Man's life is dark
as coal: tattered night,
miserable bread, harsh day.

I walked the world at length,
but on the roads or in
cities, I've never seen
mankind more abused.
Twelve sleep to a room.
The dwellings have roofs
of nondescript odds-and-ends:
pieces of tin, stones,
cardboard, wet paper.
In the wet steam of the
cold season, children and dogs
crowd together to kindle the fire
of the poor life that will be
hunger and darkness for another day.

The Torments

Another strike, salaries
fall short, women weep
in the kitchens, one by one
miners join hands
and sorrows.
              It's the strike
of those who excavated beneath the sea,
spread out in the wet cave,
and extracted the mines' black clump
with sweat and blood.
This time the soldiers came.
They ransacked their houses, at night.
They marshaled them to the mines
as to a prison and plundered
the poor wheat they'd saved,
the grain of rice for their children.

Then they beat their walls down,
exiled them, crushed them,
corralled and branded them
like beasts, and on the roads,
in a sorrowful exodus,
the captains of coal
saw their children thrown out,
their wives offended
and hundreds of miners
deported to Patagonia
and jailed, in the antarctic cold,
or in the deserts of Pisagua.

The Traitor

And atop these calamities
a smiling tyrant
spits on the betrayed
miners' hopes.

Every nation has its sorrows,
every struggle its torments,
but come here and tell me
if among the bloodthirsty,
among all the unbridled
despots, crowned with hatred,
with scepters of green whips,
there was ever another like Chile's?
This man betrayed trampling

his promises and smiles,
his scepter was made of filth,
he danced on the poor
affronted people's grief.

And when the black eyes
of the offended and aggrieved
were gathered in the prisons
filled by his disloyal decrees,
he danced in Viña del Mar, surrounded
by jewelry and wineglasses.

But the black eyes stare
through the black night.

What did you do? Did your word ever come
for your brother of the deep mines,
for the grief of the betrayed,
did your fiery syllable ever come
to plead for your people and defend them?

**I
Accuse**

Then I accused the man
who had strangled hope,
I called out to America's corners
and put his name in the cave
of dishonor.
          Then they reproached
me for crimes, that pack
of flunkies and hired hoodlums:
the "secretaries of government,"
the police, wrote their murky insult
against me with tar,
but the walls were watching
when the traitors
wrote my name in large letters,
and the night erased,
with its innumerable hands,
hands of the people and the night,
the ignominy that they try
in vain to cast on my song.

Then they went at night to burn
my house (the fire now marks

the name of he who sent them),
and all the judges joined together
to condemn me, to summon me,
to crucify my words
and punish these truths.

They closed Chile's cordilleras
so that I couldn't leave
to tell what's happening here,
and when Mexico opened its doors
to welcome me and protect me,
Torres Bodet, pitiful poet,
demanded that I be delivered
to the furious jailers.

But my word's alive,
and my free heart accuses.

How will it end, how will it end?
In Pisagua's night, jail, chains,
silence, the country debased,
and this bleak year, year of blind rats,
this bleak year of rage and rancor,
you ask, you ask me how it will end?

The Victorious
People

My heart's in this struggle.
My people will overcome. All the peoples
will overcome, one by one.
                         These sorrows
will be wrung like handkerchiefs until
all the tears shed on the desert's
galleries, on graves, on the steps
of human martyrdom, are squeezed dry.
But the victorious time's nearby.
Let hatred reign so that punishment's
hands won't tremble,
                    let the hour hand
reach its timetable in the pure instant,
and let the people fill the empty streets
with fresh and firm dimensions.

Here's my tenderness for that time.
You'll know it. I have no other flag.

V

González
Videla,
Chile's
Traitor
(Epilogue)
1949

From the ancient cordilleras executioners
    protruded
like bones, like American spines on the hirsute
    back
of a genealogy of catastrophes: they were
    established,
encysted in the misery of our communities.
Every day blood stained their fringes.
From the cordilleras they were procreated
like bony monsters by our black clay.
Those were the saber-toothed saurians, the glacial
    dynasts,
recently emerged from our caverns and defeats.
And so they disinterred Gómez's maxillaries
beneath the roads stained by fifty years of our
    blood.

The beast darkened the lands with his ribs
when, after executions, he twisted his moustache
beside the North American ambassador, who
    served him tea.

These monsters vilified, but weren't villainous.
    Now,
in the corner that the light reserved for purity,
in the snow-capped white country of Araucania,
a *traitor* smiles on a corrupt throne.

In my country villainy presides.

González Videla is the rat who shakes
his hair matted with manure and blood
on my land, which he sold. Every day
he withdraws stolen money from his pockets,
wondering if tomorrow he'll sell territory
or blood.
    He has *betrayed* everything.
He climbed like a rat to my people's shoulders
and there, gnawing on my country's sacred
flag, he twitches his rodent's tail
telling landowners and foreigners, the owners
of Chile's subsoil: "Drink all this

nation's blood, I'm the overseer
of anguish."
                    Wretched clown, miserable
mixture of monkey and rat, whose tail
is combed with a gold pomade on Wall Street,
it won't be long before you fall from your tree
and become the pile of conspicuous filth
that pedestrians will bypass on the street corners!

And so it has been. *Betrayal* was Chile's
    Government.
A traitor has bequeathed his name to our history.
Judas flourishing a grinning skull
sold out my brother and sister,
                                poisoned my
        country,
founded Pisagua, demolished our star,
profaned the colors of a pure flag.

Gabriel González Videla. Here I leave your name,
so that when time has erased
ignominy, when my country cleans
its face illuminated by wheat and snow,
those who later seek here the heritage
that I leave in these lines like a hot green coal
will also find the name of the traitor who brought
the glass of agony that my people refused.

My people, my people, raise your destiny!
Break the bonds, open the walls that enclose you!
Crush the ferocious passage of the rat that governs
from the Palace: raise your lances to the dawn,
and from the loftiest heights let your angry star
shine forth, illuminating America's roads.

VI

AMERICA, I DO NOT INVOKE YOUR NAME IN VAIN

I

**From
Above
(1942)**

The journey's end, the indefinable
air, the moon of craters,
dry moon poured
upon scars,
the torn tunic's calcareous hole,
frozen veins of foliage, the panic
of quartz, wheat, the dawn,
keys spread out in secret rocks,
the terrifying line
of the dismembered South,
sulphate asleep in its stature
of long geography,
and turquoise dispositions
rotating round the extinguished light,
the incessantly blossoming pungent bouquet,
the spacious night of density.

II

An
Assassin
Sleeps

The waist stained by wine
when the vile god steps
on broken wineglasses and dishevels
the unbridled dawn's light:
the rose watered in the little
prostitute's sob, the feverish days' wind
entering the paneless windows
where the victim sleeps with his shoes on,
in an acrid smell of pistols,
in a blue color of lost eyes.

III

On the
Coast

In Santos, amid the bittersweet smell of plantains
that, like a river of soft gold opened in the back,
leaves the stupid saliva of
unhinged paradise on the shores,
and the iron clamor of shadows, water and
    locomotive,
a current of sweat and feathers,
something that descends and flows from the
    depths
of burning leaves as from a pulsing armpit:
a crisis of flights, a remote
foam.

IV

Winter
in the
South, on
Horseback

I've penetrated the bark a thousand
times assailed by the austral blows:
I've felt the horse's neck grow numb
beneath the cold stone of the South's night,
quiver in the naked mountain's compass,
ascend in the pale cheek that begins:
I know the end of the gallop in the mist,

the poor transient's tatters:
and for me there's no god but dark sand,
the interminable spine of stone and night,
the unsociable day
with an advent
of miserable clothes, of exterminated soul.

V

Crimes   On dark nights, perhaps you've traced
the stabbing cry, footsteps in the blood:
the solitary edge of our cross a thousand times
trampled,
heavy blows on the silent door,
the abyss or thunderbolt that swallowed the
    assassin
when dogs bark and the violent police
enter among the sleeping
to forcefully twist the tear's threads
plucking them from the terrified eyelid.

VI

Youth   A perfume like an acid plum
sword on a road,
sugary kisses on the teeth,
vital drops trickling down the fingers,
sweet erotic pulp,
threshing floors, haystacks, inciting
secret hideaways in spacious houses,
mattresses asleep in the past, the pungent green
    valley
seen from above, from the hidden window:
all adolescence becoming wet and burning
like a lantern tipped in the rain.

VII

Climates
In autumn, high arrows, renewed
oblivion, fall from the poplar:
feet plunge into the pure blanket:
the aroused leaves' coldness
is a dense fountain of gold,
a spiny splendor sets the dry
candelabras of bristling stature near the sky,
and the yellow jaguar scents a live droplet
between its claws.

VIII

Varadero in Cuba
From the electric coast Varadero glows
when, shattering, it receives on its hip the
Antilles,
the greatest blow of glowworm and water,
the radiant infinity of phosphorous and moon,
the intense cadaver of dead turquoise:
and the dark fisherman extracts from the metals
a tail bristling with marine violets.

IX

The Dictators
There's a lingering smell in the sugarcane fields:
a mixture of blood and body, a penetrating,
nauseous petal.
Amid the coconut palms graves are filled
with demolished bones, smothered gasps.
The delicate satrap chats
with wineglasses, collars and gold braid.
The little palace shines like a wristwatch
and smart gloved laughter
occasionally drifts across the hallways
to join dead voices
and freshly buried blue mouths.
The sob is hidden like a plant

whose seed falls ceaselessly to the ground
and makes its great blind leaves grow without
    light.
Hatred has been formed scale by scale,
blow by blow, in the terrible water of the swamp,
with a snout full of clay and silence.

X

**Central
America**

What moon of bloody rifle butts,
what branch of whips,
what atrocious light of plucked eyelids
make you moan without voice or mouth,
O, central waistline, O, paradise
of implacable wounds.
Night and day I see martyrdom,
day and night I see the enchained—
Whites, Blacks, Indians—
writing on the night's interminable
walls with bruised phosphoric hands.

XI

**Hunger in
the South**

I see the sob in Lota's coal
and the humiliated Chilean's wrinkled shadow
picking the innards' bitter vein, dying,
living, born stooped
in the hard ash, fallen as if the world
entered and departed so,
amid black dust, amid flames,
and just the winter cough, a horse
moving through black water, where a eucalyptus
leaf has fallen like a dead knife.

XII

Patagonia
Seals are calving
in the depths of the frozen zones,
in crepuscular grottoes that form
the ocean's uttermost muzzles:
Patagonia's cows
stand against the day
like a tumult, like heavy steam
in the cold, raising its hot column
to the wastelands.

You're deserted, America, like a bell:
filled inside with a song that doesn't rise:
herdsmen, plainsmen, fishermen
have no hand, ear, piano
or cheek nearby: the moon shepherds them,
space augments them, night stalks them,
and an old day, slow like the others, dawns.

XIII

**A
Rose**
I see a rose beside the water, a little cup
of red eyelids
sustained aloft by an ethereal sound:
a green-leaved light touches the headsprings
and transfigures the forest with solitary beings
with transparent feet:
the air's full of bright vestments
and the tree establishes its dormant magnitude.

XIV

**Life and
Death
of a
Butterfly**
The butterfly from Muzo flies in the tempest:
all the equinoctial threads,
the emeralds' frozen paste,
everything flies in the thunderbolt,

the air's ultimate consequences are shaken,
then a rain of green stamens
and the emerald's startled pollen rises:
its great velvets of wet fragrance
fall on the cyclone's blue shores,
merge with the fallen terrestrial leavens,
return to the homeland of leaves.

XV

**The Man
Buried in
the Pampa**

From tango to tango, if I could
circumscribe the dominion, the grasslands,
if now asleep
the wild wheat rising from my mouth,
if on the prairies I heard
a thunderclap of horses,
a furious tempest of hooves
passing over my buried fingers,
lipless I'd kiss the seed
and bind to it the vestiges
of my eyes
to see the gallop that my turbulence loved:
O kill me, Vidalita,
kill me and let my substance flow
like the harsh metal of the guitars.

XVI

**Sea
Workers**

In Valparaiso, the sea workers
invited me: they were small and rugged,
and their weathered faces were the Pacific
Ocean's geography: a current
within the immense waters, a muscular wave,
a bouquet of sea wings in the tempest.
It was beautiful to see them like poor little gods,
semi-naked, malnourished, it was beautiful
to see them struggling and throbbing with other
    men from overseas,

209

other men from other miserable seaports, and to
hear them:
it was the same language of Spaniards and
Chinese,
the language of Baltimore and Kronstadt,
and when they sang "The Internationale" I sang
with them:
a hymn rose to my heart, and I tried to tell them:
"Brothers,"
but I had only tenderness transformed into song
that went with their song from my mouth to the
sea.
They acknowledged me, embraced me with their
powerful stare
without speaking, just staring at me and singing.

XVII

**A
River**

I want to drift the Papaloapan
as so many times the earthy mirror,
touching the powerful water with my fingernails:
I want to drift toward the matrices, toward the
contexture of its original branches of crystal:
to drift, to wet my brow, plunging skin, thirst
and dream into the
dew's secret confusion.
Shad leap from the water
like a silver violin,
and ashore atmospheric flowers
and motionless wings
in the heat of space defended
by blue swords.

XVIII

America

I am, I am surrounded
by honeysuckle and wasteland, by jackal and
lightning,
by the enchained perfume of lilacs:
I am, I am surrounded

by days, months, waters that I alone know,
by fingernails, fish, months that I alone
    establish,
I am, I am surrounded
by the slender combatant foam
of the seaboard full of bells.
The scarlet shirt of Indian and volcano,
the road, which the naked foot raised amid the
    leaves
and thorns amid the roots,
comes to my feet at night that I may walk it.
Dark blood like autumn
poured on the ground,
the dreadful banner of death in the jungle,
invading footsteps dissolving, the warriors'
cry, the dormant spear twilight,
the soldiers' startled sleep, the great
rivers in which the alligator's peace splashes,
your recent cities of unforeseen mayors,
the chorus of birds of indomitable custom,
in the jungle's rank day, the firefly's
tutelary glow,
when I exist in your womb, in your beaconed
evening, in your repose, in the uterus of your
    births, in the
earthquake, in the peasants' ox cart, in the ash
that falls from the glaciers, in space,
in pure space, inapprehensible trajectory,
in the condors' bloody talons, in Guatemala's
humiliated peace, in the blacks,
on Trinidad's docks, in La Guayra:
all is my night, all is
my day, all is
my air, all is
whatever I live, suffer, raise and agonize.
America, the syllables that
I sing aren't made of night or light.
The empowered matter of my victory's
radiance and bread is made of earth,
and my dream's not dream but earth.
I sleep surrounded by spacious clay
and when I live a fountain of boundless
lands flows through my hands.
And what I drink is not wine but earth,
hidden earth, my mouth's earth,
earth of agriculture with dew,

a gale of luminous vegetables,
cereal stock, granary of gold.

XIX

America, I do not invoke your name in vain.
When I hold the sword to my heart,
when I endure the leaks in my soul,
when your new day
penetrates me through the windows,
I'm of and I'm in the light that produces me,
I live in the shade that determines me,
I sleep and rise in your essential dawn,
sweet as grapes and terrible,
conductor of sugar and punishment,
soaked in the sperm of your species,
nursed on the blood of your legacy.

CANTO GENERAL
OF CHILE

Eternity

I write for a land recently dried, recently
fresh with flowers, pollen, mortar,
I write for some craters whose chalk cupolas
repeat the round void beside the pure snow,
I suddenly decree for that which barely
conveys the iron vapor recently emerged from the abyss,
I speak for meadows that know no name
other than the lichen's little bell or the burned stamen
or the harsh density where the mare burns.

Where am I from, but these seedlings, blue
matter that entangles or curls or uproots
or clamorously sows or somnolently spreads,
or climbs and forms the tree's bulwark,
or sinks and binds the copper's cell,
or springs to the rivers' branch, or succumbs
in the coal's buried stock or gleams
in the grape's green darkness?

At night I sleep like the rivers, incessantly
on the move, surging ahead, overtaking
the swimming night, raising hours

to the light, groping for secret
images unearthed by lime, rising through bronze
to the recently disciplined cascades, and I touch
in a river network all that it doesn't distribute
except the unborn rose, the drowned hemisphere.
The earth's a cathedral of pale eyelids,
eternally bound and gathered in a
tempest of segments, in salt domes,
in a final color of forgiven autumn.

You've never, you've never touched
what the naked stalactite determines,
the fiesta amid the glacial lamps,
the black leaves' lofty coldness,
you've never entered with me the fibers
hidden by the earth,
after death you've never again climbed
the steps of sand grain by grain
until the crowns of dew
cover a blooming rose again,
you cannot exist with the hand-me-downs
of happiness without dying a slow death.

But I'm the metallic nimbus, the ring
chained to space, clouds, spheres,
that touches hurtling mute waters,
and again defies the infinite inclemency.

I
———

Hymn and
Homecoming
(1939)

O country, my country, I return my blood to
    you.
But I implore you, as a baby cries
to its mother.
          Welcome
this blind guitar,
this lost brow.
I went to find children for your land,
I went to embrace the hopeless with your snowy
    name,
I went to build a home with your pure wood,
I went to take your star to the wounded heroes.

I Want to Return to the South (1941)

Now I want to sleep in your substance.
Give me your vibrant night of penetrating strings,
your ship's night, your starry stature.

My country: I want to change shadows.
My country: I want to change roses.
I want to envelop your slender waist,
sit on your stones blackened by the sea,
stop the wheat and see it from within.
I'm going to pick the nitrate's slender flower,
I'm going to spin the bell's glacial stamen,
and beholding your illustrious and solitary foam,
I'll weave a tideland bouquet to extol your beauty.

O country, my country
all enveloped by assailing water
and assailed snow,
in you the eagle and sulphur unite,
and in your antarctic hand of ermine and sapphire
a drop of pure human light shines forth
lighting the enemy sky.

Guard your light, O country!, maintain
your hope's hard spike of grain amid
the blind fearsome air.
All this difficult light has fallen on your
remote land, this destiny of mankind
that makes you defend a mysterious flower
alone, in the immensity of slumbering America.

II

I Want to Return to the South (1941)

Ill in Veracruz, I remember a day,
in the South, my land, a day silvery
as a darting fish in the water of the sky.
Loncoche, Lonquimay, Carahue, sown
from above, surrounded by silence and roots,
seated on their thrones of leather and wood.
The South's a shipwrecked horse
crowned with slow trees and dew,
when it raises its green muzzle raindrops fall,
the shade from its tail soaks the great archipelago

and venerated coal grows in its intestine.
Will you never again—tell me, shade, never again,
    tell me,
hand, never again, tell me, foot, door, leg,
    combat—
disturb the forest, roads, spikes of grain,
mist, the cold, whatever, blue, determined
every one of your footprints, incessantly
    consumed?
Sky, someday let me go from star to star
treading light and gunpowder, destroying my
    blood,
until I reach the rain's nest!
                         I want to
follow the wood down the fragrant
River Toltén, I want to leave the sawmills,
enter the cantinas with wet feet,
be guided by the electric hazel tree's light,
stretch out beside the cowpies,
die and revive chewing wheat.
                      Ocean, bring me
a day from the South, a day embracing your
    waves,
a wet-tree day, bring a polar-
blue wind to my cold flag!

III

Melancholy
Near
Orizaba
(1942)

What is there for you in the South but a river, a
    night,
some leaves that the cold air manifests
and spreads until they cover the sky's shores?
Is it because love's hair flows
like another snow or water from the broken
    archipelago,
like another subterranean movement of fire,
and waits again in the sheds,
where the leaves fall trembling
so many times, devoured by that dense mouth,
and the rain's sparkle closes its vine,
from the gathering of secret grain
to the foliage full of bells and raindrops?

Where springtime brings a wet voice
that drones in the sleeping horse's ear,
then the milled wheat's gold falls
and a transparent finger appears in the grape.
What's waiting for you—where, without hallways,
without walls, does the South call you?
Like the plainsman you hear the earth's cup
in your hand, putting your ear in the roots:
from afar a wind from a fearsome hemisphere,
the gallop in the police's hoarfrost:
where the needle stitches time with fine water,
and its disjoined seam disintegrates:
what is there for you in the wild-flanked night,
howling with its mouth brimming with blue?

There's a day perhaps arrested, a thorn
jabs its degraded spine into the old day
and its ancient nuptial flag is rent.
Who has preserved a black forest day, who
has awaited some stone hours, who
envelops the legacy wounded by time, who flees
without disappearing in midair?
A day, a day full of desperate leaves,
a day, a light shattered by cold sapphire,
yesterday's silence preserved in yesterday's
hollow, in the absent territory's reserve.

I love your tangled leathery hair,
your antarctic beauty of inclemency and ash,
your painful combatant sky's weight: I love
the flight of the air of the day when you await
    me,
I know the earth's kiss doesn't change, and it
    doesn't change,
I know the leaf doesn't fall from the tree, and it
    doesn't fall:
I know that the same lightning arrests its metals
and the forsaken night is the same night,
but it's my night, but it's my plant, the water
of the glacial tears that know my hair.

Let me be what awaited me yesterday in mankind:
whatever in laurel, ash, quantity, hope,
develops its eyelid in blood,
in the blood that fills kitchen and forest,

factories that the iron covers with black plumes,
mines drilled by sulphuric sweat.

Not only pungent vegetable air awaits me:
not only thunder over the snowy splendor:
tears and hunger rise like two shivers
to the country's bell tower and toll:
so amid the fragrant sky,
so when October explodes, and the antarctic
springtime overflows the wine's splendor,
there's one lament and another lament and another
until they cut across snow, copper, roads, ships,
penetrating night and land,
to my parched throat that hears them.

My people, what do you say? Sailor,
peon, mayor, nitrate miner, do you hear me?
I hear you, dead brother, living brother, I hear
    you,
whatever you desired, whatever you buried,
        everything,
the blood you spilt in the sand and the sea,
the battered heart that resists and startles.

What is there for you in the South? Where does
    the rain fall?
And from the interstice, what corpses has it
    lashed?
My people, those from the South, the lonely
    heroes,
bread disseminated by bitter rage,
long grief, hunger, harshness and death,
leaves have fallen upon them, the leaves,
the moon upon the soldier's breast, the moon,
the miserable blind alley, man's
silence everywhere, like a hard mineral
whose cold vein freezes my soul's light
before building the bell in the heights.
O country full of seeds, don't call me, I can't
sleep without your crystal gaze and darkness.
Your hoarse cry of waters and beings shakes me
and I sleepwalk on the fringe of your solemn
        foam
to the uttermost isle of your blue waist.
You call me sweetly like a poor bride.
Your long steel light blinds me and seeks me

like a sword filled with roots.
O country, esteemed land, burned-out light still
    aglow:
like the coal within your fire that precipitates
your dreadful salt, your naked shadow.
Let me be whatever awaited me yesterday, and let
    me resist
tomorrow in a fistful of poppies and dust.

IV

Ocean

If your naked and green appearance,
if your boundless apple, if
in the darkness your mazurka, where's
your source?
Night
sweeter than night,
            mother
salt, blood salt, curve-mother of the water,
planet traversed by foam and pith:
titanic sweetness of stellar longitude:
night with a single wave in the hand:
tempest against the sea eagle,
blind beneath the unfathomable sulphate's hands:
storeroom entombed in so many nights,
cold corolla, all invasion and sound,
cathedral buried by blows in the star.

There's the wounded horse, substituted by
glacial fire, trotting on the age of your seashore,
there's spruce transformed into plumage
and shattered in your hands of atrocious crystal,
and the incessant rose assailed in the islands
and the diadem of water and moon that you
    establish.
My country, all this dark sky
to your land!
All this universal fruit, all this
delirious crown!
For you this glass of foam where lightning
becomes lost like a blind albatross, and where
the South's sun rises beholding your sacred
    condition.

V

Saddlery   For me this saddle designed
like a heavy rose in silver and leather,
gently sloped, smooth and durable.
Every cut is a hand, every
stitch a life in which the unity
of forest lives, a chain of eyes
and horses, lives on.
Grains of wheat shaped it,
woodlands and water hardened it,
the opulent harvest gave it pride,
metal and wrought morocco leather:
and so from misfortune and dominion,
this throne set forth through the meadowlands.

**Pottery
Shop**   Crude dove, clay piggy bank,
on your grieving back a sign, something
that barely deciphers you. My people,
how—shouldering your sorrows,
beaten and subdued—how did you manage
to accumulate naked science?
Black prodigy, magic matter
raised to the light by blind fingers,
minute statue in which the earth's most
secret essence unlocks its languages for us,
Pomaire's earthen pitcher in whose kiss
earth and skin congregate, infinite
forms of clay, vessels' light,
shape of a hand that was mine,
movement of a shadow that calls me,
you're a gathering of hidden dreams,
indestructible, ceramic dove!

Looms   You know that there the snow tending
the valleys, or rather
the South's dark springtime, black birds
to whose breasts but a droplet of blood
came to tremble, a great
winter mist that spread its wings,

so too the territory, and its fragrance
rises from poor flowers, demolished
by the weight of copper and cordilleras.
And there the loom, seeking thread by thread,
reconstructed the flower, raised the feather
to its imperial scarlet, interweaving
blues and saffrons, the skein
of fire and its yellow power,
the lineage of violet lightning,
the lizard's sandy green.
My people's hands on the looms,
poor hands that weave, one by one,
the starry feathers that your
skin lacked, dark-colored Country,
substituting the sky fiber by fiber
so that man may sing his loves
and kindle grain on the gallop!

VI

Floods   The poor live below waiting for the river
to rise at night and take them to sea.
I've seen little cradles afloat, remains
of houses, chairs, and an august rage
of livid waters in which sky and terror are fused.
It's only for you, poor man, for your wife and
     offspring,
for your dog and your tools, so that you can learn
     to beg.
The water doesn't rise to the homes of the
     gentlemen
whose snow-clad collars fly from the laundries.
Eat this devastating mud and these ruins that
     swim
with your dead, gently drifting to sea,
amid humble tables and lost trees
that tumble downstream displaying their roots.

Earthquake   I awakened when dreamland gave way beneath
     my bed.

A blind column of ash tottered in the middle
of the night,
                    and I ask you: am I dead?
Hold my hand in this rupture of the planet
while the scar of the purple sky becomes a star.
Ah!, but I remember, where are they?, where are
      they?
Why does the earth boil, gorging on death?
O masks beneath the devastated dwellings, smiles
untouched by fear, beings dismembered
under the beams, blanketed by night.
And today you dawn, O blue day, dressed
for a dance, with your gold tail
above the listless sea of debris, fiery,
seeking the lost faces of the unburied.

VII

Atacama

Insufferable voice, disseminated
salt, substituted
ash, black bouquet
on whose extreme dewdrop the blind moon
rises, through grieving galleries of copper.
What matter, what hollow swan
plunges its naked agony into the sand
and hardens its slow liquid light?
What hard thunderbolt shatters its emerald
amid the indomitable stones until
the lost salt congeals?
Land, land
above the sea, above the air, above the gallop
of the horsewoman full of coral:
heaping granary where wheat
sleeps in the bells' tremulous root:
O mother of the ocean!, maker
of blind jasper and golden silica:
upon your pure skin of bread, far from the forest,
nothing but your secret lines,
nothing but your sandy brow,
nothing but mankind's days and nights,
but beside the thistle's thirst, where
there's a submerged and forgotten paper, a stone

marks the deep cradles of sword and cup,
indicates the calcium's sleeping feet.

VIII

Tocopilla

From Tocopilla to the south, to the north: sand,
fallen quicklime, barges, broken
boards, twisted iron.
Who added broken utensils and filth
to the planet's pure line, golden and baked,
sleep, salt and gunpowder?
Who made the roof sag, who left the walls
open, with a cluster
of trampled papers?
Lugubrious light of the dismissed man in you,
always returning to the hollow of your calcareous
    moon,
ill-received by your lethal sand!
Rarefied gull of the work sites, herring,
curly petrel,
fruits, you, children of the bloody trawl line
and the tempest, have you seen the Chilean?
Have you seen the human being, between the
    double lines
of cold and water, beneath the coastline's
teeth, in the bay?

Lice, seething lice attacking the salt,
lice, lice of seacoast, towns, miners,
from the desert's scar to another,
against the moon's coast, be gone!,
treading the cold ageless seal.
Beyond the pelican's feet, when neither
water nor bread nor shade touch the harsh phase,
saltpeter's exercise appears
or copper's statue decides its stature.
Everything's like buried stars,
like bitter points, like infernal white
flowers,
snowstorms of tremulous light
or a green and black branch of heavy radiance.
What's needed there is not the pen but the obscure

Chilean's battered hand—doubt is useless there.
Just blood. Just that hard hammering
that seeks man in the vein.
In the vein, in the mine, in the tunneled cave
without water and without laurels.

O little
compatriots burned by this light bitterer
than the bath of death, heroes obscured
by the dawning of salt on earth,
where do you build your nest, migrant children?
Who has seen you amid the desolate
seaport's broken filaments?
                              Beneath
the briny mist
or behind the metallic coast,
or perhaps or perhaps,
beneath the desert now, beneath
its dusty word
forever! .
Chile, Metal and Sky,
and you, Chileans,
seed, hard brothers and sisters,
all disposed in order and silence
like the permanence of stones.

IX

Peumo Tree

I broke a glossy woodland leaf: a sweet
aroma of cut edges
brushed me like a deep wing that flew
from the earth, from afar, from never.
Peumo, then I saw your foliage, your minute,
curly verdure, cover its earthly trunk
and your fragrant breadth with its impulses.
I thought how you're my entire land: my flag
must have a peumo's aroma when it unfurls,
a smell of frontiers that suddenly
enter you with the entire country in their current.
Pure peumo, fragrance of years and hair
in the wind, in the rain, beneath the mountain's

curvature, with the sound of water running
down to our roots, O love, O wild time
whose perfume can be born, issuing
from a leaf and filling us until we flood
the earth, like old buried pitchers!

**Quila
Bamboo**

Amid the erect unsmiling leaves
you hide your nursery of clandestine spears.
You didn't forget. When I pass through your
    foliage
hardness whispers, and wounding words,
syllables that nurse spines, awaken.
You don't forget. You were mortar mixed
with blood, you were columns of home and war,
you were flag, my Araucanian mother's roof,
wild warrior's sword, Araucania
bristling with flowers that wounded and killed.
Harshly you hide the lances that you manufacture,
known by the wild region's wind,
the rain, the eagle of the burned forests,
and the furtive inhabitant, recently dispossessed.
Perhaps, perhaps: tell no one your secret.
Save me a wild lance, or an arrow
shaft. I haven't forgotten either.

**Drimis
Winterei**

Nameless plants, leaves
and mountainous tendons,
branches woven with green air, freshly
embroidered threads, limbs of dark metals,
innumerable coronary flora
of the moisture, the vast vapor, the immense
    water.
And among all the forms that this bower sought,
among these leaves whose intact mold
poised its prodigy in the rain,
O tree, you awakened like a thunderclap,
and in your crown filled with all the verdure
winter slumbered like a bird.

X

**Untilled
Zones**

Forsaken limit! Frenzied line
on which wildfire or enraged thistle
form layers of electrified blue.

Stones hammered by
the copper's needles, roads
of silent matter, branches submerged
in the stones' salt.

Here I am, here am I,
a human mouth abandoned to the pale passage
of a time arrested like a wineglass or hip,
a central penitentiary of impounded water,
tree of a demolished corporal flower,
nothing but deaf and brusque sand.
My country, earthly and blind as
newborn spurs of sand, for you all
my soul's foundation, for you my blood's
perpetual eyelids, for you my
plate of poppies home again.

Give me at night, amid the earthly plants,
the sullen rose of dew that sleeps in your flag,
give me of moon or earth your bread dusted
with your frightful dark blood:
beneath your sandy light
there are no corpses, but long cycles of salt, blue
branches of mysterious dead metal.

XI

**House
Wrens**

Please don't be distrusting: it's summer,
water bathed me and raised desire
like a branch, my song sustains me
like a wrinkled trunk, with certain scars.
Minuscule, beloved, come perch on my head.
Nest on my shoulders, where the lizard's
splendor promenades, on my thoughts,
where so many leaves have fallen,

O minute circles of sweetness, grains
of winged wheat, little feathered egg,
purest forms on which
the unerring eye aims flight and life—
here, nest in my ear, distrustful
and diminutive: help me:
every day I want to be more bird.

**Red-Breasted
Meadowlark**

Beside me, bloodstained, but absent.
With your cruel mask and warrior's eyes,
amid the clods of earth, hopping from treasure
to treasure, in the pure and wild plenitude.
Tell me how, among all,
among all our woodlands' dark
nesting formation which the rain
tinged with its laments, how your
breast alone absorbs all the world's rouge?
Ah, you're sprinkled by red summer,
you've entered the scarlet pollen's grotto
and your stain gathers all the fire.
And that stare—more than the firmament
and the snowy night in its Andean bulwark—
when it opens its daily fan, nothing
stops it: just your briar that
keeps on blazing without burning the earth.

**Chucao
Tapaculo**

In the cold multiplied foliage, suddenly
the chucao's call as if nothing existed
but that cry of all the wilds combined,
like that call of all the wet trees.
The cry, slower and deeper than flight, passed
trembling and dark over my horse: I stopped—
where was I? What days were those?
All that I lived galloping in those
lost seasons, the world of rain
on windows, the puma in the elements,
prowling round with two points of bloody fire,
and the sea of channels, amid green tunnels
of drenched beauty, the solitude, my first
love's kiss beneath the hazel trees,
all surged up suddenly when in the jungle the cry
of the chucao passed by with its wet syllables.

XII

Botany   The sanguinary litre and the beneficent
boldo tree disseminate their style
in irritating emerald animal kisses or
anthologies of dark water around the stones.

Mistletoe establishes its white teeth
in the treetops
and the wild hazel tree builds its castle
of pages and raindrops.
Mugwort and grama grass circle
the oregano's eyes
and radiant borderlands laurel
perfumes the distant intendencies.

Quila and quelenquelén in the morning.
Cold language of fuchsias
wending its way through the tricolored stones
shouting "Viva Chile" with the foam!

Golden foxglove waits for
the snow's fingers
and time rolls on without its matrimony
that would join the angels of fire and sugar.

The magic Winter's bark
bathes its family branches in the rain
and hurtles its green ingots
beneath the vegetable water of the South.

Laden with flowers,
the ulmo's sweet limb
raises the droplets of the red copihue
to meet the sun of the guitars.

Wild delgadilla
and celestial spearmint
dance on meadows with young dew,
recently arranged by the River Toltén.

The indecipherable doca
decapitates its purple in the sand
and conducts its marine triangles
toward the dry littoral moons.

The burnished poppy,
lightning and wound, dart and mouth,
puts its scarlet punctuations
upon the burning wheat.

The evident patagua
decorates its dead
and weaves its families
with springwater and river medallions.

Paico arranges lanterns
in the climate of the South, forsaken,
when the ever sleepless
sea night falls.

The southland beech sleeps alone,
very vertical, very poor, very frazzled,
very decisive in the pure meadow
with its shabby down-and-outer's suit
and its head full of solemn stars.

XIII

**Araucaria
Pine**

The entire winter, the entire battle,
all the nests of wet iron
rise up in your wild citadel,
in your air-pierced fortitude.

The renegade prison of stones,
the spine's submerged threads,
transform your barbed hair into
a pavilion of mineral shadows.

Bristling tears, eternity of water,
scaly mount, thunderbolt of horseshoes,
your tormented house is built
with petals of pure geology.

Midwinter kisses your armor
and covers you with ravaged lips:
violent-smelling springtime

tears its net in your implacable statue:
and solemn autumn waits in vain
to pour gold on your green stature.

XIV

**Tomás
Lago**

Others went to bed between the pages sleeping
like Elzeviran insects, disputing
(as in football) recently printed books among
themselves, scoring goals of wisdom.
We sang then in the springtime,
beside rivers that dredge the Andes' stones,
and we were entwined with our women sipping
more than one honeycomb, devouring even the
    world's sulphur.
Not only that but much more: we shared
life with humble friends whom we loved
and who taught us with the wine's vintage
the sand's honorable alphabet, the repose
of those who've managed to rise
from adversity singing. O days when
we visited the cellars and dives together,
destroying spiderwebs, and wandering
the shores of the South beneath the night
and its stirred mortar:
all was flower and fleeting countryside,
all was rain and misty matter.
What a wide road we walked, stopping
over in the inns, turning
our attention to an extreme sunset, a stone,
a wall scribbled with charcoal, a group
of stokers who suddenly
taught us all the winter songs.
Not only the caterpillar, bathed in cellulose,
metamorphosed on our windows, ever more
celestial in its role of bookworm,
but the man of steel, the enraged, the cowboy
who tried to rob us at gunpoint,
threatening us with devouring our mothers
and pawning our possessions
(calling all this *heroism* and other things).
We watched them go their merry way, they
    couldn't

squeeze a cent out of us or make us bat an eyelid,
and each went off to his grave
of European newspapers or Bolivian pesos.
Our lanterns, still lit, burn
brighter than paper and bandits.

**Rubén
Azócar**

"To the islands!" we said. Those were confident
        days,
and we were sustained by illustrious trees:
nothing seemed distant to us, on the spur of a
        moment
anything could become entwined in the light we
        produced.
We arrived with thick leather shoes: it rained
and rained in the islands, and that's how the
        territory
was maintained like a green hand, like a glove
whose fingers floated
                            amid the red kelp.
We filled the archipelago with tobacco, smoked
into the wee hours at the Hotel Nilsson, and fired
fresh oysters at all the cardinal points.
The city had a religious factory.
On sleepy afternoons, a black procession
filed out of its great doors like a long beetle
with cassocks, beneath the sad rain:
we hastened to all the burgundies, filled
paper with signs of hieroglyphic sorrow.
Suddenly I slipped away: for many years, faraway,
in other climes that claimed my passions,
I remembered the boats beneath the rain, with
        you,
for there you remained so that your bushy
        eyebrows
could strike their wet roots in the islands.

**Juvencio
Valle**

Juvencio, nobody knows like you and me
the Boroa forest's secret: nobody
knows certain paths of red earth
on which the hazel tree's light dawns.
When people don't hear us they don't know
that we're listening to the rain on trees and zinc

roofs, that we're still in love with the telegraphist,
that girl, that girl who knows,
like us, the sinking cry of winter
trains, in the country.
                              Silent, you alone
entered the aroma distilled by rain,
incited the flora's golden increase,
harvested the jasmine before it blossomed.
The sad clay, in front of the stores,
the clay ground by solemn ox carts
like the black sludge of certain sufferings,
is, who knows better than you?, scattered
behind the deep springtime.
                              We've
kept other secret treasures too:
leaves that cover the earth like
scarlet tongues and stones worn smooth
by the currrent, river stones.

Diego Muñoz

We not only defended ourselves, it seems, with
        discoveries
and signs drawn over tempestuous paper,
but, captains, we corrected
the malignant streets with fists
and then amid accordions raised
our spirts with water and riggings.
Sailor, now you've returned from your seaports,
from Guayaquil, odors of dusty fruits,
and all the earth a steely sun
that made you sow victorious swords.
Today an hour has arrived above the country's
coal—the sorrows and love we shared—
and from the sea a thread of fraternity vaster
than the earth rises above your voice.

XV

Rider in the Rain

Fundamental waters, walls of water, clover
and assailed oats,
cordage now bound to the net of a wet,
dripping, savagely spun night,
rending raindrop repeated in lament,

diagonal rage cutting sky.
Horses drenched in perfume gallop
underwater, pounding the water, charging it
with their red branches of hair, stone and water:
and steam like a demented milk accompanies
the hardened water with fleeting doves.
There's no day, but cisterns
of harsh climate, green movement,
and hooves bind swift earth and flux
amid bestial aroma of horse with rain.
Blankets, saddles, sheepskins bunched
in dark pomegranates upon the
burning sulphur backs that pound
the jungle, telling it:
                         Beyond, beyond, beyond,
beyond, beyond, beyond, beyooooond,
riders demolish the rain, riders
pass beneath the bitter hazel trees, rain
twists its sempiternal wheat in tremulous rays.
There's light from the water, blurred lightning
cast on the leaf, and a flightless water, wounded
by the earth, rises from the very sound of the
      gallop.
Wet reins, arbored vault,
tunnels of pounding hoofbeats, vegetable
nocturne of stars shattered like ice or moon,
      cyclonic horse
covered by arrows like a frozen specter,
full of new hands born in fury,
throbbing apple besieged by fear
and the frightful banner of its great monarchy.

XVI

**Chile's
Seas**
  In faraway regions I bathed
your foamy feet, your scattered shore,
with furious exiled tears.

Today I come to your mouth, today to your
      brow.

I didn't disclose your respectful secret
or syllable to the sanguinary coral,

to the burned star
or the incandescent and battered waters.
I safeguarded your enraged voice, a petal
of tutelary sand
amid the furniture and old clothes.

A dust of bells, a wet rose.

And it was often Arauco's
selfsame water, hard water:
but I preserved my submerged stone
and in it, the pulsing sound of your shadow.

O, Chilean sea, O, water
soaring and encircling like a raging wildfire,
pressure and dream and sapphire fingernails,
O, earthquake of salt and lions!
Fountainhead, source, planet's
seashore, your eyelids
open the earth's noontide
attacking the stars' blue.
Salt and movement are released from you,
distributing ocean to mankind's grottoes
until your weight breaks beyond the islands
and extends a bouquet of total substances.
Sea of the northern desert, sea that hammers the
        copper
and advances the foam toward the hand
of the harsh solitary inhabitant,
amid pelicans, rocks with cold sun and dung,
coast burned by the passage of an inhuman dawn!

Sea of Valparaíso, wave
of lonely nocturnal light,
window of the ocean
from which my country's
statue looks out,
gazing with eyes still blind.

Sea of the South, sea ocean,
sea, mysterious moon,
in Imperial, terror of the southland beech,
in Chiloé anchored to blood,
and from Magellan to the limit
all the whistling salt, all the mad moon,
and the stellar streaking horse of the ice.

XVII

O, yes, imprecise snow,
O, yes, trembling in full snowy blossom,
boreal eyelid, little frozen ray,
who, who called you to the ashen valley,
who, who dragged you from the eagle's beak
down to where your pure waters touch
my country's terrible tatters?
River, why do you convey
cold secret water,
water that the stones' hard dawn
preserved in its inaccessible cathedral,
to the wounded feet of my people?
Return, return to your chalice of snow, bitter
        river,
return, return to your chalice of spacious frost,
submerge your silvery root in your secret source
or plunge and burst in another tearless sea!
Mapocho River, when night falls
and, like a black recumbent statue,
sleeps under your bridges with a black cluster
of heads smitten by cold and hunger
like two immense eagles, O river,
O harsh river born of the snow,
why don't you rise like an immense phantom
or a new cross of stars for the forsaken?
No, your brusque ash now runs
beside the sob cast into the black water,
beside the torn sleeve that the cruel wind
makes shiver beneath the iron leaves.
Mapocho River, where do you carry
plumes of ice forever wounded,
will the wild flower blossom forever
bitten by lice beside your purple banks,
with your cold tongue rasping
my naked country's cheeks?
                            O, let it not be so,
O, let it not be so, and let a drop of your black
        foam
leap from the loam to the flower of fire
and precipitate mankind's seed!

THE EARTH'S
NAME IS JUAN

I

**Cristóbal
Miranda
(Shoveler,
Tocopilla)**

I met you, Cristóbal, on the barges
in the bay, when the saltpeter
comes down, to the sea, in the scorching
attire of a November day.
I remember that static bearing,
the metal hills, the still water.
And the bargeman alone, bathed
in sweat, moving snow.
Nitrate snow, poured
on the shoulders of sorrow, falling
into the ships' blind bellies.
There, shovelers, heroes of an
acid-etched dawn, subject
to the fates of death, firm,
receiving the torrential nitrate.
Cristóbal, this keepsake for you.
For the shovel comrades,
in whose breasts acid enters,

and murderous emanations,
bloating hearts like vanquished
eagles, until man falls,
until man tumbles into the streets,
into the pampa's broken crosses.
Enough said, Cristóbal, now this
paper remembers you, all of you—
bargemen in the bay, man
blackened by the ships—my eyes
accompany you on this shift
and my soul's a shovel that rises
loading and unloading blood and snow,
beside you, desert lives.

II

Jesús
Gutiérrez
(Agrarian)

My Father, Genovevo Gutiérrez,
died in Monterrey. He left
with Zapata. At night, horses
beside the house, government troops'
smoke, gunshots in the wind,
the hurricane that rises from the corn,
rifle slung across his chest,
from the lands of Sonora,
sleeping on the run, we measured
rivers and forests, on horseback,
amid corpses, to defend
the land of the poor, beans,
tortilla, guitar, we rolled on
to the limits—we were dust,
the gentry took an early lead,
until our rifles
rose from every stone.
Here's my house, my little
parcel of land, the certificate
signed by my general
Cárdenas, turkeys,
ducklings in the pond,
the fighting's over now,
my father remained in Monterrey
and hanging here on the wall
beside the door my cartridge belt,

rifle ready, horse ready,
for the land, for our bread,
tomorrow perhaps on the gallop,
if my general so advises.

III

**Luis Cortés
(from Tocopilla)**

Comrade, my name's Luis Cortés.
When the repression came, they arrested me
in Tocopilla. They threw me into Pisagua.
You know, comrade, what that's like.
Many fell ill, others
went mad. It's González
Videla's worst concentration camp.
I saw Angel Veas die of heart failure
one morning. It was terrible
to see him die in that murderous sand,
surrounded by barbed wire, after all
his generous life. When I too developed
heart problems, they transferred me
to Garitaya. You can't imagine, comrade.
It's high up, on the border with Bolivia.
A desolate outpost, at 5,000 meters elevation.
There's brackish drinking water, saltier
than seawater, full of sand fleas
that seethe like pink maggots.
It's cold and the sky atop
the solitude seemed to fall on us,
on my heart that could bear it no more.
Even the police took pity,
and against orders to let us die
without ever attempting to send a stretcher,
they bound me to a mule and we came down the
      mountains:
26 hours the mule walked, and my body
endured no more, comrade, amid the roadless
      cordillera,
and my heart bad, so here I am, look at
the bruises, I don't know how long I'll last,
but it's up to you, I don't intend to ask for
      anything,

comrade, tell them what the scoundrel's doing to
    the people,
to those of us who carried him to the top where
    he laughs
like a laughing hyena over our sorrows,
tell it, tell it like it is, comrade, neither my death
    nor
our suffering is important because the struggle is
    long,
but speak out about this suffering,
speak out, comrade, don't forget.

IV

**Olegario
Sepúlveda
(Shoemaker,
Talcahuano)**

My name is Olegario Sepúlveda.
I'm a shoemaker, crippled
since the great earthquake.
Part of the hill on the tenement
and the world on my leg.
I called out there for two days,
but my mouth was full of earth,
my call grew fainter
until I dozed off to die.
The earthquake was a great silence,
terror in the hills,
washwomen wept,
a mountain of dust
buried words.
So here I am with this shoe sole,
facing the sea, the only clean thing —
the waves shouldn't
come blue to my door.
Talcahuano, your filthy slipways,
your corridors of poverty,
foul water in the hills,
broken wood, black caves
where the Chilean kills and dies.
(Oh! sorrows of misery's
open vein, leprosy of the world,
slums of corpses, accusing
and venomous gangrene!
Have you come from the somber
Pacific, at night, to the seaport?

Have you touched, amid the pustules,
the child's hand, the rose
spattered by salt and urine?
Have you raised your eyes
through the tortuous steps?
Have you seen the beggar woman
tremble like wire in the garbage,
rise from her hands and knees
and gaze up from the bottom where
there are no more tears or hatred left?)
I'm a shoemaker in Talcahuano.
Sepúlveda, in front of the great Dike.
Any time, sir, the poor
never shut their doors.

V

Arturo
Carrión
(Seaman,
Iquique)

June 1948. Dear Rosaura, I'm
here in Iquique, in jail, send me a shirt
and tobacco. I don't know
how long this dance will last.
When I shipped out on the *Glenfoster*
I thought about you, I wrote you from Cádiz,
where they executed at will, then it was
grimmer in Athens, that morning
in the jail they shot two hundred
seventy-three youths to death.
The blood ran outside the wall,
we saw Greek officers
with American commanders come out laughing:
they enjoy the people's blood,
but there was something like a pall of smoke
in the city, the weeping, anguish and mourning
were hidden,
I bought you a card file, there
I met a countryman from Chiloé
who owns a little restaurant, he told me
that things are bad, there's hatred:
then it was better in Hungary,
the peasants have land,
they distribute books, in New York
I got your letter, but they all
gang up to pound on the poor,

so, you see, I'm an old sailor
and since I'm a union member,
no sooner had they taken me from the deck
than they asked me
stupid questions, arrested me,
police everywhere,
tears on the pampa too:
everyone wonders how long
these things will last, nowadays
the poor keep taking a pounding,
they say they're two thousand in Pisagua,
I wonder what's happening to the world,
but the police say we're not allowed to question
these things: don't forget the tobacco, speak with
    Rojas
if he's not in jail, don't cry,
the world has too many
tears, something else is needed
and I hope to see you soon,
hugs and kisses from your loving husband,
Arturo Carrión Cornejo,
Iquique jail.

VI

**Abraham
Jesús Brito
(People's
Poet)**

His name is Jesús Brito, Jesús Parrón or People,
and he kept turning into water through his eyes,
and through his hands he kept turning into roots,
until they planted him again where he was
before he came to be, before he rose
from the territory, amid the poor stones.

And amid mine and mariner he was
a knotty bird, a patriarchal saddler
of the terrible homeland's smooth bark:
the colder it was, the bluer he found it:
the harder the ground, the more the moon rose
    from him:
the hungrier he was, the more he sang.

And he opened the entire world of the railways
with his key and his gnarled lyre,
and walked through the country's foam

filled with starry little packages,
he, the tree of copper, kept watering
every little clover in his path,
dreadful crimes, fires,
and the branch of tutelary rivers.

His voice was hoarse cries
drowned in a night of kidnappings,
he bore torrential bells
gathered at night in his hat,
and he gathered the people's
bursting tears in his tattered sack.
He journeyed the sandy branch lines,
through the sunken expanse of saltpeter,
through the harsh coastal hills
building his ballad clef by clef,
and tile by tile erecting his verse:
endowing it with the grime from his hands
and the leaks of his orthography.

Brito, along the capital walls,
amid the cafés' murmurings,
you wandered like a migrant tree
seeking soil with deep feet,
until you turned yourself into roots,
stone and clump and dark mining.

Brito, your majesty was beaten
like a majestic leather drum
and your dominion of woodlands and people
was a monarchy exposed to the elements.

Drifting tree, now your roots
sing beneath the land, and in silence.
You're a little deeper now.
Now you have land and you have time.

VII

Antonio
Bernales
(Fisherman,
Colombia)

The Magdalena River moves like the moon,
leisurely through the planet of green leaves,
a red bird wails, the whirring sound
of aged black wings, the riverbanks

tinge the coursing of waters upon waters.
Everything is river, every life river,
and Antonio Bernales was river.
Fisherman, carpenter, oarsman, netting
needle, nail for the planks,
hammer and song, Antonio was everything
while the Magdalena dredged the torrent
of river lives like a leisurely moon.
Higher up in Bogotá, flames, fire,
blood, Gaitán is dead, or so
it's rumored. Amid the leaves,
like a jackal, Laureano's laughter
fans the flames, the people's
tremor penetrates the Magdalena
like a shiver.
Antonio Bernales is the culprit.
He never left his shack.
He spent those days sleeping.
But the lawyers so decree,
Enrique Santos wants blood.
They all join beneath their frock coats.
Antonio Bernales has fallen
murdered in revenge,
he fell open-armed into the river,
returned to his river as to mother water.
The Magdalena washes his corpse to sea
and from the sea to other rivers, to other waters
and other seas and other little rivers
spinning round the earth.
                              Again
he enters the Magdalena, they're the riverbanks
that he loves, he opens arms of red water,
passes amid shadows, amid dense light,
and again continues his waterway.
Antonio Bernales, no one can
distinguish you in the riverbed, but I remember
      you
and hear the tow of your name that cannot
die, that envelops the earth,
just a name, people, amid names.

VIII

I'm dead. I'm from María Elena.
I spent my entire life on the pampa.
We gave our blood to the North American
Company, my parents before, my brothers and
    sisters.
Without striking, without reason, they surrounded
    us.
The entire Army came, at night,
they went from house to house awakening people,
taking them to the concentration camp.
I hoped that we wouldn't go.
My husband worked so hard for the Company,
and for the President, he did the most
to get votes here, he's so loved,
no one has anything bad to say about him, he
    fights
for his ideals, few are so pure
and honorable. Then Colonel Urízar
ordered them to come to our door,
and they dragged him away half-dressed and
    shoved
him violently into the truck that departed in the
    night
for Pisagua, for darkness. Then
I felt I could no longer breathe, I felt
the ground give way beneath my feet,
there's so much betrayal, so much injustice,
that something like a sob that wouldn't let me live
rose to my throat. My friends brought me food,
and I told them: "I won't eat until he returns."
On the third day they spoke to Mr. Urízar,
who roared with laughter, they sent
telegram after telegram that the tyrant in Santiago
never acknowledged. I kept sleeping and dying,
not eating, clenching my teeth in order to refuse
even soup or water. He never returned, he never
    returned,
and little by little I died away, and they buried
    me:
here, in the cemetery of the nitrate works.
That afternoon there was a windstorm,

the aged and the women wept and sang
the song that I'd sung so often with them.
If I'd been able, I would have looked to see if
    Antonio,
my husband, was there, but he wasn't, he wasn't,
they didn't even allow him to attend my death:
    now
I'm here, dead, in the pampa cemetery
there's nothing but solitude about me, for I no
    longer am,
I'll no longer be, without him, ever again,
    without him.

IX

**José Cruz
Achachalla
(Miner, Bolivia)**

Yes, Sir, José Cruz Achachalla,
from Sierra de Granito, south of Oruro.
And that's where my mother
Rosalía must still be living:
she works for some folks,
washing their clothes.
We went hungry, captain,
and they beat my mother
daily with a switch.
That's why I became a miner.
I escaped through the great sierras,
a little leaf of coca, sir,
some branches on my head
and walk, walk, walk. Vultures
followed me from the sky,
and I thought: they're better
than the white folks from Oruro,
and so I walked to the mining
territory.
        It's been
forty years, I was
a starving child then. The miners
took me in. I was an apprentice
and in the dark galleries,
fingernail by fingernail against the earth,
I gathered the hidden tin.
I don't know where or why
the silvery ingots are dispatched:

we live poorly, in broken-down houses,
and hunger, again, sir,
and when
we joined together, captain,
for another peso of salary,
the red wind, the club, fire,
the police pounded us,
so here I am, captain,
fired from work,
and where can I go,
no one knows me in Oruro,
I'm old as the stones,
I can no longer cross the mountains,
what can I do on the road,
I'm stuck here now,
let them bury me in the tin,
the tin alone knows me.
Yes, José Cruz Achachalla,
don't keep moving around,
you've reached the end of the line, the end,
Achachalla, you've reached the end of the line.

X

**Eufrosino
Ramírez
(Casa Verde,
Chuquicamata)**

We had to take the hot sheets
of copper with our hands, and feed them
to the power shovel. They emerged red-hot,
heavy as the world, we were overfatigued
transporting the slabs of mineral, occasionally
one of them fell on a foot, shattering it,
on a hand, turning it into a stump.
The gringos came and said: "The faster
you carry them the sooner you go home."
With great difficulty, in order to leave earlier,
we did the job as told. But they returned:
"Now that you work less, you earn less."
Casa Verde went on strike, a ten-week
strike, and when we returned to work,
I was given the gate with a pretext:
"Where are your tools?" Look at these hands,
turned into callouses by the copper,
listen to my heart, can you hear it
murmur?, the copper crushes it,

247

and I can hardly walk from place to place
searching, hungrily, for work that I can't find:
It seems that they see me stooped, carrying
invisible sheets of the copper that's killing me.

XI

**Juan Figueroa
("María Elena"
Iodine Works,
Antofagasta)**

Are you Neruda? Come in, comrade.
Yes, at the Iodine Works, there are no others
living now. I'm hanging on.
I know that I'm no longer alive, that the pampa
earth awaits me. It's four hours
a day, at the Iodine Works.
It comes through some pipes, and emerges like
        dough,
like purple rubber. We take it
from tub to tub, wrapped
like a baby. Meanwhile,
the acid eats away at us, saps us,
entering our eyes and mouths,
our skin, our fingernails.
You don't leave the Iodine Works
singing, my friend. And if we ask
them to raise our salaries a few pesos
for our shoeless children, comrade,
they say, "Moscow's their mastermind,"
and declare a state of siege, corral us
like animals and beat us,
and that's how these sons of bitches are, comrade.
So here I am, now I'm the last:
where's Sánchez? where's Rodríguez?
Rotting beneath the dust of Dustville.
Death finally gave them what we requested:
their faces have masks of iodine.

XII

**Maestro Huerta
(from the "La
Despreciada" Mine,
Antofagasta)**

When you visit the North, sir,
go to the mine "La Despreciada,"
and ask for maestro Huerta.

From afar you'll see nothing
but gray sandbanks.
Then you'll see structures,
the cableway, mounds of rubble.
Fatigue, suffering,
aren't visible, they're moving
underground, crushing beings,
or they're at rest, stretched out,
silently transforming themselves.
Maestro Huerta was a "pickman."
He measured 6'5".
Pickmen are the people who break
the earth down to the lower ground
when the vein's level decreases.
1600 feet below,
with water up to the waist,
the pickman keeps picking away.
He only leaves the inferno
once every forty-eight hours,
after the drilling
in the rock, in the darkness,
in the mud, leaves the pulp
wherever the mine meanders.
Maestro Huerta, a great pickman,
seemed to fill the shaft
with his shoulders. He entered
singing like a captain.
He emerged pocked, yellow,
hunchbacked, withered, and his eyes
were those of a corpse.
Then he shuffled through the mine.
He could no longer descend the shaft.
Antimony consumed his innards.
He grew so thin that it was frightening.
He couldn't even walk.
His legs seemed pierced
by knifepoint, and since he was
so tall he looked
like a starving ghost
begging without begging, you know.
He didn't reach his thirtieth birthday.
Ask where he's buried.
No one can tell you,
because the sand and wind batter
and bury the crosses, afterward.

It's up in "La Despreciada,"
where maestro Huerta worked.

XIII

**Amador Cea
(from Coronel,
Chile, 1949)**

Since they had arrested my father,
and the President we elected passed through
and said we were all free, I asked them to release
        my dad.
They took me and beat me all day long.
I don't know anyone in the jail. I don't know, I
        can't
even remember their faces. It was the police.
Whenever I lost consciousness, they threw
water on my body and kept beating me.
In the afternoon, before leaving,
they dragged me into a bathroom,
shoved my head into the toilet
bowl filled with excrement. I gagged.
"Now, go ask the President, who sends you
this gift, for freedom," they told me.
I feel battered, they broke this rib.
But inside I'm the same as before, comrade.
They'll only break us by killing us.

XIV

**Benilda
Varela
(Concepción,
University City,
Chile, 1949)**

I made lunch for the kiddies and left.
I tried to enter Lota to see my husband.
As you know, the police are in command,
and no one can enter without their permission.
They didn't like the looks of my face. It was
        ordered
by González Videla, before he began
to give his speeches, so that our people
would be afraid. And so it was: they seized me,
stripped me, beat me to the ground.
I passed out. I came to on the floor,
naked, with a wet sheet covering
my bleeding body. I recognized one henchman:

the beast's name is Víctor Molina.
As soon as I opened my eyes, they continued
to beat me with pieces of rubber. My body's
    black
with blood, and I can't move.
There were five, and the five of them beat me
like a sack. And that went on for six hours.
If I haven't died, it's to be able to tell you,
    comrades:
we must fight much harder, until these butchers
disappear from the face of the earth.
Let the people become familiar with their speeches
on "freedom" in the UN,
while the outlaws beat women to death
in cellars, without anyone being aware.
Nothing happened here, they'll say, and Mr.
    Enrique
Molina will lecture us about the triumph of the
    "spirit."
But all this will not go on forever.
A phantom ranges the world, and they can begin
    to beat again
in the cellars: they'll soon pay for their crimes.

XV

**Calero,
Banana Worker
(Costa Rica,
1940)**

I don't know you. In the pages of Fallas I read
    about
your life, dark giant, abused, tattered and drifting
    child.

From those pages your laughter and songs fly
amid the banana workers, in the somber mud,
    rain and sweat.
What a life we lead, what ravaged happiness,
what strength destroyed by loathsome food,
what songs demolished by tumbledown shacks,
what powers of mankind undone by man!

But we'll change the earth. Your happy shadow
    won't go
from puddle to puddle toward naked death.
We'll change, joining your hand with mine,

the night that cloaks you with its green dome.

(The hands of the dead that fell
with these and other hands that build
are sealed, like the Andean heights
with their depths of buried iron.)

We'll change life that your kin
may survive and build their organized light.

XVI

Catastrophe
in Sewell

Sánchez, Reyes, Ramírez, Núñez, Álvarez.
These names are like Chile's foundations.
The people are the country's foundation.
If you let them die, the country keeps collapsing,
keeps bleeding until it is drained.
Ocampo has told us: every minute
there's a wound, and every hour a corpse.
Every minute and every hour
our blood falls, Chile dies.
Today it's smoke from the fire, yesterday
    firedamp,
the day before the cave-in, tomorrow the sea or
    the cold,
machinery and hunger, the unforeseen or acid.
But there where the seaman dies,
but there where people from the pampa die,
but there in Sewell where they disappeared,
everything is maintained—machinery, glass,
iron, papers—
except man, woman or child.
It's not the gas: it's greed that kills in Sewell.
That tap turned off in Sewell so that not even a
    drop
of water for the miners' poor coffee would fall,
there's the crime, the fire's not to blame.
Everywhere they turn off the people's tap
so that the water of life won't be distributed.
But the hunger and cold and fire that consume
our race (the flower, Chile's foundations),
the tatters, the miserable house,
they're not rationed, there's always enough
so that every minute there's a casualty

and every hour a corpse.
We have no gods to turn to.
Poor mothers dressed in black
already wept all their tears while they prayed.

We don't pray.
Stalin said: "Our best treasure
is mankind,"
the foundations, the people.
Stalin erects, cleans, builds, fortifies,
preserves, ponders, protects, nourishes,
but he punishes too.
And that's what I wanted to tell you, comrades:
punishment is needed.
This human cave-in cannot be,
this bleeding of the beloved country,
this blood that falls from the people's heart
every minute, this death
of every hour.
My name's the same as theirs, as the ones who
    died.
I, too, am Ramírez, Muñoz, Pérez, Fernández.
My name's Álvarez, Núñez, Tapia, López,
    Contreras.
I'm related to all those who die, I'm people,
and I mourn for all the blood that falls.
Compatriots, dead brothers, from Sewell, Chile's
dead, workers, brothers and sisters, comrades,
as you're silent today, we're going to speak.
And may your martyrdom help us
to build a severe nation
that will know how to flower and punish.

XVII

The
Earth's
Name Is
Juan

Juan followed upon the liberators
working, fishing and fighting,
in his carpentry work or in his damp mine.
His hands have plowed the earth and measured
the roads.
      His bones are everywhere.
But he's alive. He returned from the earth. He
was born.

He was born again like an eternal plant.
All the impure night tried to submerge him
and today he affirms his indomitable lips in the
    dawn.
They bound him, and he's now a determined
    soldier.
They wounded him, and he's still hearty as an
    apple.
They cut off his hands, and today he pounds with
    them.
They buried him, and he sings along with us.

Juan, the door and the road are yours.
                                    The earth
is yours, people, truth was born
with you, with your blood.
                    They couldn't exterminate you.
    Your roots,
tree of humanity,
tree of eternity,
are today defended with steel,
are today defended with your own grandeur
in the Soviet land, armored
against the snaps of the moribund wolf.

People, order was born of suffering.

Your victorious flag was born of order.

Hoist it with all the hands that fell,
defend it with all the hands that are joined:
and let the unity of your invisible faces
advance to the final struggle, to the star.

LET THE
WOODCUTTER
AWAKEN

*. . . And thou, Capernaum, which art
exalted to heaven, shalt be thrust down
to hell . . .*

Saint Luke, X, 15

I

**Let the
Woodcutter
Awaken**

West of the Colorado River
there's a place that I love.
I hasten there with every pulsing thing
that transpires in me, with all
that I was, that I am, that I sustain.
There are some high red stones, the wild
thousand-handed air
that made them edified structures:
the blind scarlet rose from the abyss
and became copper, fire and strength in them.
America stretched out like a buffalo skin,
aerial and clear night of the gallop,

there toward the starry heights,
I drink your glass of green dew.
Yes, through acrid Arizona and knotty Wisconsin,
to Milwaukee raised against the wind and snow,
or in the burning swamps of West Palm,
near Tacoma's pine groves, in your forests'
heavy smell of steel,
I wandered treading mother earth,
blue leaves, cascade stones,
hurricanes that trembled like all the music,
rivers that prayed like monasteries,
mallards and apples, lands and waters,
infinite quietude that the wheat might come forth.

There, in my central stone, I could extend to the
    air
my eyes, ears, hands, until I heard
books, locomotives, snow, struggles,
factories, graves, vegetable movements,
and from Manhattan the moon on the ship,
the song of the spinning machine,
the iron scoop that eats earth,
the drill with its condor's blow
and whatever cuts, presses, runs, sews:
beings and wheels repeating and being born.

I love the farmer's little house. Recent mothers
    sleep
scented like tamarind syrup, the linens
freshly ironed. Fire
burns in a thousand homes ringed with onions.
(When the men sing at the riverside they have
a hoarse voice like stones from the riverbed:
tobacco rose from its broad leaves
and reached these homes like a fire sprite.)
Come into Missouri, behold the cheese and wheat,
fragrant boards, red as violins,
man navigating the barley,
the newly mounted blue colt smells
the aroma of bread and alfalfa:
bells, butterflies, blacksmith shops,
and in the dilapidated wild movie houses
love opens its teeth
in the dream born of the earth.
It's your peace that we love, not your mask.
Your warrior's face is not beautiful.

You're beautiful and spacious, North America.
You're of humble stock like a washwoman,
beside your rivers, white.
Built in the unknown, your
honeycomb peace is your sweetness.
We love your man with his red hands
of Oregon clay, your black child
who brought you music born
in the ivory lands: we love
your city, your substance,
your light, your mechanisms, the West's
energy, the peaceful
honey, from hive and hamlet,
the gigantic lad on the tractor,
the oats that you inherited
from Jefferson, the whispering wheel
that measures your earthly ocean,
factory smoke and a new
colony's thousandth kiss:
we love your laborer's blood:
Your folk hand full of oil.

Beneath the prairie night the song
of all that I was before I came to be,
of all that we were, has long since rested
on a buffalo skin, in a solemn silence of syllables.
Melville's a spruce tree, a careen's curve
is born of his branches, an arm
of wood and ship. Whitman innumerable
as grain, Poe in his mathematical
darkness, Dreiser, Wolfe,
fresh wounds of our own absence,
recent Lockridge, bound to the depths,
how many others, bound to shadow:
above them burns the same dawn of the
        hemisphere
and what they made of it is what we are.
Powerful infantrymen, blind captains,
at times intimidated amid events and bombast,
interrupted by happiness and sorrow,
beneath the meadowlands crisscrossed by traffic,
how many casualties on fields never before visited:
tormented innocents, recently printed prophets,
on the buffalo skin of the meadowlands.

From France, from Okinawa, from the atolls
of Leyte (Norman Mailer has documented it),
from the enraged air and the waves,
almost all the boys have returned.
Almost all . . . the story of mud and sweat
was green and bitter: they didn't hear
the coral reefs' song enough
or touch, except perhaps to die on the islands, the
     crowns
of splendor and fragrance:
                         blood and manure
pursued them, filth and rats,
and a weary and anguished heart that fought on.
But now they've returned,
                    you've welcomed them
in the open spaces of outstretched lands
and they've closed (those who've returned) like a
     corolla
of innumerable anonymous petals
to be reborn and to forget.

II

But they've found
a house guest besides,
or they've brought new eyes (or they were blind
     before)
or the bristling branches tore their eyelids
or there are novel things in America's lands.
Those blacks who fought beside you, rugged
and spirited, look:
                they placed a burning cross
in front of their dwellings,
they've hanged and burned your blood brother:
they made him a combatant, today they deny him
voice and decision: the hooded
hangmen join forces
at night, with their crosses and whips.
                    (Something
else was heard fighting overseas.)
               A guest,
     unexpected
as a worn old octupus,

immense, all–enveloping,
occupied your house, poor soldier:
the press distills ancient poison, cultivated in
    Berlin.
The periodicals (*Time, Newsweek,* etc.) have been
    turned
into yellow leaves of indictment: Hearst,
who sang the Nazis a love song, grins
and files his fingernails so that you'll ship out
    again
to the reefs or steppes
to fight for this guest who inhabits your house.
They give you no respite: they want to keep
    selling
steel and bullets, to prepare new gunpowder
and sell it fast, before the fresh
gunpowder advances and falls into new hands.

The masters installed in your mansion
extend their phalanges everywhere,
they love black Spain and offer you a glass of
    blood
(one execution, one hundred): the *Marshall cocktail.*
Select young blood: China's
peasants, prisoners
from Spain,
blood and sweat from Cuba's sugar bowl,
women's tears
from Chile's coal and copper mines,
then stir vigorously,
like beating with a baton,
not forgetting the ice cubes and a few dashes
of the song *We Defend Christian Culture.*
Is this a bitter brew?
You'll soon get used to drinking it, poor soldier.
Anywhere in the world, in the moonlight,
or in the morning, in a luxury hotel,
request this drink that invigorates and refreshes
and pay for it with a bona fide bill
with Washington's image.

You've also found that Charlie Chaplin, the
    world's
last father of tenderness,
should flee, and that writers (Howard Fast, etc.),
scholars and artists

in your land
must sit to be judged for "un-American" thoughts
before a tribunal of merchants enriched by the
    war.
Fear has reached the uttermost parts of the earth.
My aunt reads this news, alarmed,
and all the earth's eyes witness
these tribunals of shame and revenge.
They're the witness stands of the bloody Babbits,
the slavers, Lincoln's assassins,
they're the new inquisitions raised now,
not by the cross (and then it was horrible and
    inexplicable)
but by the round gold that rings
on the tables of brothels and banks
and has no right to sit in judgment.

In Bogotá Moriñigo, Trujillo, González Videla,
Somoza, Dutra, joined together and applauded.
You, young America, don't know them: they're
the dark vampires of our sky,
the shadow of their wings is bitter:
                      shackles,
martyrdom, death, hatred: the petroleum
and nitrate lands of the South
conceived monsters.
              At night in Chile, in Lota,
in the miners' humble and wet houses,
the hangman's order arrives. The children
awaken crying.
         Thousands
imprisoned, they estimate.
             In Paraguay
the dense forest shadow hides
the assassinated compatriot's bones, a gunshot
echoes
in the summer phosphorescence.
                Truth
died there.
        Why didn't Mr. Vandenberg,
Mr. Armour, Mr. Marshall, Mr. Hearst,
intervene in Santo Domingo to defend the West?
In Nicaragua, why did the President,
awake at night, tormented, have
to flee to die in exile?

(There are bananas to defend there, not *liberties*,
and that's why Somoza suffices.)
                                        The *grand*
victorious ideals are in Greece
and in China for the relief
of governments soiled like filthy rugs.
                    Ah, poor soldier!

III

Beyond your lands, America, I also wend my way
and make my wandering house: I fly about, pass
        through,
sing and chat for days on end.
And in Asia, in the USSR, in the Urals I stop
and stretch out my soul drenched in wilds and
        resin.

In the open spaces I love whatever
man has created by dint of love and struggle.
The pines' ancient night
still surrounds my house in the Urals,
and silence like a towering column.
Here wheat and steel were born
of mankind's hand and breast.
And a song of hammers cheers the ancient forest
like a new blue phenomenon.
From here I see extensive zones of humanity,
geography of children and women, love,
factories and songs, schools
that glow like gillyflowers in the forest
where only yesterday the wild fox thrived.
From this point my hand on the map embraces
the meadowlands' green, smoke
from a thousand workshops, textile
aromas, the wonder
of harnessed energy.
In the afternoon I return
on recently charted new roads
and enter kitchens
where cabbage simmers and a new
fountainhead rises for the world.

Here, too, the boys returned,
but countless millions remained behind,

strung up, hanging from the gallows,
burned in special ovens,
savaged until nothing was left of them
except a name in memory.
Their towns were annihilated too:
the Soviet land was annihilated:
millions of glass shards and bones fused,
cows and factories, until springtime
vanished, engulfed by the war.
But the boys returned,
and love for the homeland founded
had mingled in them with so much blood
that they say *Motherland* with their veins,
sing Soviet Union with their blood.
The voice of the conquerors of Prussia and
Berlin was loud when they returned
so that the cities, animals
and springtime would be reborn.
Walt Whitman, raise your beard of grass,
look with me from the forest,
from these perfumed magnitudes.
What do you see there, Walt Whitman?
I see, my deep brother tells me,
I see how the factories run,
in the city that the dead remember,
in the pure capital,
in resplendent Stalingrad.
From the field contested
through suffering and fire,
I see, rising in the morning moisture,
a tractor whirring toward the prairies.
Give me your voice and the weight of your
    buried breast,
Walt Whitman, and the solemn
roots of your face
to sing these reconstructions!
Let's sing together whatever arises
from all the sorrows, whatever surges
from the great silence, from the solemn
victory:
        Stalingrad, your steely voice surges,
floor by floor hope's reborn
like a collective house,
and there's a new tremor on the march
teaching,

singing
and building.

From the blood Stalingrad surges
like an orchestra of water, stone and iron,
and bread's reborn in the bakeries,
springtime in the schools,
it raises new scaffolds, new trees,
while the old iron Volga pulses on.
                             These books,
in fresh pine and cedar boxes,
are gathered over
the dead executioners' grave:
these theaters made in the ruins
blanket martyrdom and resistance:
books transparent as monuments:
a book above each hero,
above each millimeter of death,
above each petal of this immutable glory.

Soviet Union, if we joined
all the blood spilt in your struggle,
all that you gave like a mother to the world
that moribund freedom might live,
we'd have a new ocean,
greater than any,
deeper than any,
alive as all the rivers,
active as the Araucanian volcanoes' fire.
Plunge your hand into that sea,
mankind from every land,
then raise it to drown
the one who forgot, the one who defiled,
the one who lied and the one who soiled,
the one who joined a hundred little curs
from the rubbish heap of the West
to insult your blood, Mother of the free!

From the fragrant smell of the Ural pines
I see the library born
in the heart of Russia,
the laboratory where silence
labors, I see trains that transport
wood and songs to the new cities,
and in this balmy peace a throbbing swells
as in a new breast:

girls and doves return
to the steppeland waving whiteness,
orange groves are filled with gold:
today the market has
a new aroma
every dawn,
a new aroma that comes from the high lands
where martyrdom was unmatched:
engineers make the map of the prairies
tremble with their numbers
and the pipelines are wrapped like long serpents
in the lands of the new vaporous winter.

In three rooms of the old Kremlin
lives a man named Joseph Stalin.
His bedroom light is turned off late.
The world and his country allow him no rest.
Other heroes have given birth to a nation,
he helped to conceive his as well,
to build it
and defend it.
His immense country is, then, part of himself
and he cannot rest because it's never at rest.
In times past snow and gunpowder
found him facing the old bandits
who wanted (then as now) to revive
the *knut*, and misery, the slaves' anguish,
the slumbering sorrow of millions of poor.
He opposed those who, like Wrangel and
        Deniken,
were sent from the West to "defend Culture."
There those defenders of executioners
left their hides behind, and in the USSR's
spacious terrain, Stalin worked night and day.
But later the Germans fattened by Chamberlain
advanced in a wave of lead.
Stalin confronted them on all the vast frontiers,
on all the retreats, on all the advances,
and entered Berlin with his children like a
        hurricane
of peoples and brought Russia's spacious peace.
Molotov and Voroshilov
are there, I see them
with the others, the high generals,
the indomitable.
Firm as snowy oak groves.

None of them has palaces.
None has regiments of slaves.
None became rich in the war
selling blood.
None struts like a peacock
to Rio de Janeiro or Bogotá
to direct the little satraps stained with torture:
none has two hundred suits:
none has stocks in weapons factories,
and all have
stocks
in the happiness and construction
of the vast country where the dawn risen
on the night of death resounds.
They said "Comrade" to the world.
They made a king of the carpenter.
A camel won't be threaded through that needle.
They washed the villages.
They distributed land.
They raised the serf.
They expunged the beggar.
They annihilated the cruel.
They gave light to the spacious night.

That's why I address you, young lady from
    Arkansas, or
you, golden youth from West Point or best
you mechanic from Detroit or rather
you stevedore from old Orleans, to all
I speak and say: steady your step,
open your ears to the vast human world,
it's not the State Department dandies
or the ferocious owners of steel
speaking to you
but a poet from the far South of America,
son of a railwayman from Patagonia,
American as the Andean air,
today fugitive of a country where
prison, torment, anguish prevail
while copper and petroleum are slowly
turned into gold for foreign kings.
                You're not
the idol that bears gold in one hand
and in the other a bomb.
           You're
what I am, what I was, what we should

shelter, purest America's
fraternal subsoil, humble
humanity of the roads and streets.
My brother Juan sells shoes
like your brother John,
my sister Juana peels potatoes,
like your cousin Jane,
and my blood's miner and mariner
like your blood, Peter.

You and I are going to open the doors
so that air from the Urals
can breach the ink curtain,
you and I are going to tell the enraged:
"My dear guy, you've reached the limit,"
on this side the land belongs to us
so that we won't be hearing the hiss
of a machine gun but rather a
song, and song after song.

IV

But if you arm your hordes, North America,
to destroy that pure frontier
and bring the butcher from Chicago
to govern the music and the order
that we love,
   we'll rise from the stones and the air
to bite you:
   we'll rise from the last window
to pour fire on you:
   we'll rise from the deepest waves
to sting you with spines:
   we'll rise from the furrow so that the seed
will pound like a Colombian fist,

   we'll rise to deny you bread and water,
   we'll rise to burn you in hell.

So do not set foot, soldier,
on sweet France, because we'll be there
so that the verdant vineyards will yield vinegar
and humble girls will show you the spot

where German blood is fresh.
Do not ascend Spain's dry sierras
because every stone will be transformed into fire,
and the brave will fight there for a thousand
     years:
do not stray amid the olive groves because you'll
never return to Oklahoma, and do not enter
Greece, because even the blood that you're
     shedding today
will rise from the earth to arrest you.
Do not come to fish in Tocopilla
because the swordfish will recognize your spoils
and the obscure miner from Araucania
will seek the cruel ancient arrows
that await, buried, new conquerors.
Do not count on the gaucho singing a *vidalita*
or the worker in the meat-packing plants. They'll
be everywhere with eyes and fists,
like the Venezuelans who'll then be waiting for
     you
with a bottle of petroleum and a guitar in their
     hands.
Do not, do not enter Nicaragua either.
Sandino's asleep in the jungle awaiting that day,
his rifle has become filled with vines and rain,
his face has no eyelids,
but the mortal wounds with which you murdered
     him are alive
like Puerto Rico's hands that await
the knife's light.
                  The world will be implacable for
     you.
Not only will the islands be deserted but the air
that now knows the words that it loves.

Do not come to request high Peru's
human flesh: in the monuments' corroded mist
our blood's sweet ancestor sharpens
his swords of amethyst against you,
and in the valleys the hoarse battle conch
congregrates the warriors and slingmen,
children of Amaru. Don't seek men in the
Mexican cordilleras to take them to combat the
     dawn:
Zapata's rifles are not asleep,
they're oiled and aimed at the lands of Texas.

Do not enter Cuba, because from the marine
    splendor
of the sweaty canefields
there's just one dark stare that awaits you
and just one cry until they kill or die.
                              Do not
    approach
the partisans' land in whispering
Italy: do not step beyond the columns of
    waistcoated soldiers
that you keep in Rome, do not step beyond Saint
    Peter:
beyond, the villages' saintly rustics,
the fish's saintly seamen
love the great country of steppelands
where the world flowered again.
                         Do not touch
Bulgaria's bridges, Rumania's rivers
won't let you cross, we'll cast boiling blood into
    them
so that they'll burn the invaders:
do not greet the peasant who today knows
the feudal lords' grave and stands guard
with his plow and his rifle: do not stare at him
because he'll burn you like a star.
                         Do not
    disembark
in China: the Mercenary Chiang will no longer be
surrounded by his corrupt court of Mandarins:
there'll be a forest of peasant sickles
and a volcano of gunpowder awaiting you.

In other wars there were moats with water
and then wire entanglements, with barbs and
    claws,
but this moat is greater, these waters are deeper,
these wires more invincible than all the metals.
They're atom after atom of human metal,
they're one knot and a thousand knots of lives
    upon lives:
they're the old sorrows of peoples
from all the remote valleys and kingdoms,
from all the flags and ships,
from all the caves where they were huddled
    together,
from all the nets that set forth against the tempest,

from all the earth's harsh wrinkles,
from all the infernos of hot boilers,
from all the textile mills and foundries,
from all the locomotives lost or congregated.
This wire encircles the world a thousand times:
it seems divided, exiled,
and suddenly its magnets are united
until they fill the earth.
But even
further beyond, radiant and determined,
steely, smiling,
men and women from tundra and taiga
await you
to sing or to fight,
Volga warriors who vanquished death,
children from Stalingrad, giants from the Ukraine,
all the vast and towering wall of stone and blood,
iron and songs, courage and hope.
If you touch this wall you'll fall,
burned like coal from the factories,
Rochester's smiles will turn to darkness
that the steppeland air will then scatter
and the snow will then bury forever.
Those who've fought since Peter to the new
    heroes
who astonished the earth will come
and turn their medals into cold little bullets
that will whistle without respite from
all the vast earth that today is happiness.
And from the laboratory covered with vines
the unleashed atom will also set forth
toward your proud cities.

V

Let none of this come to pass.
Let the Woodcutter awaken.
Let Abraham come with his ax
and his wood plate
to eat with the peasants.
Let his head of bark,
his eyes seen in the boards,
in the oak's wrinkles,

return to behold the world
rising above the treetops,
higher than the sequoias.
Let him go shopping in the drugstores,
let him take a bus to Tampa,
let him bite into a yellow apple,
let him go to the movies, let him talk
with all the common people.

Let the Woodcutter awaken.

Let Abraham come, let his old
yeast swell Illinois's
gold and green earth,
and let him heft his people's ax
against the new slavers,
against the slave's whip,
against the poison press,
against the bloody merchandise
that they want to sell.
Let the white youth, the black youth,
march singing and smiling
against the walls of gold,
against the manufacturer of hatred,
against the merchant of their blood,
singing, smiling and conquering.

Let the Woodcutter awaken.

VI

Peace for the coming twilights,
peace for the bridge, peace for the wine,
peace for the letters that seek me
and that rise in my blood entwining
the old song with land and loves,
peace for the city in the morning
when bread rises, peace for the
Mississippi River, river of roots,
peace for my brother's shirt,
peace in the book like a stamp of air,
peace for Kiev's great kolkhoz,
peace for the ashes of these fallen,

and these other fallen, peace for Brooklyn's
iron black, peace for the mailman
from house to house like the day,
peace for the choreographer who shouts
to the vines with a megaphone,
peace for my right hand,
which only wants to write Rosario:
peace for the Bolivian secretive
as a tin stone, peace
that you may marry, peace for all
the Bío-Bío's sawmills,
peace for the broken heart
of warring Spain:
peace for Wyoming's little Museum
whose sweetest thing
is a pillow with an embroidered heart,
peace for the baker and his loves
and peace for the flour: peace
for all the wheat that need bring forth,
for all the love that will seek foliage,
peace for all the living: peace
for all lands and waters.

Here I say good-bye, I'm returning
home, in my dreams,
I'm returning to Patagonia where
wind pounds the stables
and the Ocean spatters ice.
I'm nothing but a poet: I love you all,
I've wandered the world that I love:
in my homeland they imprison miners
and soldiers command the judges.
But I love even the roots
of my cold country.
If I had to die a thousand times
I want to die there:
if I had to be born a thousand times
I want to be born there,
near the wild araucaria,
the south wind's bluster,
the newly purchased bells.
Let no one think about me.
Let's think about the whole earth,
pounding with love on the table.
I don't want blood to soak
the bread, beans, music,

again: I want the miner,
the little girl, the lawyer, the doll
manufacturer to accompany me,
let's go to the movies and set out

to drink the reddest wine.

I don't want to solve anything.

I came here to sing
so that you'd sing with me.

THE
FUGITIVE

I

**The
Fugitive
(1948)**

Through the dead of night, through my entire
    life,
from tear to paper, from clothes to clothes,
I paced these trying days.
I was the fugitive from justice:
and in the crystal hour, in the fastness
of solitary stars,
I crossed cities, forests,
small farms, seaports,
from the door of one human being to another,
from the hand of one being to another being, and
    another.
Solemn's the night, but man
has disposed his fraternal signs,
and groping my way along roads and shadows
I reached the lit doorway, the little
point of star that was mine,

the bread crumb that the wolves in the forest
had not devoured.

Once, in the countryside,
at night, I reached a house, where
I'd never seen anyone before that night
or even imagined those lives.
Whatever they did, their hours
were new in my consciousness.
I entered, they were a family of five:
all had arisen as on the night
of a fire.
                    I shook
hand after hand, saw face after face,
that said nothing to me: they were doors
that I didn't see before in the street,
eyes that didn't know my face,
and in the dead of night, after
welcoming me, I succumbed to fatigue,
to sleep my country's anguish.

As sleep approached,
the innumerable echo of the earth
with its hoarse barking and filaments
of solitude, the night advanced,
and I thought: "Where am I? Who
are they? Why are they sheltering me today?
Why do they, who never saw me before today,
open their doors and defend my song?"
And no one answered
except the rustling of a leafless night,
a fabric of crickets building up:
the entire night barely
seemed to tremble in the foliage.
Nocturnal land, you came
to my window with your lips
that I might sleep peacefully,
like falling on thousands of leaves,
from season to season, from nest to nest,
from branch to branch, until I suddenly
slumbered like a corpse in your roots.

II

It was the grape autumn.
The numerous arbor trembled.
The white clusters, veiled,
frosted their sweet fingers,
and the black grapes filled
their replete little udders
with a secret round river.
The owner of the house, a thin-faced
craftsman, read me
the pale earthy book
of crepuscular days.
His kindness knew the fruit,
the main trunk and the pruning
work that gives the tree
its naked form of a wineglass.

He spoke to the horses
as to immense children: the five
cats and the dogs of that house
followed behind him,
some arched and slow,
others running wildly
beneath the cold peach trees.
He knew each branch,
each scar of those trees,
and his ancient voice taught me
caressing the horses.

III

And so I turned to the night again.
As the Andean night crossed the city,
the brimming night opened its rose
on my suit.
                    It was winter in the South.
The snow had
climbed to its high pedestal, the cold
burned with a thousand frozen points.

The Mapocho River was black snow.
And I, amid street after street of silence
through the tyrant's soiled city.
Ah! I was the essence of silence
seeing how much love upon love fell
from my eyes on my breast.
Because that street and the other and the snowy
night's threshold, and the nocturnal
solitude of beings, of my people,
submerged, dark, in their slums of corpses,
everything, the last window
with its little bouquet of false light,
the crammed black coral
of room after room, my country's
never-spent wind,
everything was mine, everything
raised to me in the silence
a loving mouth filled with kisses.

IV

A young couple opened a door
that I didn't know before either.
                                    She was
golden as the month of June,
he an engineer with lofty eyes.
From then on I shared bread and wine
with them,
            little by little
I reached their unknown intimacy.
They told me: "We were
separated,
our dissension was now eternal:
today we joined to welcome you,
today we awaited you together."
There, united
in the little room,
we embodied silent fortitude.
I kept silence even in my sleep.
I was in the dead
center of the city, I almost heard
the Traitor's footsteps, beside the walls
that separated me, I heard

the jailors' filthy voices,
their crooked laughter, their drunk
syllables inserted amid bullets
in my homeland's waist.
The belches of Holgers and Pobletes
almost brushed my silent skin,
their footsteps, shuffling along, almost
touched my heart and its bonfires:
they, consigning my people to torment,
I preserving my swordlike health.
And again, in the night, good-bye, Irene,
good-bye, Andrés, good-bye, new friend,
good-bye to the scaffolds, to the star,
good-bye perhaps to the unfinished house
which in front of my window seemed
to become filled with linear phantoms.
Good-bye to the minute speck of mountain
that gathered in my eyes every afternoon,
good-bye to the green neon light that opened
every new night with its lightning.

V

Again, another night, I went farther.
The entire cordillera of the coast,
the wide strand to the Pacific Ocean,
and then amid tortuous streets,
bystreets and blind alleys, Valparaíso.
I entered a house of seamen.
The mother was expecting me.
"I didn't know until yesterday," she told me.
"My son called me, and Neruda's name
ran through me like a shiver.
But I asked him: what amenities
can we offer him?" "He belongs
to us, the poor," he replied,
"he doesn't ridicule or disdain
our poor life, he upholds it
and defends it." "I told him: so be it,
this is his house from this day on."
No one knew me in that house.
I looked at the clean tablecloth, the pitcher of
	water

pure as those lives that from the depths
of night came to me
like crystal wings.
I went to the window: Valparaíso opened a
     thousand
trembling eyelids, the nocturnal
sea air entered my mouth,
the lights from the hills, the tremor
of the maritime moon on the water,
darkness like a monarchy
adorned with green diamonds,
all the new repose that life
offered me.
          I looked: the table was set,
bread, napkin, wine, water,
and a fragrance of earth and tenderness
moistened my soldier's eyes.
Beside that window from Valparaíso
I spent days and nights.
My new home's navigators
searched daily
for a ship to leave on.
          They were
deceived time and again.
                    The *Antomena*
couldn't take them, the *Sultan*
either. They explained to me:
They paid the bite or bribe
to one boss after another. Others
paid more.
          Everything was corrupt
like the Palace in Santiago.
Here they opened the pockets
of the foreman, the Secretary,
not so deep as the
President's pockets, but they gnawed
the poor's skeleton.
Sad republic lashed
by thieves like a dog,
howling alone on the roads,
beaten by the police.
Sad Gonzalized nation
cast into the informer's
vomit by petty crooks,
sold on broken-down street corners,
dismantled in public auction.

Sad republic in the hands
of him who sold his own daughter
and surrendered his own country
wounded, mute and manacled.
The two seamen returned
and left again to load
sacks, bananas, foodstuffs,
longing for the waves' salt,
seabiscuits, the towering sky.

On my solitary day the sea
receded: then I beheld
the hills' vital flame,
every house perched precariously, the
pulse of Valparaíso:
the high hills brimming
with lives, doors painted
turquoise, scarlet and pink,
toothless steps,
clusters of poor doors,
dilapidated dwellings,
fog, mist extending its
nets of salt over things,
desperate trees
clinging to the ravines,
clothes hanging from the arms
of inhuman hovels,
the hoarse whistle, abrupt
creature of the vessels,
the sound of brine,
of the fog, the sea voice,
made of strokes and murmurs,
all this enfolded my body
like a new earthly suit,
and I inhabited the mist from above,
the towering city of the poor.

VI

Window of the hills! Valparaíso,
cold tin,
shattered in cry after cry of popular stones!
Behold with me from my hideaway

the gray seaport trimmed with boats,
slightly shifting lunar water,
immobile depositories of iron.
In another distant hour,
the sea was filled, Valparaíso,
with the slender ships of pride,
the Five-Masters with the whisper of wheat,
the disseminators of saltpeter,
those that came to you from
the nuptial oceans, filling your holds to the brim.
Lofty windships of the maritime day,
commercial crusaders, banners
swollen by the seafaring night,
with you ebony and the pure
clarity of ivory, the aromas
of coffee and of night in another moon,
came to your perilous peace,
Valparaíso, enveloping you in perfume.
The Potosí trembled with its nitrates
advancing on the sea—fish and arrow,
blue turgidity, delicate whale—
toward the earth's other black seaports.
How many a night from the South upon furled
sails, upon the erect nipples
of the ship's figurehead,
when Valparaíso's entire night,
the world's austral night, descended
upon the vessel's Lady,
face of those rolling prows.

VII

It was the dawning of saltpeter on the pampas.
The fertilizer's planet palpitated
until Chile was filled like a ship
of snowy holds.
Today I behold whatever remained of all those
who passed leaving no tracks
in the Pacific's sands.
                    Behold what I behold,
the sullen detritus
that the shower of gold left on my country's
throat, like a necklace of pus.

Wayfarer, may you be accompanied
by this steadfast piercing stare,
bound to Valparaíso's sky.

The Chilean lives
amid trash and tempest, obscure
offspring of the harsh Homeland.
Shattered glass, broken roofs,
obliterated walls, leprous quicklime,
buried door, dirt floor, barely clinging
to the vestige of the ground.
Valparaíso, filthy rose,
pestilential marine sarcophagus!
Don't wound me with your spiny streets,
with your crown of bitter alleyways,
don't let me see the child wounded
by your mortal swamp's misery!
You make me grieve for my people,
all my American homeland,
all that they've gnawed from your bones,
deserting you, girdled by the foam,
like a miserable mangled goddess
on whose sweet broken breast
the famished dogs urinate.

VIII

I love, Valparaíso, everything you enfold,
and everything you irradiate, seabride,
even beyond your mute nimbus.
I love the violent light with which you turn
to the sailor on the sea night,
and then, orange-blossom rose,
you're luminous and naked, fire and fog.
Let no one come with a turbid hammer
to pound what I love, to defend you:
none but my being for your secrets:
none but my voice for your open
rows of dew, for your steps
on which the sea's brackish maternity
kisses you, none but my lips
on your cold siren's crown,
raised in the air of the heights,

oceanic love, Valparaíso.
Queen of all the world's coasts,
true headquarters of waves and ships,
you're in me like the moon or like
the bearing of the wind in the treetops.
I love your criminal alleyways,
your daggerlike moon upon the hills,
and amid your plazas the seafolk
decking springtime in blue.

Please understand, I beg you, my seaport,
that I'm entitled
to write you the good and the evil
and I'm like bitter lamps
when they illuminate broken bottles.

IX

I've ranged the far-famed seas,
the nuptial stamen of each island,
I'm a great paper seafarer
and I ran, ran, ran,
to the uttermost foam,
but your penetrating sea love
was marked in me as in no other.
You're the mountainous
head capital
of the great ocean,
and on your celestial centaur's rump
your outskirts display the red and blue
paint of the toy shops.
You'd fit in a sailor's flask
with your miniature houses and the *Latorre*
like a gray iron on a sheet
if it weren't because the great tempest
of the most immense sea,
                                    the green blow
of the glacial squalls, the martyrdom
of your quaking lands, the subterranean
horror, the entire
sea surging against your torch,
made you magnitude of shadowy stone,
tempestuous church of the foam.

I declare my love to you, Valparaíso,
and once again I'll live your crossroads,
when you and I are free
again, you on our throne
of sea and wind, I on my wet
philosophers' lands. We'll see how freedom
surges between the sea and the snow.
Valparaíso, sole Queen,
alone in the solitude of the
Ocean's South,
                I beheld every yellow
spire of your heights,
I touched your torrential pulse, your portwoman's
hands that gave me the embrace
for which my soul summoned you in the
    nocturnal hour
and I remember you reigning in the sparkling
blue fire that your kingdom sprays.
There's none like you above the sand,
Swordfish of the South, Queen of the water.

X

And so, from night to night,
that long hour, the entire Chilean
seaboard engulfed in darkness,
I fled from door to door.
Other humble homes, others hands
in every crease of the country
awaited my footsteps.
                You passed
a thousand times by that door that said nothing to
    you,
by that unpainted wall, by those
windows with wilted flowers.
The secret was for me:
it was pulsing for me,
it was the zones of coal
soaked in martyrdom,
it was in the coastal seaports
beside the antarctic archipelago,
perhaps it was (listen) in that
sonorous street, amid the midday

music of the streets,
or beside the park, that window
that no one distinguished amid the other
windows, and that awaited me
with a bowl of clear soup
and its heart on the table.
All the doors were mine,
they all said: "It's my brother,
bring him to this humble home,"
while my country stained itself
with so much punishment,
like a press of bitter wine.
The little tinsmith came,
the mother of those girls,
the ungainly farmer,
the man who made soap,
the sweet lady novelist, the young man
pinned like an insect
to the desolate office
came, and there was a secret sign
on their doorway, a key
defended like a tower
that I might enter abruptly
at night, afternoon or day
and not knowing anyone
I could say: "Brother, you know who I am,
I think you were expecting me."

XI

What can you do, scoundrel, against the air?
What can you do, scoundrel, against everything
that flowers and surges and is silent and watches
and awaits me and judges you?
Scoundrel, you bought everything with
your betrayals, you must constantly irrigate
everything with your coins.
Scoundrel, you can
exile, imprison and torture
and pay on the double
before the sellout repents,
you'll only be able to sleep
surrounded by hired guns

while I, fugitive of the night,
live in my country's bosom!

How pitiful your transient little
victory! While Aragon, Ehremburg,
Eluard, the poets
of Paris, the brave
writers
of Venezuela and untold others
are with me,
you, Scoundrel,
amid Escanilla and Cuevas,
Peluchoneaux and Poblete!
I, on ladders that my people assume,
in corridors that my people conceal,
upon my country and its dove's wing,
sleep, dream and demolish your borders.

XII

To all, to you
silent beings of the night
who took my hand in the darkness, to you,
lamps
of immortal light, star lines,
staff of life, secret brethren,
to all, to you,
I say: there's no giving thanks,
nothing can fill the wineglasses
of purity,
nothing can
contain all the sun in the invincible
springtime's flags,
like your quiet dignity.
I only
think
that I've perhaps been worthy of so much
simplicity, of a flower so pure,
that perhaps I'm you, that's right,
that bit of earth, flour and song,
that natural batch that knows
whence it comes and where it belongs.
I'm not such a distant bell

or a crystal buried so deep
that you can't decipher, I'm just
people, hidden door, dark bread,
and when you welcome me, you welcome
yourself, that guest
repeatedly beaten
and repeatedly
reborn.
                    To all, to all,
to whomever I don't know, to whomever never
heard this name, to those who dwell
all along our long rivers,
at the foot of the volcanoes, in the sulphuric
shadow of copper, to fishermen and farmhands,
to blue Indians on the shores
of lakes sparkling like glass,
to the shoemaker who at this very hour questions,
nailing leather with ancient hands,
to you, to the one who unknowingly has awaited
        me,
I belong and acknowledge and sing.

XIII

American sand, solemn
plantation, red cordillera,
children, brothers and sisters stripped
by the old storms,
let's join each living kernel
before it returns to the earth,
and may the new corn that comes forth
have heard your words
and repeat them and multiply.
And may they sing to one another day and night,
and bite and consume one another,
and be scattered throughout the earth,
and become, suddenly, silence,
plunge beneath the stones,
find the nocturnal doors,
and again rise to be born,
to be sown, to perform
like bread, like hope,
like the ships' air.

The Fugitive (1948)

The corn brings you my song,
risen from my people's
roots, to be born,
to build, to sing,
and to be seed again,
more numerous in the storm.

Here are my lost hands.
They're invisible, but you
see them through the night,
through the invisible wind.
Give me your hands, I see them
through the rasping sands
of our American night,
and I choose yours and yours,
that hand and that other hand,
the one that rises to struggle
and the one that's sown again.

I don't feel alone in the night,
in the darkness of the land.
I'm people, innumerable people.
I have in my voice the pure strength
to penetrate silence
and germinate in the dark.
Death, martyrdom, shadow, ice,
suddenly shroud the seed.
And the people seem to be buried.
But the corn returns to the earth.
Its implacable red hands
pierced the silence.
From death we're reborn.

THE FLOWERS
OF PUNITAQUI

I

**The Valley
of Stones
(1946)**

Today, April 25, the rain, the long-awaited
water of 1946, has fallen on the
fields of Ovalle.

On this first wet Thursday, a steamy day
builds its gray foundry on the hills.
It's this Thursday of little seeds
that hungry peasants store in their pockets:
today they'll hurriedly break the earth and
drop their little grains of green life into it.

Only yesterday I ascended the Hurtado River:
high up, amid harsh querulous hills,
bristling with spines, because the great Andean
    cactus,
like a cruel candelabra, strikes root here.

And over its barren spines, like scarlet
clothing, or like a stain with a terrible flush,
like blood from a body dragged over a thousand
    barbs,
red mistletoe lights its bloody lanterns.

The rocks are immense bags congealed
in the age of fire, blind sacks of stone
that rolled until they were fused in these
implacable statues that stand vigil over the valley.

The river bears a sweet and moribund murmur
of final waters amid the foliage's
willowdark multitude and poplars
drip their slender yellow.

It's the autumn of Norte Chico, belated autumn.

Here light blinks more in the cluster.

Like a butterfly, the transparent sun
bides its time until the grape is formed,
and its muscatel patches shine above the valley.

II

**Brother
Pablo**

But today peasants come to see me: "Brother,
    there's
no water, brother Pablo, there's no water, it
    hasn't rained.

And the river's
scant current
circulates seven days, runs dry seven days.

Our cattle died in the cordillera.

And the drought begins to kill children.
Up above, many have nothing to eat.
Brother Pablo, speak to the Minister."

(Yes, brother Pablo will speak to the Minister, but
    they don't know
how those armchairs of ignominious leather
receive me,
and then the ministerial wood, rubbed
and polished by servile saliva.)
The Minister will lie, he'll wash his hands,
and the livestock of the poor commoner,
with his burro and his dog, will fall,
from hunger to hunger, amid threadbare rocks.

III

Hunger
and
Rage

Good-bye, good-bye to your homestead, to the
    shade
you've earned, to the transparent
bough, the hallowed land,
the ox—good-bye, stingy water,
good-bye, headsprings, music
that didn't come in the rain, to the pale sash
of the parched and stony dawn.

Juan Ovalle, I gave you my hand, a waterless
    hand,
a stone hand, a hand of wall and drought.
And I told you: curse the drab sheep, the bitterest
stars, the moon like a purple thistle,
the broken bouquet of nuptial lips,
but don't touch man, don't spill man yet,
striking his veins, don't stain the sand yet,
don't light the valley with the tree
of fallen arterial branches.

Juan Ovalle, don't kill. And your hand
answered me: "These lands
want to kill, they seek revenge
at night, the old amber air
in bitterness is poisonous air,
and the guitar's a hip
of crime, and the wind a knife."

IV

**They
Steal
Their
Land**

For behind the valley and the drought,
behind the river and the slender leaf,
stalking clump of earth and crop,
the landrobber.

Look at that tree of resounding purple,
contemplate its flushed banner,
and behind its matinal lineage,
the landrobber.

Like the reef's salt you hear
the crystal wind in the walnut trees,
but above each day's blue,
the landrobber.

Between the germinal layers you feel
wheat pulsing in its golden shaft,
but between bread and man there's a mask:
the landrobber.

V

**Toward
the
Minerals**

Then I climbed
to the high stones
of salt and gold, to the buried
republic of metals:
they were sweet walls on which one
stone is bound to another
with a kiss of dark clay.

A kiss between stone after stone
along the tutelary roads,
a kiss of earth upon earth
between the large red grapes,
and like one tooth next to another tooth
the earth's teeth,
the dry-stone walls of pure matter,
those that bear the interminable

kiss of river stones
to the road's thousand lips.

Let's climb from agriculture to gold.
The towering flintstones are here.

The weight of the hand is like a bird.
A man, a bird, a substance of air,
obstinacy, flight, agony,
perhaps an eyelid, but combat.

And from the transverse cradle of gold,
there in Punitaqui, face-to-face,
with the silent brakemen
of the shaft, of the shovel, come,
Pedro, with your leathery peace,
come, Ramírez, with your burning
hands that questioned the uterus
of the confined mine works,
hello! on the steps, in
the gold's calcareous subways,
down in its matrices,
where your digital tools
were imprinted with fire.

VI

**The
Flowers
of
Punitaqui**

There the homeland was hard as before.
Gold was a lost salt,
                           it was
a ruddy fish and in the wrathful clump
its minuscule crushed minute
was born, was being born of bloody fingernails.

Amid the dawn, like a cold almond,
beneath the cordillera's teeth,
the heart drills its hole,
searches, gropes, suffers, climbs, and at
the most essential, most planetary heights,
appears with a torn undershirt.

Brother with a burned-out heart,
join this shift in my hand,
and let's descend again to the slumbering strata

in which your hand gripped like tongs
the live gold that tried to fly
even deeper, ever farther down.

And there with some flowers
the women from there, Chileans from above,
the mine's mineral daughters,
deposited a bouquet in my hands,
some flowers from Punitaqui,
some red flowers,
geraniums, poor flowers
from that harsh land,
as if they'd been found in the deepest mine,
as if those flowers, daughters of red water,
had returned from the buried depths of mankind.

I took their hands and their flowers, broken
mineral earth, perfume
of profound petals and sorrows.
When I saw them I knew they'd come
from the hard solitude of gold.
Like drops of blood they showed me
their scattered lives.

In their poverty they were
flowering fortitude, the bouquet
of tenderness and its remote metal.

Flowers from Punitaqui, arteries, lives, at
my bedside, in the night, your aroma
rises and guides me through the most subterranean
corridors of grief,
through the pocked heights, through the snow,
    and even
through the roots, penetrated by tears alone.

Flowers, lofty flowers,
flowers from mine and stone, flowers
from Punitaqui, daughters
of the bitter subsoil: in me, never forgotten,
you remained alive, building
immortal purity, a corolla
of stone that doesn't die.

VII

Gold

Gold had that day of purity.
Before plunging its structure again
into the dirty debut that awaits it,
recently arrived, recently extracted
from the solemn statue of the earth,
it was purged by fire, enveloped
by man's sweat and hands.

There the gold's people said good-bye.
And their contact was earthy, pure
as the gray mother of emerald.
The sweaty hand that scoured
the snarled ingot was like
the stock of soil reduced
by the infinite dimension of time,
the earthly color of seeds,
the ground charged with secrets,
the earth that fashions clusters.

Lands of unstained gold, human
stock, immaculate metal
of the people, virginal veinstones
that touch without seeing one another in
the implacable junction of their two roads:
man will keep biting the dust,
he'll keep being flinty soil,
and gold will rise above his blood
until it wounds and rules over the wounded.

VIII

**Gold's
Road**

Welcome, sir, buy country and land,
dwellings, blessings, oysters,
you've come to the place where everything's for
　　sale.
There's no tower that won't fall in your
　　gunpowder,

there's no presidency that will refuse anything,
there's no net that won't reserve its treasure.

As we're "free" as the wind,
you can buy the wind, the waterfall,
and in the processed cellulose
ordain impure opinions
or reap love without free will,
dethroned in the mercenary linen.

Gold changed clothes using
patterns of rags, frayed paper,
cold edges of an invisible blade, belts of gnarled
    fingers.

The gap-toothed father took
to the maiden in her new castle
the plate of bills
which the beauty devoured, disputing it
on the floor, wreathed in smiles.
To the Bishop it raised the investiture
of the golden centuries, it opened the door
of the judges, maintained the carpets,
made night tremble in the brothels,
ran with its hair in the wind.

(I've lived the age in which it ruled.
I've witnessed consumptive poverty,
pyramids of dung swamped
by honor: ebb and flow
of the purulent rain's caesars,
convinced of the weight they put
on the scales, stiff
dolls of death, blackened
by their harsh devouring ash.)

IX

I went beyond the gold. I entered the strike.
There the delicate thread that
joins beings endured, there the pure ribbon
of mankind was alive.
                  Death bit them,
gold, acid teeth and poison

strained toward them, but the people
put their flintstones in the doorway,
they were a solidary clump that let
tenderness and combat flow
like two parallel waters,
                                              threads
of roots, waves of consanguinity.

I saw the strike in the joined arms
that expel distrust
and in a tremulous pause of struggle
I first saw the only thing alive!
The unity of mankind's lives.
In the kitchen of resistance
with their poor stoves, in the womens'
eyes, in the noble hands that
reached awkwardly
toward the leisure of a day
like an unknown blue sea,
in the fraternity of meager bread,
in the unbreakable union, in all
the seeds of stone that surged forth,
in that valorous pomegranate
raised in the salt of abandonment,
I found at last the lost foundation,
the remote city of tenderness.

X

**The
Poet**

I used to wander through life amid
an ill-starred love: I used to keep
a little page of quartz
to rivet my eyes to life.
I bought kindness, I was in the market
of greed, I inhaled envy's
most sordid waters, the inhuman
hostility of masks and beings,
I lived a sea-swamp world
in which the flower, the lily, suddenly
consumed me in their foamy tremor,
and wherever I stepped my soul slid
toward the teeth of the abyss.
That's how my poetry was born, barely

freed from the nettles, clutched
above solitude like a punishment,
or its most secret flower sequestered
in the garden of immodesty until it was buried.
And so isolated like the dark water
that inhabits its deep corridors,
I fled from hand to hand, to each
being's alienation, to daily hatred.
I knew that was how they lived, hiding
half of their beings, like fish
from the strangest sea, and in the murky
immensities I encountered death.
Death opening doors and roads.
Death gliding along the walls.

XI

**Death
in the
World**
Death kept dispatching and reaping
its tribute in sites and tombs:
man with dagger or with pocket,
at noon or in the nocturnal light,
hoped to kill, kept killing,
kept burying beings and branches,
murdering and devouring corpses.
He prepared his nets, wrung dry,
bled white, departed in the morning
smelling blood from the hunt,
and upon returning from his triumph he was
    shrouded
by fragments of death and abandonment,
and killing himself, he then buried
his tracks with sepulchral ceremony.

The homes of the living were dead.
Slag, broken roofs, urinals,
wormy alleyways, hovels
awash with human tears.
"You must live like this," said the decree.
"Rot in your substance," said the Foreman.
"You're filthy," reasoned the Church.
"Sleep in the mud," they told you.
And some of them armed the ash
to govern and decide,

while the flower of mankind beat
against the walls built for them.

The Cemetery possessed pomp and stone.
Silence for all and stature
of lofty tapered vegetation.

At last you're here, at last you leave
us a hollow in the heart of the bitter jungle,
at last you lie stiff between walls
that you won't breach. And every day
the flowers, like a river of perfume,
joined the river of the dead.
The flowers untouched by life
fell on the hollow that you left.

XII

Mankind   Here I found love. It was born in the sand,
it grew without voice, touched the flintstones
of hardness, and resisted death.
Here mankind was life that joined
the intact light, the surviving sea,
and attacked and sang and fought
with the same unity of metals.
Here cemeteries were nothing but
turned soil, dissolved sticks
of broken crosses over which
the sandy winds advanced.

XIII

The   The idle factory was eerie.
Strike   A silence in the plant, a distance
between machine and man, like a thread
cut between planets, a void
in man's hands which spend
time building, and naked
dwellings without work or sound.
When man abandoned the turbine's

dens, when he detached his arms
from the blast and the furnace's
innards failed, when he removed his eyes
from the wheel and the vertiginous light
stopped in its invisible circle,
of all the mighty powers,
of all the pure circles of potency,
the awesome energy,
a mountain of useless steel remained,
and in the rooms without man, the widowed air,
the solitary aroma of oil.

Nothing existed without that pounded
fragment, without Ramírez,
without the man with tattered clothes.
There was the motors' skin,
amassed in impotent might,
like black cetaceans in the pestilent
depths of a waveless sea,
or mountains suddenly plunged
beneath the planet's solitude.

XIV

**The
People**

The people paraded their red flags
and I was among them on the stone
they struck, in the thunderous march
and in the struggle's lofty songs.
I saw how they conquered step by step.
Their resistance alone was road,
and isolated they were like broken bits
of a star, mouthless and lusterless.
Joined in the unity made silence,
they were fire, indestructible song,
the slow passage of mankind on earth
turned into depths and battles.
They were dignity that fought
whatever was trampled, and they awakened
like a system, the order of lives
that touched the door and sat down
in the main hall with their flags.

XV

**The
Letter**

So it was. And so it will be. In the limy
sierras, and on the brink
of the smoke, in the workshops,
there's a message written on the walls
and the people, the people alone, can see it.
Its transparent letters were formed
with sweat and silence. They're written.
You, the people, kneaded them on your road
and they're above the night like the scorching
hidden fire of dawn.
Enter, O people, the shores of the day.
March like an army, united,
and pound the earth with your footsteps
and with the same sonorous identity.
Let your road be uniform like
sweat in combat is uniform,
uniform the dusty blood
of people murdered on the roads.

Above this clarity, farms, cities,
mines will bring forth,
and above this unity like firm
germinant earth, creative permanence
has been disposed, the seed
of the new city for lives.
Light from the abused trade unions,
homeland kneaded by metallurgic hands,
order rising from fishermen
like a bouquet from the sea, walls erected
by burgeoning masonry,
grain schools, structures
of factories forged by mankind.
You return, exiled peace, shared
bread, dawn, sorcery
of earthly love, built
above the four winds of the planet.

THE RIVERS
OF SONG

I

**Letter to
Miguel Otero
Silva, in
Caracas
(1948)**

A friend delivered me your letter written
with invisible words, on his suit, in his eyes.
How happy you are, Miguel, how happy we are!
No one's left in a world of stuccoed ulcers
except us, indefinably happy.
I see the crow pass by and it can't harm me.
You observe the scorpion and clean your guitar.
We live among wild beasts, singing, and when we
    touch
a man, the substance of someone in whom we
    believed,
and he crumbles like rotten pastry,
you in your Venezuelan patrimony rescue
whatever can be salvaged, while I defend
the live coal of life.
              What happiness, Miguel!

You wonder where I am? I'll tell you
—giving only details *useful* to the government—
that on this coast full of wild stones,
sea and countryside merge: waves and pines,
eagles and petrels, foam and meadows.
Have you seen from very close up and all day
      long
how the seabirds fly? It seems as if
they carried the world's letters to their
      destinations.
Pelicans cruise by like windships,
other birds that fly like arrows and bring
the messages of deceased kings, of princes
entombed with turquoise threads on the Andean
      coasts,
and gulls made of round whiteness,
that constantly forget their messages.
How blue life is, Miguel, when we've put into it
love and struggle, words that are bread and wine,
words that they cannot yet dishonor,
because we take to the streets with shotgun and
      songs.
They're lost with us, Miguel.
What can they do but kill us, and even so
it's a poor bargain for them, they can only
try to rent a flat in front of us and shadow us
to learn to laugh and weep like us.
When I wrote love lyrics, which sprouted
from all my pores, and I pined away,
aimless, forlorn, gnawing the alphabet,
they told me: "How great you are, O
      Theocritus!"
I'm not Theocritus: I took life,
stood before it, kissed it until I conquered it,
and then I went through the mine galleries
to see how other men lived.
And when I emerged with my hands stained with
      filth and grief
I raised and displayed them on gold chains,
and I said: "I'm not an accomplice to this crime."
They coughed, became very annoyed, withdrew
      their welcome,
stopped calling me Theocritus, and ended up
insulting me and sending all the police to imprison
      me,

because I didn't continue to be preoccupied
    exclusively with metaphysical matters.
But I had conquered happiness.
Ever since I've awakened to read letters
that seabirds bring from afar,
letters delivered wet, messages that little by little
I keep translating leisurely and confidently: I'm
meticulous as an engineer in this strange craft.
And suddenly I go to the window. It's a square
of transparency, the distance of grasses
and pinnacles is pure, so I keep working
amid things that I love—waves, stones, wasps—
with an intoxicating marine cheerfulness.
But no one likes us to be happy, to you they
    assigned
a fool's role: "But don't overdo it, relax,"
and they tried to pin me in an insect collection
    amid the tears,
so that I'd drown and they could make their
    speeches on my grave.
I remember a day on the sandy nitrate
pampa, there were five hundred men
on strike. It was the scorching afternoon
of Tarapacá. And when their faces had drawn
all the sand and the dry bloodless desert sun,
I saw old melancholy approach my heart,
like a wineglass of hatred. That critical hour,
in the desolate salt marshes, in that frail minute
of struggle, in which we could have been
    defeated,
a pale little girl from the mines
recited with a plaintive voice composed of crystal
    and steel
one of your poems, one of your old poems that
    rolls between the wrinkled eyes
of all the workers and farmhands of my country,
    of America.
And that fragment of your song suddenly beamed
on my mouth like a purple flower
and ran down to my blood, filling it again
with a surging happiness born of your song.
And I thought not only of you but of your bitter
    Venezuela.
Years ago, I saw a student whose ankles bore

the scar of the chains that a general had put on
    him,
and he told me how chain gangs worked on the
    roads
and people disappeared in the prisons. Because
    that's how our America has been:
a prairie with devouring rivers and constellations
of butterflies (in some places, emeralds are thick as
    apples),
but always, all night long and along the rivers
there are bleeding ankles, near the petroleum
    before,
today near the nitrate, in Pisagua, where a dirty
    despot
has buried the flower of my country so that it
    will perish, and he can market the bones.
That's why you sing, that's why, so that
    dishonored and wounded America
will make its butterflies flutter and will harvest its
    emeralds
without punishment's ghastly blood, clotted
on the hands of hangmen and merchants.
I realized how happy you'd be, beside the
    Orinoco, singing,
for sure, or perhaps buying wine for your home,
occupying your place in the struggle or in
    happiness,
broad shouldered, like the poets of our times
—with light-colored suits and walking shoes.
Ever since, I've been thinking that sometime I'd
    write you,
and when the friend arrived, chock-full of your
    stories
that fell from his entire suit and were
scattered under the chestnut trees in my garden,
I told myself: "Now," yet I still didn't sit down
    to write you.
But today has been too much: not just one but
    thousands
of seabirds passed by my window, and I collected
the letters which no one reads and which they
    carry
around the world's seacoasts, until they lose them.
And then, in each one I read your words

and they were like those that I write and dream
        and sing,
and so I decided to send you this letter, which I
        sign off now
in order to gaze through the window at the world
        that is ours.

II

**To
Rafael Alberti
(Puerto Santa
María, Spain)**

Rafael, before I arrived in Spain your poetry,
        literal rose,
beveled cluster, crossed my path,
and to this day it has been not a memory for me
but fragrant light, emanation of a world.

You brought the dew that time had forgotten
to your land scorched by cruelty,
and Spain awakened with you on its waist,
crowned again with morning dewdrops.

You'll remember what I brought: dreams
dissolved by implacable acids, permanences
in exiled waters, in silences
from which bitter roots rose forth
like tree trunks burned in the forest.
How can I forget that time, Rafael?

I arrived in your country like someone who lands
on a stone moon, finding eagles from the barrens,
dry spines, everywhere,
but there, seaman, your voice was waiting
to welcome me and give me the gillyflower's
fragrance, honey from the fruits of the sea.

And your poetry was on the table, naked.

Pine groves from the South, vinestocks
gave your cut diamond its resins, and on
touching such beautiful clarity, much of the
        shadow
that I brought to the world melted away.

Architecture made in the light, like petals,
through your verses of intoxicating aroma,
I saw the waters of yesteryear, the hereditary
     snow,
and I owe Spain to you more than anyone.
With your fingers I touched honeycomb and
     wasteland,
I knew shores worn away by the people
as by an ocean, and the steps
on which poetry kept spangling
all its clothing with sapphires.

You know that no one teaches but one's brother.
     And in that
hour you taught me not only that,
not only the extinguished pomp of our stock,
but the rectitude of your destiny,
and when blood struck Spain once again
I defended the patrimony of the people who were
     mine own.

Now you know, now everyone knows these
     things.
I just want to be with you,
and today, since half your life remains,
your homeland, to which you're more entitled
     than a tree,
today, since not only the country's calamities,
the mourning of the one we love, but your
     absence, too,
cover the legacy of the olive tree that the wolves
     devour,
I want to give you, O! if only I could, big
     brother,
the starry happiness that you gave me then.

Between the two of us poetry
touches like celestial skin,
and with you I like to pick a cluster,
this tendril, that root of darkness.

The envy that opens doors in beings
couldn't open your door or mine. It's beautiful,
like when the raging wind
unleashes its dress outdoors
and the bread, wine and fire are with us,

to let the vendor of rage howl,
to let the one who passed between your feet
    whistle,
and to raise the wineglass full of amber
with the whole rite of transparency.

Someone wants to forget that you're first?
Let him set sail and he'll find your face.
Someone wants to give us a quick burial?
That's fine, but he'll be obliged to fly.

They'll come, but who can shake the harvest
that raised autumn's hand
until it stained the world with the tremor of wine?

Give me that wineglass, brother, and listen: I'm
    surrounded
by wet and torrential America, sometimes
I lose the silence, I lose the nocturnal corolla,
and hatred surrounds me, perhaps nothingness, the
    void
of a void, the twilight
of a dog, of a frog,
and then I regret that so much of my land
    separates us,
and then I want to go to your house where I
    know you await me,
just to be good-natured as we alone
can be. We owe nothing.

And they really owe you, and it's a country: just
    wait.

You'll return, we'll return. Someday I want to
    walk
along your shores with you, enraptured with
    gold,
to your seaports, seaports of the South that I
    never saw.
You'll show me the sea where sardines
and olives dispute the sands,
and those fields with green-eyed bulls
that Villalón (a friend who didn't come
to see me either, for he was buried)
owned, and the kegs of sherry, cathedrals

in whose Gongorene hearts
topaz burns with pale fire.

We'll go, Rafael, where he lies in rest—
he who sustained Spain's waist
with his hands and yours.
The corpse that couldn't die, the one for whom
    you stand
in vigil
because your existence alone defends him.

There lies Federico, but there are many more
    who, sunken, buried,
amid the Spanish cordilleras, unjustly
fallen, dispersed,
lost grain in the mountains,
are ours, and we're in their clay.

You're alive because you were always a
    miraculous god.
For you alone they searched, the wolves
wanted to devour you, to crush your authority.
Each one wanted to be a maggot in your death.

Well, they were mistaken. It's perhaps the
    structure
of your song, intact transparency,
your sweetness' armed decision,
hardness, delicate fortitude,
that spared your love for the earth.

I'll accompany you to taste the water
of the Genil, of the dominion you gave me,
to see in the sailing silver
the slumbering effigies that founded
the blue syllables of your song.

We'll also enter the smithies: now
the people's metal is waiting there
to be born in knives. Singing, we'll pass
beside the red nets that the firmament moves.
Knives, nets, songs will expunge the sorrows.
Your people will bear with hands burned
by gunpowder, like meadowland laurel,
whatever your love kept winnowing in misery.

To Rafael Alberti (Puerto Santa María, Spain)

Yes, the flower's born of our exile, the form
of the homeland that the people reconquer with
     thunderbolts,
and it's not just one day that elaborates
the lost honey, the truth of the dream,
but each root that becomes song
until it fills the world with its leaves.

You're there, there's nothing that the diamond
moon that you left can't stir:
solitude, wind in the corners,
everything touches your pure territory,
and the last corpses, those who fell
in prison, executed lions,
and those of the guerrillas, captains
of the heart, are moistening
your own crystalline investiture,
your own heart with their roots.

Time has passed since those days when we shared
sorrows that left a radiant moon,
the warhorse trampled the village
with its horseshoes, shattering the glass.
All that was born beneath the gunpowder,
all that is waiting for you to raise the spike of
     grain,
and in that birth the smoke and tenderness
of those trying days will envelop you again.

Spain's skin is wide and your spur
endures in it like a sword with a shining hilt,
and there's no forgetting, no winter that can
     expunge you,
radiant brother, from the lips of the people.
And so I address you, forgetting perhaps a word,
answering at long last letters that you don't
     remember,
which reached my solitude
when the climates of the East covered me
like a scarlet aroma.
                         May your golden brow
find in this letter a day of another time,
and another time of a day that will come.
                              I say
                              good-bye

today, December sixteen, 1948,
from some point of America from which I sing.

III

**To
González
Carbalho
(in Río de
la Plata)**

When night devoured human sounds, and cast
its shadow line by line,
we heard, in the heightened silence, beyond
    beings,
González Carbalho's river murmur,
his profound and permanent water, his course that
    seems
still as the growth of tree or time.

This great fluvial poet accompanies the silence of
    the world,
with sonorous austerity, and whoever wants to
    hear it amid
the hustle-bustle, let him (like the explorer lost in
    the
forests or prairies) put his ear
to the earth: and even in the middle of the street,
    he'll hear
this poetry rise amid the passing din: the deep
voices of earth and water.

Then, beneath the city's onslaught, beneath the
    lamps
with scarlet shades, like wheat coming forth,
    erupting in
every latitude, this singing river.

Above his riverbed, startled twilight
birds, flushed throats dividing space,
purple leaves descending.

All those who dare to face solitude:
those who pluck the abandoned string, all the
immensely pure, and those who, from the ship,
    heard
salt, solitude and night merge,
will hear González Carbalho's chorus rise high and
    crystalline

from his nocturnal springtime.
Do you remember another? Prince of Aquitaine:
he substituted his abolished tower,
in the initial hour, for the corner of tears
that millennial man decanted wineglass by
    wineglass.
And let the one who didn't look at those faces
    know it, victor
or vanquished:
preoccupied with the sapphire wind or the bitter
    wineglass:
beyond street after street, beyond one hour,
touch that darkness, and let's continue together.

Then, on the disorderly map of small lives
with blue ink: the river, the river of singing
    waters,
made of hope, lost suffering,
anguish–free water that rises to victory.

My brother made this river:
these solemn sounds drenched in silence
were constructed of his lofty subterranean song.
My brother's this river that envelops things.

Wherever you may be, night or day, on the road,
atop the sleepless trains of the meadowland,
or beside the cold dawn's dewy rose,
or perhaps
amid suits, touching
the twister,
bend to the ground, let your face receive
this great throb of secret water that circulates.

Brother, you're the longest river on earth:
behind the orb your solemn river voice resounds,
and I bathe my hand on your breast
faithful to a treasure never interrupted,
faithful to the transparency of a sublime tear,
faithful to mankind's beseiged eternity.

IV

When a man like Silvestre Revueltas
returns definitively to the earth,
there's a murmur, a wave of voice and
weeping that prepares and propagates his
    departure.
The little roots tell the grains: "Silvestre died,"
and wheat ripples his name on the slopes
and then the bread knows.
Now all America's trees know
and our arctic region's frozen flowers too.

Drops of water transmit it,
the indomitable rivers of
                  Araucania now know the
    news.
From glacier to lake, from lake to plant,
from plant to fire, from fire to smoke:
everything that burns, sings, blossoms, dances and
    revives,
everything permanent, lofty and profound of our
    America embraces him:
pianos and birds, dreams and sounds, the
    palpitating net
that links all our climates in the air,
trembles and transfers the funeral choir.
Silvestre is dead, Silvestre has entered his total
    music,
his sonorous silence.

Son of the earth, child of the earth, from this day
    on you enter time.
From this day on, when your country is tolled,
    your name resonant with music will fly as
    from a bell,
with an unfamiliar sound, with the sound of what
    you were, brother.

Your cathedral heart covers us in this instant, like
    the firmament,
and your great grandiose song, your volcanic
    tenderness,

fills all the heights like a burning statue.
Why have you spilt your life? Why
have you poured
your blood into every wineglass? Why
have you searched
like a blind angel, bumping into the dark doors?

Ah, but music rises from your name,
and crowns of fragrant laurel
and apples of aroma and symmetry
rise from your music, as from a market.

On this solemn day of parting you're the traveler,
but you no longer hear,
your noble brow is absent and it's as though a
     great tree
were missing in the middle of mankind's house.

But the light we see is another light from this day
     on,
the street we take is a new street,
the hand we touch has your strength from this
     day on,
everything acquires vigor in your repose
and your purity will rise from the stones
to show us the clarity of hope.

Rest, brother, your day has ended,
you filled it with your sweet and powerful soul,
with light loftier than daylight
and a sound blue as the sky's voice.
Your brother and your friends have asked me
to repeat your name in America's air,
to let the bull of the pampa know it, and the
     snow,
to let the sea carry it away, to let the wind discuss
     it.

Now America's stars are your homeland
and from this day on the Earth your doorless
     home.

V

To
Miguel
Hernández,
Murdered
in the
Prisons
of Spain

You came to me directly from the Levant. You
    brought me,
goatherder, your wrinkled innocence,
the scholasticism of old pages, an aroma
of Fray Luis, of citrus blossoms, of manure
    burned
on the mountains, and on your mask
the cereal asperity of reaped oats
and a honey that measured the earth with your
    eyes.

You also brought the nightingale in your mouth.
A nightingale spotted with oranges, a thread
of incorruptible song, of naked force.
Ah, youth, gunpowder supervened in the light
and you, with nightingale and rifle, strolling
beneath the moon and the sun of combat.

Now you know, dear friend, how much I
    couldn't do, now you
know that for me, of all poetry, you were the
    bluest fire.
Today I put my face on the earth and I hear you,
I hear you, blood, music, moribund honeycomb.

I haven't seen a dazzling race like yours,
or roots so hard, or soldier's hands,
nor have I seen anything alive as your heart
burning in the purple of my own flag.

You live, eternal youth, commoner of yesteryear,
inundated by germs of wheat and springtime,
wrinkled and dark as innate metal,
waiting for the minute that will elevate your
    armor.

I'm not alone since you died. I'm with those who
    seek you.
I'm with those who'll come someday to avenge
    you.
You'll recognize my footsteps among those
that will hurtle over Spain's breast,

crushing Cain so that he'll return
the buried faces to us.

Let those who murdered you know that they'll
    pay with blood.
Let those who tormented you know that they'll
    see me someday.
Let the wretches who today include your name
in their books—the Dámasos, the Gerardos, the
    sons
of bitches, silent accomplices of the executioner—
know that your martyrdom won't be expunged,
    that your death
will fall on their entire moon of cowards.
And to those who denied you in their rotten
    laurel,
on American soil, the space that you mantle
with your fluvial crown of bled lightning,
let me give them contemptuous oblivion
for they tried to mutilate me with your absence.

Miguel, far away from the Osuna prison, far
    away
from cruelty, Mao Tse-tung directs
your poetry dismembered in combat
toward our victory.
                        And humming Prague
building the sweet hive that you sang,
green Hungary cleans its granaries
and dances beside the river that awakens from
    slumber.
And rising from Varsovia, the naked siren that
    edifies
brandishes its crystalline sword.
And further beyond the earth becomes gigantic,
                                    the earth,
which your song visited, and the steel
that defended your country are secure,
spreading over the firmness
of Stalin and his children.
                        Now the light
approaches your dwelling.
                        Miguel from Spain, star
from razed lands, I won't forget you, dear friend,
I won't forget you, dear friend!
                        But I learned life

317

with your death: my eyes were slightly blurred,
and within myself I found
not tears but
inexorable arms!
                    Wait for them! Wait for me!

NEW YEAR'S CHORALE FOR THE COUNTRY IN DARKNESS

I

**Greetings
(1949)**

Happy year, Chileans, to the country in darkness,
happy year to all, to all but one,
we're so few, happy year, compatriots, brothers
    and sisters,
men, women, children, today my voice flies to
    Chile,
to you, it knocks on your window
like a blind bird, and calls to you from afar.

Homeland, summer blankets your sweet hard
    body.
The arrises from which the snow has set forth,
galloping to the ocean with turbulent lips,
look blue and high like coal from the sky.
Perhaps today, at this hour, you're wearing the
    green tunic
that I adore: forests, water, and wheat on your
    waist.

And beside the sea, beloved, marine homeland,
    you move
your iridescent universe of sands and oysters.

Perhaps, perhaps . . . Who am I to touch your
    ship,
your perfume, from afar? I'm part of you: a secret
wood circle taken by surprise in your trees,
growth mute as your smooth sulphur,
stentorean ash from your subterranean soul.

When I departed from you, persecuted, bristling
with beard and poverty, without clothing, without
    paper
to write the letters that are my life, with
nothing but a little knapsack, I brought two books
and a section of hawthorn recently cut from the
    tree.
(The books: a geography
and the Book of the Birds of Chile.)

Every night I read your description, your rivers:
they guide my dream, my exile, my frontier.
I touch your trains, run my hand through your
    hair,
stop to ponder the iron
skin of your geography, lower my eyes
to the lunar sphere of wrinkles and craters,
and as I sleep my silence journeys to the South
    enveloped
in your final thunderclaps of shattered salt.

When I awaken (the air is different, the light,
different streets, fields, stars) I touch
the disk of your hawthorn that accompanies me,
cut in Melipilla from a tree that they gave me.

And in the hawthorn's cuirass I behold your
    name,
rugged Chile, homeland, heart of bark:
in your form, hard as earth, I see the faces
of those who I love and who offered me their
    thorny hands,
men of the desert, nitrate and copper.

The thorny tree's heart
is a circle smooth as burnished metal,
ochre like a spot of hard dry blood,
ringed by firewood's sulphurous iris,
and touching this pure prodigy of the forest,
I recall its hostile curly flowers
when the violent perfume of your power
casts you through the thorny dense wreaths.
And so my country's lives and smells haunt me,
live with me, kindle their stubborn fire
within me, consuming me and rising forth.
In other lands they see through my clothing,
stare at me like a lamp that passes through the
    streets,
shedding a marine light that penetrates the doors:
it's the flaming sword that you gave me and that I
    keep,
like the hawthorn, pure, powerful, indomitable.

II

**The
Men from
Pisagua**

But the hand that caresses you stops
beside the desert, along the seashore,
in a world scourged by death.
Is it you, Homeland, is this you, is this your face?
This martyrdom, this red crown
of wires rusted by brackish water?
Is Pisagua now your face too?
Who hurt you, how did they pierce
your naked honey with a knife?

Above all, my greetings to them,
to the men, to the plinth of sorrows,
to the women, maniu tree branches,
to the children, transparent schools,
who on the sands of Pisagua
were the persecuted country, were
all the honor of the land that I love.
It will be tomorrow's sacred honor
to have been cast on your sands,
Pisagua: to have been suddenly
rounded up on the night of terror
at the order of the vile felon
and to have come to your scorching inferno
for having defended mankind's dignity.

I won't forget your lifeless coast where
the hostile sea's dirty teeth
slash the walls of torment
and the bulwarks of the infernal
barren hills rise abruptly:
I won't forget how you gaze at the water,
toward the world that forgets your faces,
I won't forget when with eyes full
of questioning light, you turn your face
toward the pale lands of Chile,
governed by wolves and thieves.

I know how they've thrown your food
to the ground, as to mangy dogs,
until you made plates out of
empty little tin cans:
I know how they shoved you to sleep
and how, in single file, you received,
solemnly and courageously,
the foul beans
that you threw so often to the sand.
I know how, when you receive
clothing, food gathered
from every corner of the country,
you felt proudly
that perhaps, perhaps you weren't alone.
Courageous, steely compatriots
who give the earth a new meaning:
they selected you in the hunt
so that through you all the people
would suffer in exiled sands.
And selecting hell they examined
the map, until they found
this brackish jail, these walls
of solitude, of overwhelming
anguish, so that you'd crush your heads
beneath the contemptible tyrant's feet.

But they didn't encounter their own substance:
You're not made of manure like the putrid,
wormy traitor: their reports
lied, they encountered
the people's metallic firmness,
the heart of copper and its silence.

It's the metal that the country will found
when the stranded people's wind
expels that captain of filth.

Firm, be firm brothers,
firm when in trucks, assaulted
at night in your shacks, shoved,
arms bound with wire,
unawake, just startled
and battered, you were taken
to Pisagua by armed jailors.

Then they returned
and loaded trucks with helpless
families, beating the children.

And a weeping of sweet children still
haunts the desert night, a weeping
of thousands of infant mouths,
like a chorus seeking the harsh wind
so that we'll hear, so that we won't forget.

III

**The
Heroes**

Félix Morales, Angel Veas,
murdered in Pisagua,
Happy New Year, brothers,
beneath the hard earth that you loved,
that you defended. Today you're
beneath the salt marshes that crackle
pronouncing your pure names,
beneath the outstretched roses
of saltpeter, beneath the cruel
sand of the boundless desert.

Happy New Year, my
brothers, what love
you've shown me, what
expanse above tenderness
you've embraced in death!

You're like the islands born
suddenly in the middle of the ocean,

sustained by space
and submarine firmness.

I learned the world from you:
the purity, the infinite bread.
You showed me life, the area
of salt, the cross of the poor.
I crossed the desert lives
like a ship on a dark sea
and you showed me man's
toil nearby, the land,
the tattered house, the wail
of misery on the plains.

Félix Morales, I remember you
painting a tall portrait, refined,
svelte and young like a tamarugo
sapling in the thirsty
expanses of the pampa.

Your shock of wild hair struck
your pale brow, you were painting
the portrait of a demagogue
for the upcoming elections.

I remember you perched
on the footladder,
imparting life to your painting,
sketching all his sweet youth.

You were portraying your
hangman's smile on the canvas,
adding white, measuring,
giving light to the mouth
that later ordered your agony.

Angel, Angel, Angel Veas,
worker of the pampa, pure
as unearthed metal,
now they've murdered you, now you're
where the owners of Chile's land
wanted you to be:
beneath the devouring stones
that you lifted with your hands
so many times toward greatness.

Nothing purer than your life.

Just the air's eyelids.

Just the water's mothers.

Just inaccessible metal.

Throughout my life I'll bear
the honor of having shaken
your noble combatant hand.

You were tranquil, you were wood
trained in suffering
until you became pure tool.
I remember you when Iquique's
Intendancy was honored by you,
workman, ascetic, brother.

Bread, flour ran short. So
you rose before daybreak
and with your hands distributed
bread to everyone. I never
saw you greater, you were bread,
you were the people's bread, broken
with your heart in the earth.

And late in the workday, when
you returned shouldering the load
of the day's terrible toil,
you smiled like flour,
you entered your breaden peace,
and distributed yourself again,
until sleep restored
your husked heart.

IV

**González
Videla**

Who was that? Who's there? where am I, they ask
    me
in other lands where I drift about.
In Chile, fists in the wind, they don't ask,

eyes in the mines are focused on one point,
on a vicious traitor who wept with them
when he requested their votes to ascend the
    throne.
These men from Pisagua, the rugged titans of
    coal,
saw him: he shed tears,
poured forth promises,
embraced and kissed the children who now
scour the trace of his pustule with sand.
In my nation, in my land we know him. The
    sleeping
farmhand dreams of the day when his hard hands
will encircle the lying dog's throat,
and the miner in the shadow of his wakeful
    cavern
stretches his foot out, dreaming that he squashed
this malignant, insatiable, perverted louse.

He knows the man who speaks behind a curtain
of bayonets, or behind livestock,
or behind the new merchants,
but never behind the people who seek him
to speak for an hour with him, his last hour.

He uprooted my people's hope—smiling,
he sold them in the shadows to the highest
    bidder,
and instead of fresh houses and freedom, they
    were injured,
beaten in the mineshaft,
their salary dictated at gunpoint,
while a social set governed dancing
with the pointed fangs of nocturnal alligators.

V

**I
Didn't
Suffer**

But didn't you suffer? I didn't suffer. I only
suffer my people's suffering. I live
within, within my country, a cell
of its infinite and burning blood.
I have no time for my sorrow.

Nothing makes me suffer but these lives
that gave me their pure trust,
which a traitor had rolled to the bottom
of a lifeless pit, from which
we must raise the rose again.

When the hangman pressured the
judges to condemn
my heart, my resolute swarm,
the people opened their immense labyrinth,
the cellar where their loves sleep, guarding
even the entry of light and air.
They told me: "You owe it to us,
you're the one to put the cold brand
on the wretches' dirty names."
And I suffered nothing but not having suffered.
But now having probed the dark
jails of brother upon brother,
with all my passion like a wound,
and every broken footstep rolled toward me,
every blow on your back struck me,
every drop of martyrdom's blood
trickled toward my bleeding song.

VI

**In These
Times**

Happy year . . . Today you who have
my land on both sides of you, you're happy,
   brother.
I'm a drifting child of all that I love.
Answer me, suppose that I'm with you
questioning you, suppose that I'm the January
   wind,
Puelche wind, wizen wind of the mountains
that visits you when you open the door,
not entering, airing its swift questions.
Tell me, have you entered a field of wheat or
   barley,
are they golden? Speak to me about a day of
   plums.
Far from Chile I aspire to a round day,
purple, transparent, with sugar in clusters,

thick with blueberries that drip
their wineglasses laden with delight into my
　　　mouth.
Tell me, did you bite into the pure crupper
of a peach today, sating yourself with immortal
　　　ambrosia,
until you too were the earth's fountain,
fruit after fruit granted to the world's splendor?

VII

They
Spoke
to Me
Before

I traversed these same foreign lands
in another time: my homeland's name shone
like the starry secrets of its sky.
Persecuted in all latitudes, blind,
overwhelmed by foreboding and ignominy,
I touched my hands, I told myself: "Chilean"
in a voice tinged with hope. Then
your voice echoed like a hymn, your
sandy heads were small, homeland, but they
　　　covered
more than one wound, redeemed
more than one desolate springtime.
You store within all that hope,
repressed in your peace, beneath the earth,
spacious seed for all mankind,
true resurrection of the star.

VIII

Chile's
Voices

Before, Chile's voice was the metallic voice
of freedom, of wind and silver,
before, it resounded in the heights
of the newly scarred planet,
of our America assailed
by thickets and centaurs.
Even the intact snow, in vigil,
raised your chorus of honorable leaves,
your rivers' song of free waters,

the blue majesty of your decorum.
It was Isidoro Errázuriz pouring
his combatant crystalline star,
upon obscure and fettered towns,
it was Bilbao with his tumultuous
little planet's brow,
it was Vicuña Mackenna transporting
his innumerable germinal foliage
impregnated with signs and seeds
through other towns where the window
was closed to the light. They entered
and lit the lamp in the night,
and in the bitter day of other towns
they were the snow's loftiest light.

IX

**The
Liars**

Today their names are Gajardo, Manuel Trucco,
Hernán Santa Cruz, Enrique Berstein,
Germán Vergara: those who, prepaid,
say they speak, O Homeland, in your sacred
name and claim to defend you plunging
your lion's legacy into the filth.
Dwarfs concocted like pills
in the traitor's drugstore, budget
mice, little
liars, pickpockets
of our strength, poor
mercenaries with outstretched hands
and slanderous rabbit tongues.

They're not my homeland, I so declare
to whoever will hear me in these lands,
they're not the nitrate's great man,
they're not the salt of the transparent people,
they're not the deliberate hands that build
the monument of agriculture,
they're not, they don't exist, they lie and
    rationalize
in order to continue, nonexistent, to collect.

X

**They
Shall Be
Named**

As I write my left hand reproaches me.
It tells me: why name them, what are they, what
        meaning
have they? Why not leave them in their
        anonymous winter
mud, in the mud that horses urinate?
And my right hand answers: "I was born
to pound on doors, to clench blows,
to light the uttermost shadows
where poisonous spiders feed."
They shall be named. Homeland, you didn't grant
        me
the sweet privilege of naming just
your flowers and your foam,
you didn't give me words, homeland, to address
        you
just with names of gold, of pollen and fragrance,
in order to scatter the dewdrops
that fall from your imperious black hair:
with milk and flesh you gave me the syllables
that will also name the pale worms
that crawl in your womb,
that prey on your blood, plundering your life.

XI

**The
Forest's
Worms**

Something from the ancient forest fell. Perhaps
it was the storm, purifying growth and strata,
and in the fallen trunks mushrooms fermented,
slugs crisscrossed their loathsome threads,
and the dead wood that fell from the heights
was filled with holes and hideous larvae.
That's how your side is, homeland, the wretched
governance of insects that fill your wounds,
the stout traffickers that chew wire,
those from the Palace that deal in gold,
the worms that amass buses and fisheries,
those that gnaw something cloaked by the robe

of the traitor who dances his dazzling samba,
the journalist who jails his colleagues,
the filthy informer who serves the government,
the fatuous boor who appropriates a fatuous
    magazine
with gold stolen from the Yaguans,
the admiral dumb as a tomato, the gringo
who spits a purse of dollars at his vassals.

XII

**Homeland,
They Want
to Parcel
You Out**

"They called him Chilean," say these larvae,
    referring to me.
They want to remove the country from beneath
    my feet,
they desire to cut you for themselves like a dirty
    deck
and parcel you among themselves like greasy
    meat.
I don't love them. Now they believe that you're
    dead,
quartered, and in the orgy of their dirty designs
they spend you like owners. I don't love them.
    Let me
love your land and people, let me pursue my
dreams on your boundaries of sea and snow,
let me harvest all your bitter perfume
that I carry on the roads in a wineglass,
but I cannot be with them, don't ask me,
when you move your shoulders and they fall to
    the ground
with their germinations of corrupt animals,
don't ask me to believe that they're your
    offspring.
My country's venerable wood is another.
                      Tomorrow
you'll be in your narrows of a beseiged vessel,
between your two tides of ocean and snow,
the most beloved, the bread, the land, the child.
By day the noble rite of liberated time,
by night the starry entity of the sky.

XIII

They Receive Orders Against Chile

But we must search behind them all, there's
something behind the gnawing traitors and rats,
there's an empire that sets the table,
serves meals and bullets.
They want to do with you what they're doing to
    Greece.
Greek dandies at the banquet, and bullets
to the people in the mountains: they must clip the
    wings
of the new victory of Samothrace, they must
    hang,
murder, destroy, plunge the murderous knife
clutched in New York, they must open fire
on man's pride, which appears
everywhere as if it were born
of the earth bathed in blood.
They must arm Chiang and the infamous Videla,
they must give them money for prisons, wings
to bomb compatriots, they must give them
a dunce, some dollars, they'll do the rest:
they lie, corrupt, dance upon the dead,
and their wives sport the most expensive "minks."
The people's agony is unimportant, the master—
owners of copper need this martyrdom: the facts:
generals retire from the army to serve
as Staff assistants in Chuquicamata,
and in the nitrate works the "Chilean" general
commands, sword in hand, what the pampa's
offspring can request for a salary raise.
That's how they govern from above, from the
    purse of dollars,
that's how the treacherous dwarf receives orders,
that's how the generals serve as police,
that's how the country's tree trunk rots.

XIV

I Recall the Sea

Chilean, have you gone to the sea lately?
Go in my name, wet your hands and raise them

and from other lands I'll adore those drops
that fall on your face from the infinite water.
I know, I've lived all my seacoast,
the heavy sea of the North, of the barrens, to
the tempestuous weight of foam in the islands.
I recall the sea, the pocked iron coasts
of Coquimbo, the imperious waters of Tralca,
the solitary waves of the South, that formed me.
I recall in Puerto Montt or in the islands, at night,
or returning along the beach, the boat waiting,
and our feet left fire in their tracks,
the mysterious flames of a phosphorescent god.
Each footstep was a streak of phosphorous.
We were writing the earth with stars.
And the boat, skimming the sea, shook
a branch of marine fire, of glowworms,
an innumerable wave of eyes that awakened
once and slept again in their abyss.

XV

**There's
No
Forgiving**

I want land, fire, bread, sugar, flour,
sea, books, homeland for all, that's why
I wander about: the traitor's judges pursue me
and his thurifers, like trained monkeys,
try to muddy my reputation.
And I went with *him*, the man who presides,
to the mineshaft, to the desert of the forgotten
　　　dawn,
I went with him and told my poor brothers:
"You won't save the threads of tattered clothes,
you won't have this breadless day, you'll be
　　　treated
as if you were the country's children." "Now
we're going to distribute beauty, and womens'
eyes won't weep for their children."
And when instead of distributing love, in the
　　　night
they took that same man off to hunger and
　　　martyrdom,
that one who heeded *him* and surrendered
his powerful tree's strength and tenderness,
then I wasn't with the little satrap,

333

but with that nameless man, with my people.
I want my country for mine own, I want
equal light above
my fiery country's hair,
I want the day's and plow's love,
I want to erase the line they draw
with hatred to segregate the people's bread,
and the man who switched the country's line
until (like a jailor) he delivered it,
handcuffed, to those who pay to hurt it,
I'm not going to sing or silence this,
I'm going to leave their numbers and names
nailed to the wall of dishonor.

XVI

**You Will
Struggle**

This new year, compatriot, is yours.
It was born of you more than of time, choose
the best of your life and surrender it to combat.
This year that has fallen like a corpse in its tomb
cannot rest with love and with fear.
This expired year is a year of sorrows that accuse.
And in the hour of festivity, in the night,
when its bitter roots break away and fall
and another ignored crystal rises to the void
of a year that your life will gradually fill,
give it the dignity required by my country,
yours, this narrowness of volcanoes and wines.
I'm not a citizen of my country: I'm told
that the indecorous clown who governs has
        scratched
my name with thousands of others
from the lists that were the law of the Republic.
My name is scratched so that I won't exist,
so that the dungeon's grisly vulture can vote
and the bestial agents who deliver
blows and torment in government
vaults can vote, so that the stewards,
foremen and partners of the merchant
who surrendered the Country will pledge their
        vote.
I'm forced to wander, I live the anguish of being
        far

from prisoners and flowers, from mankind and
    land,
but you'll struggle to change life,
you'll struggle to scratch the spot
of manure from the map, you'll doubtlessly
    struggle
so that the shame of these times will end
and the people's prisons will open and the wings
of betrayed victory can soar.

XVII

**Happy Year
to My
Country in
Darkness**

Hapy year to you, this year, to all
mankind and lands, beloved Araucania.
Between you and my existence a new night
separates us, and forests and rivers and roads.
But my heart gallops toward you
like a dark horse, my little land:
I enter deserts of pure geography,
pass green valleys where the grape accumulates
its green alcohols, the sea of its clusters.
I enter your communities of enclosed gardens,
white as camelias, the pungent smell
of your sawmills, and like a log,
I penetrate the water of rivers that tremble,
quivering and singing with bursting lips.

I remember, on the roads, perhaps at this time,
or else in autumn, they set golden
ears of corn to dry on roofs,
and how many times I was like an enraptured
    child
seeing gold on the roofs of the poor.

I embrace you, now I must
return to my hideaway. I embrace you
without knowing you: tell me who you are, do
    you recognize
my voice in the chorus of all that's being born?
Among all the things that surround you, do you
    hear

my voice, don't you feel yourself surrounded by
    my accent,
emanating from the earth like natural water?

It's me embracing the entire sweet surface,
my homeland's flowery waist, and I call you
so that we can talk when happiness expires
and to hand you this hour like a closed flower.
Happy New Year to the country in darkness.
Let's walk together, the world is crowned with
    wheat,
the lofty sky races along, bowling and dashing
its pure towering stones against the night: the new
wineglass has just been filled with a minute
bound to join the river of time that bears us.
This time, this wineglass, this land are yours:
conquer them and hark the dawning of the day.

XIV

THE GREAT OCEAN

I

The Great Ocean

Ocean, if I could destine my hands a measure, a
     fruit, a ferment
of your gifts and destructions,
I'd choose your distant repose, your steely lines,
your extension guarded by air and night,
and the energy of your white language
that destroys and topples its columns
in its own shattered purity.

It's not the last wave with its salty weight
that pulverizes coasts and produces
the sandy peace that envelops the world:
it's the central volume of force,
the extended potency of waters,
the motionless solitude brimming with life.
Time, perhaps, or accumulated cup
of all movement, pure unity

unsealed by death, green gut
of the burning totality.

Of the submerged arm that raises a drop
nothing remains but the salt's kiss. Of man's
corpses on your shores the dewy fragrance
of a wet flower endures. Your energy
seems to flow unconsumed,
seems to return to its repose.

The wave that you release
—arch of identity, starry plume—
when it broke it was just foam
and it rose again without expiring.

All your force becomes origin again.
You only deliver crushed debris,
detritus removed from your cargo,
whatever the action of your abundance expelled,
everything that ceased to be cluster.

Your statue stretches beyond the waves.
Living and orderly like breast and cloak
of a single human being and its breaths,
raised in the light's matter,
prairies heaved up by the waves
form the planet's naked skin.
You fill your own being with your substance.

You brim the curvature of silence.

The cup, universal cavity of water,
trembles with your salt and honey,
and nothing lacks in you as it does
in the flayed crater, the savage vessel:
empty peaks, scars, signs
that guard the mutilated air.

Your petals pulse against the world,
your submarine grains tremble,
smooth ova dangle their threat,
schools navigate and pullulate,
and nothing rises to the nets' thread
but the dead lightning of a fish scale,
a wounded millimeter in the distance
of your crystalline totalities.

II

Births   When the stars were transmuted
into earth and metal, when energy
was extinguished and the cup
of dawns and coal was spilt and
the fire submerged in its dwellings,
the sea plunged like a droplet burning
from distance to distance, from hour to hour:
its blue fire was transformed into sphere,
the air of its wheels was a bell,
its essential interior trembled in the foam,
and in the salt's light the flower
of its spacious autonomy was raised.

While the segregated stars
slept like lethargic lamps
thinning their immobile purity,
the sea stocked its magnitude with salt
and bites, filled the day's extension
with movement and flames,
created the earth and unleashed the foam,
left rubbery traces in its absences,
invaded the abyss with statues,
and founded blood on its shores.

Surfstar, mother water,
mother matter, invincible medulla,
tremulous church raised in mud:
in you life probed nocturnal stones,
withdrew when it reached the wound,
advanced with shields and diadems,
extended transparent teeth,
accumulated war in its belly.
Whatever formed darkness broken
by the cold substance of lightning
is living in your life, Ocean.

The earth made man its punishment.

It deposed beasts, abolished mountains,
scrutinized the eggs of death.

Meanwhile the windsails of sunken
flux survived in your age,
and the magnitude created maintains
the same scaly emeralds,
hungry spruces that devour
with the ring's blue mouths,
hair that absorbs drowned eyes,
the madrepore of combatant stars,
and in the oiled power of the cetacean
the grinding shadow glides along.
The cathedral was built without hands
by blows of innumerable tide,
salt grew thin as a needle,
became a sheet of incubatory water,
and pure beings, recently extended,
pullulated, weaving walls
until like nests clustered
with the gray attire of sponges,
the scarlet tunic slipped away,
the yellow apotheosis lived,
amaranth's calcareous flower grew.

Everything was being, tremulous substance,
murderous petals that bit,
accumulated naked quantity,
palpitation of seminal plants,
bleeding of the humid spheres,
perpetual blue wind that demolished
the abrupt limits of beings.
So the motionless light was a mouth
and its purple jewelry bit.

Ocean, it was the least harsh form,
the translucent grotto of life,
the existential mass, flowing
with clusters, tissues of ovaries,
scattered germinal teeth,
swords of matinal serum,
stinging coupling organs:
everything palpitated in you, filling the water
with cavities and convulsions.
So the cup of lives had
its turbulent aroma, its roots,
and the waves were spangled invasion:
waist and plenitude survived,

crest and latitude unfurled
the golden hosts of the foam.
And ashore, trembling forever,
the sea's voice, the water's nuptial beds,
the destructive cyclonic skin,
the star's raging milk.

III

**The Fish
and the
Drowned
Person**

Suddenly I saw intense regions
brimming with steely forms,
mouths like cutting lines,
thunderbolts of submerged silver,
mourning fish, ogival fish,
fish with studded firmament,
fish with shimmering polka dots,
fish that cruise like shivers,
white velocity, slender sciences
of circulation, oval mouths
of carnage and increase.

Beautiful the hand or waist
that, enveloped by a fleeting moon,
saw the denizens of the deep tremble,
the wet elastic river of lives,
starry growth in fish scales,
seminal opal disseminated
in the ocean's dark sheet.

He saw biting silver stones burn,
banners of tremulous treasure,
and submitting his blood he descended
to the devouring depths,
suspended by mouths that cover
his torso with bloodthirsty rings
until, disheveled and divided
like a bloody shaft of grain,
he's a tidal shield, a suit ground
by amethysts, a wounded heritage
beneath the sea, on the numerous tree.

IV

**The Men
and the
Islands**

The oceanic men awakened, waters
sang in the islands, from stone to green stone:
textile maidens crossed the enclosure
in which the entwined fire and rain
procreated diadems and drums.
                       The Melanesian
    moon
was a hard madrepore, sulphurous flowers
came from the ocean, the earth's
daughters trembled like waves
in the nuptial wind of the palms
and harpoons penetrated flesh
in pursuit of the foam's lives.

Canoes rocked on the deserted day,
from the islands like specks of pollen to
the metallic mass of nocturnal America:
diminutive unnamed stars, perfumed
like secret fountains, brimming
with feathers and coral, when
oceanic eyes discovered the dark
heights of the copper coast, the steep
tower of snow, and the men of clay
saw the wet banners
and the remote marine solitude's
atmospheric children dance,
                       the lost branch
of orange blossoms arrived, the wind
of oceanic magnolias came up, the sweetness
of the blue spur on hips,
the kiss of the metal-free islands,
pure as wild honey,
sonorous as sheets from the sky.

V

Rapa Nui
Tepito-te-henua, navel of the great sea,
workshop of the sea, extinguished diadem.

From your volcanic ash man's
brow rose above the Ocean,
the cracked stone eyes
measured the cyclonic universe,
and the hand that erected the pure
magnitude of your statues was central.

Your religious rock was cut
toward all the Ocean's lines
and the faces of man appeared,
surging from the island's womb,
rising from the empty craters
with their feet entwined to silence.

They were the sentinels and they closed
the cycle of waters that came
from all the wet dominions,
and the sea facing the masks arrested
its tempestuous blue trees.
No one but the faces inhabited
the kingdom's circle. The thread
which enveloped the island's mouth
was silent as the entry of a planet.

And so, in the light of the marine apsis
the stone fable decorates
the immensity with its dead medals,
and the little kings who raise
this entire solitary monarchy
for the eternity of the foam,
return to sea in the invisible night,
return to their sarcophagi of salt.

Only the moonfish that perished in the sand.

Only time that erodes the carved heads.

Only eternity in the sands
know the words:
the sealed light, the dead labyrinth,
the keys of the submerged cup.

VI

**The
Statue
Builders
(Rapa Nui)**

I am the statue builder. I have no name.
I have no face. Mine drifted until it overran
the brambles and rose impregnating the stones.
They have my petrified face, my land's
solemn solitude, the skin of Oceania.

They have no meaning, they wanted nothing
but to be born with all their sandy volume,
to subsist destined to silent time.

Will you ask me if the statue on which I kept
consuming so many fingernails, hands and dark
    arms
reserves a syllable of the crater for you, an ancient
aroma, preserved by a sign of lava?

There's nothing, the statues are what we were,
we are, our brow that beheld the waves,
our substance, sometimes interrupted, sometimes
continued in the stone that resembles us.

Others were malignant little gods,
fish, birds that entertained the morning,
hiding axes, breaking the stature
of the loftiest faces that the stone conceived.

If the gods so wish, let them preserve the conflict
of the postponed harvest, and nourish
the flower's blue sugar in the dance.

Let them ascend and bring down the key to the
    flour:
let them soak all the nuptial sheets
with the wet pollen that dances imperceptibly
within mankind's red springtime,
but let no one come to these walls, to this crater,
but you, O minuscule, mortal, stonecutter.

This flesh and the other will be consumed,
the flower will perhaps perish, armorless,
when—sterile dawn, dry dust—death
will come someday to the proud island's sash,

and you, statue, daughter of man, will continue
to gaze with empty eyes that rose
from hand to hand of the absent immortals.

You'll scratch the earth until firmness
is born, until the shadow falls on the structure
as upon a colossal bee that devours
its own honey lost in infinite time.

Your hands will stroke the stone until they shape
     it,
giving it the solitary energy that can
subsist, without consuming nonexistent names,
and so from one life to one death, bound
in time like a single undulating hand,
we raise the burned tower that slumbers.

The statue that grew above our stature.

Look at them today, touch this matter, these lips
possess the same silent language that sleeps
in our death, and this sandy scar,
which the sea and time have licked like sea lions,
were part of a face that wasn't demolished,
a speck of being, a cluster that defeated the ashes.

So they were born, they were lives that wrought
their own hard cells, their honeycomb in stone.
And this gaze has more sand than time has.
More silence than all death in its hive.

They were the honey of a solemn design that
     inhabited
the dazzling light that flows today in the stone.

VII

**The Rain
(Rapa Nui)**
No, don't let the Queen recognize
your face, it's sweeter
so, my love, far from the effigies, the weight
of your hair in my hands: do you remember
the tree from Mangareva whose flowers fell
on your hair? These hands don't resemble

those white petals: look at them, they're like
    roots,
like stone shoots over which the lizard
glides. Fear not, we'll wait for the rain to fall,
    naked,
the rain, the same that falls on Manu Tara.

But just as water hardens its features on stone,
it falls on us, gently bearing us
to darkness, beneath the hole
of Ranu Raraku. So don't let
the fisherman or the earthen jug see you. Bury
your twin burning breasts in my mouth,
and let your hair be my little night,
a darkness whose wet perfume blankets me.

At night I dream that you and I are two plants
that grew together, roots entwined,
that you know earth and rain like my mouth,
because we're made of earth and rain. Sometimes
I think that with death we'll sleep below,
in the depths of the effigy's feet, gazing at
the Ocean that brought us to build and to love.

My hands weren't iron when they met you, the
    waters
of another sea passed through them as through a
    net: now
water and stones sustain seeds and secrets.

Love me asleep and naked, for ashore
you're like the island: your bewildered love,
your startled love, hidden in the cavity of dreams,
is like the movement of the sea that surrounds us.

And when I too fall asleep
in your love, naked,
put my hand between your breasts so that it can
pulse along with your nipples washed in the rain.

VIII

The
Oceanics

With no gods but rotten seal hides,
honor of the sea, Yámanas lashed
by the antarctic whip, Alakalufs
smeared with oils and detritus:
amid the walls of crystal and abyss
the little canoe, in the bristling
enmity of icebergs and rain,
carried the sea lions' roving love
and the fire's coals borne
above the endmost mortal waters.

Man, if extermination
did not descend from the rivers of snow
or from the moon hardened
above the glacial vapor of the glaciers,
but from man who, even in the substance
of lost snow and the Ocean's
uttermost waters,
speculated with exiled bones
until he drove you beyond everything,
and today, beyond everything and the snow
and the unleashed tempest of ice
your dugout plies the wild salt
and furious solitude seeking
the haunts of bread, you're Ocean,
a droplet from the sea and its furious blue,
and your frazzled heart calls me
like an incredible fire that refuses to die.

I love the icy plant assailed
by the howling foamy wind,
and at the base of the gorges,
diminutive lucernarian hosts
burn above crustacean lamps
of water stirred by the cold,
and the antarctic dawn in its castle
of pale imaginary splendor.

I love even the turbulent roots
of plants burned by the dawn
of transparent hands,

but this wave
born in ruptures, driven
like love wounded beneath the wind,
rolls to you, seashade, child
of the glacial plumes, tattered oceanic.

IX

Antarctica   Antarctica, austral crown, cluster
of cold lamps, cinerarium
of ice sundered
from the earthly skin, church rent
by purity, nave opening
over the cathedral of whiteness,
immolator of shattered glass,
hurricane dashed on the walls
of nocturnal snow,
grant me your double breast stirred
by the invading solitude, the channel
of terrifying wind masked
by all the corollas of an ermine,
with all the shipwreck's horns
and the white sinking of worlds,
or your peaceful breast that cleans the cold
like a pure rectangle of quartz,
and everything that's not breathed, the infinite
transparent matter, the open air,
the solitude without land or poverty.
Kingdom of the harshest meridian,
whispery, motionless ice harp,
beside the enemy stars.

All seas are your round sea.
All the Ocean's resistences
concentrated their transparency in you,
and the salt filled you with its castles,
the ice made cities raised
on a crystal spire, the wind
ranged your salty paroxysm
like a jaguar burned by snow.

Your cupolas birthed danger
from the glaciers' vessel,

and in your desolate dorsal, life is
like a vineyard beneath the sea, burning
unconsumed, reserving fire
for the snow's springtime.

X

**Children
of the
Seacoast**

Pariahs of the sea, whipped
antarctic dogs,
dead Yaguans upon whose bones
dance the proprietors who paid
bounty for the proud necks
severed with knives.

Changos from Antofagasta and the barren coast,
pariahs, freezing sea lice,
grandchildren of Rapa, Anga-Roa's poor,
broken lemurs, Hotu-Iti's lepers,
peons from the Galápagos, coveted
castaways of the archipelagoes,
threadbare clothes whose
dirty patches reveal
the contexture of combat,
skin salted by the air, brave
fragment of human being and amber:
the shipment reached the homeland of the sea:
cordage, stamps, formalities,
the bill with a blurred profile,
detritus of bottles on the beach:
the governor came, the deputy,
and the sea heart became seam,
pocket, iodine and agony.
When they came to merchandise the dawn
was sweet, shirts
were like snow aboard the ship,
and the celestial children flashed,
flower and campfire, moon and movement.

O sea lice, eat dung now,
stalk debris, worn-out
shoes of navigators and managers,
smell like excrement and fish.
Now you've entered the circle

from which there's no escape but death.
Not a sea death, with water and moon,
but the unhinged holes
of necrology, for if you want
to forget now, you're lost.
Formerly death had territories,
transmigration, stages, seasons,
and you could rise dancing enveloped
in the diurnal dew of roses
or in the silver fish's navigation:
now you're dead forever: submerged
in the monk's gloomy decree
and just earthworms
that at best wriggle their tails
beneath the accountancy's inferno.

Come and pullulate on the
seashores: we still accept you,
you can go fishing provided
that our Fisheries Company Inc.
is guaranteed: you can survive
scratching your ribs on the docks,
carrying sacks of chick-peas,
sleeping in the coastal refuse:
you're really a menace, scabby
outcasts of the foam: it's
best, if the priest permits you,
to board the ship that awaits you,
lice and all, to bear you without coffin,
bitten by the last waves and calamities
(provided that no one has to pay for them)
to nothingness, to death.

XI

Death   Ulva-like dogfish,
naval velvet of the abyss,
like slivery moons you appear
suddenly with a purple blade:
fins oiled in darkness,
mourning and speed, vessels of fear
to which crime with its vertiginous light
ascends like a corolla,

voiceless, in a green bonfire,
in the cutlery of lightning.

Pure dark forms that glide
beneath the sea's skin, like love,
like love invading the throat,
like night shining in grapes,
like the flash of wine in daggers:
wide shadows of boundless hide
like foreboding banners: clusters
of arms, mouths, tongues that envelop
whatever they consume with an undulating
    flower.

In the slightest droplet of life
awaits an indecisive springtime
that will close whatever fell into the void
with its motionless system:
the ultraviolet ribbon that slips
a perverse phosphorous belt
onto the black agony of the lost
and the tapestry of the drowned man covered
by a forest of lances and lampreys
trembling and busy as a loom that weaves
in the devouring depths.

XII

**The
Wave**

The wave rises from the bottom with roots,
offspring of the submerged firmament.
Its elastic invasion was heaved
by the pure potency of the Ocean.
Its eternity appeared flooding
the pavilions of deep power
and each being resisted it,
shed cold fire on its waist
until its snowy might broke away
from the branches of strength.

It rises like a flower from the earth
when it advanced with resolute aroma
to the magnitude of the magnolia,
but this flower that has erupted from the sea floor

brings all the abolished light,
brings all the unburned branches
and the entire fountain of whiteness.

And so when its round eyelids,
its volume, its cups, its corals
swell the sea's skin this entire
being of submarine beings appears:
it is the unity of the sea building itself:
the sea's column rising forth:
all its births and defeats.

The school of salt opened its doors,
all the light exploded striking the sky,
the yeast of wet metal
rose from night to dawn,
all clarity became corolla,
the flower grew until it eroded the stone,
the river of foam ascended to death,
the procellous plants attacked,
the rose poured onto the steel:
the bulwarks of water buckled
and the sea collapsed without spilling
its tower of crystal and chills.

XIII

The Seaports

Acapulco, cut like a blue stone,
when the sea awakens, it dawns on your door,
nacreous and embroidered like a seashell,
and amid your stones fish pass like pulsing
thunderbolts charged by marine radiance.
You're all light, without eyelids, the day
naked, poised like a flower of sand,
amid the outstretched infinity of water
and the heights lit with lamps of clay.

Beside you lagoons granted me hot
evening love with beasts and mangroves,
nests like knots in branches from which
the flight of egrets raised foam,
and in water scarlet as crime an imprisoned
colony of mouths and roots seethed.

Topolobambo, faintly sketched on the shores
of sweet and naked maritime California,
starry Mazatlán, night seaport, I hear
the waves that pound your poverty
and your constellations, the pulse
of your passionate choirs,
your somnambulistic heart that sings
beneath the red nets of the moon.

Guayaquil, sharp syllable, blade
of equatorial star, unlatched bolt
of moist darkness that sways
like the braid of a wet woman:
iron door destroyed
by the bitter sweat
that soaks clusters,
drips ivory on foliage
and trickles into mankind's mouth,
biting like marine acid.

I ascended the white rocks of Mollendo,
arid radiance and scars,
crater whose cracked continent
imprisons its treasure amid the stones,
the narrows of man corralled
in the balds of the precipice,
shadow of metallic gullets,
yellow promontory of death.

Pisagua, painful script, stained
by torment—in your empty ruins,
in your terrifying crags,
in your prison of stone and solitude,
they sought to crush the human plant,
they tried to make a carpet out of dead
hearts, to strike calamity
like a furious brand until dignity
was broken: there in the brackish
empty back streets, the phantoms
of desolation move their mantles,
and in the offended naked fissures
history stands like a monument
pounded by the solitary foam.
Pisagua, in the emptiness of your peaks,
in the furious solitude, the force

of man's truth rises
like a naked and noble monument.

It's not just man, not just blood
that stained life on your slopes,
but all the executioners bound
to the wounded swamp of torture,
to the brushland of mourning America,
and when your desolate craggy stones
were filled with chains,
not just a flag was bitten,
it was not just a venomous bandit,
but the foul water's fauna
that repeats its teeth in history,
piercing the heart of the hapless people
with a mortal knife,
shackling the earth that made them,
dishonoring the sand of the dawn.

O sandy seaports, innundated
by nitrate, by the secret salt
that leaves sorrow in the homeland
and ships the gold to an unknown god
whose fingernails scraped the crust
of our grieving territories.

Antofagasta, whose remote voice
flows into the crystallized light,
collects in sacks and storerooms
and is dispersed toward the ships
in the morning aridity.

Parched wooden rose, Iquique,
between your white balustrades, beside
your pine walls impregnated
by the moon of the desert and the sea,
my people's blood was spilt,
truth was assassinated, hope
crushed to a bloody pulp:
the crime was buried by the sand
and distance engulfed the death gasps.

Spectral Tocopilla, beneath the mountains,
beneath the needly nakedness
the dry snow of nitrate flows
without extinguishing the light of its design

or the agony of the dark hand
that death shook in the clumps.

Forsaken seacoast, you spurn
the smothered water of human love,
hidden in your limy banks
like the major metal of shame.
Submerged man descended to your seaports
to see the light of the prostituted streets,
to unburden his heavy heart,
to forget sandpits and misery.
When you pass by, who are you, who rolls
through your golden eyes, who succeeds
in the crystals? You descend and smile,
you esteem the silence in wood,
you touch the opaque moon of the panes
and nothing more: man is guarded
by carnivorous shadows and bars,
he's stretched out in his hospital sleeping
on reefs of gunpowder.

Seaports of the South, which stripped
the shower of leaves on my brow:
bitter winter conifers
from whose needly fountain
solitude rained on my sorrows.
Puerto Saavedra, frozen on the banks
of the Imperial: sandy
inlets, glacial lament
of gulls that seemed
to soar like tempestuous orange blossoms,
without anyone rocking their foliage,
sweetlings veering toward my tenderness,
rent by the violent sea
and spattered in the wilds.

Then snow was my road
and in the slumbering homes of the Strait
in Punta Arenas, in Puerto Natales,
in the howling blue expanse,
in the whistling, unbridled
final night of the land, I saw the planks
that resisted, I lit the lamps
beneath the fierce wind, plunged my hands
into the naked antarctic springtime
and kissed the cold dust of the endmost flowers.

355

XIV

The
Ships

Silk ships borne upon the light,
raised in morning violet,
cruising the maritime sun with red pavilions
frayed like tattered stamens,
pungent smell of gilded chests
which cinnamon made resound like violins,
and cold greed which whispered in the seaports
in a tempest of rubbed hands,
the welcome green smoothness
of jade, and the pale grain of silk,
everything plied the sea like a fugue of the wind,
like a dance of anemones that disappeared.
   Slender swiftness sallied forth,
   fine sea tools, canvas fish,
   gilded by wheat, determined
   by their ashen merchandise,
   by overflowing stones that shone
   like fire falling amid the sails,
   or replete with sulphurous flowers
   gathered in salty barrens.
   Others bore races, disposed
   in the dampness of the hold, chained,
   captive eyes that cracked the ship's
   heavy wood with tears.
   Feet recently severed from ivory, bitterness
   heaped like gangrenous fruits,
   sorrows skinned like deer: heads
   fallen from the diamonds of summer
   to the depths of loathsome dung.
   Wheat-laden ships that trembled
   over the waves like cereal wind
   in shafts of grain on the prairies:
   whalers, bristling
   with hearts flinty as harpoons,
   sluggish from their haul, transporting
   their holds to Valparaíso,
   greasy sails that flapped,
   wounded by the snow and oil
   until the ship's cups brimmed
   with the blubbery harvest of the beast.
   Dismantled whale boats that crossed
   the sea fury from boom to boom

with man clinging to his memories
and the final splinters of the vessels
before the sea's flotsam bore them,
like amputated hands,
to the slender mouths that filled
the foamy sea in its agony.
Nitrate ships, trim
and sprightly as indomitable dolphins
wafted by the wind on its glorious sheets,
fine as fingers and fingernails,
swift as feathers and stallions,
navigators of the dark sea
that mines the metals of my homeland.

XV

**To a Ship's
Figurehead
(Elegy)**

In the sands of Magellan we retrieved you, weary
navigator, motionless
beneath the tempest that so often your sweet twin
    breasts
defiantly divided on your nipples.

We raised you again over the seas of the South,
    but now
you were a passenger of the dark, of the corners,
    like
the wheat and metal you safeguarded, enveloped
by the marine night, on the high seas.

Today you're mine, goddess whom the great
    albatross
brushed with its outstretched statue in flight,
like a mantle of music conducted in the rain
by your blind roving wooden eyelids.

Sea rose, bee purer than dreams,
almond-eyed woman transformed from the roots
of an oak filled with songs
into form, strength of foliage with nests,
mouth of tempests, exquisite sweetness
that would seduce the light with her hips.

When angels and queens who were born with you

slumbered covered with moss, destined
to immobility with an honor of corpses,
you rose to the slender prow of the ship
and were angel, queen and wave, tremor of the
    world.
Men's shiver rose
to your noble apple-breasted robe
while your lips, dear heart! were moistened
by other lips worthy of your wild mouth.

Beneath the strange night your waist
let the pure weight of the ship fall on the waves
cutting into the dark magnitude a path
of tumbling fire, of phosphorescent honey.
In your curls the wind opened its stormy box,
the unchained metal of its moan,
and at dawn the light received you trembling
in the seaports, kissing your wet diadem.

Sometimes you stopped short above the sea
and the trembling ship laid on her beam-ends
like a massive fruit that breaks loose and falls,
a stricken sailor embraced by the foam
and the pure movement of time and ship.
And you alone among the faces paralyzed
by the threat, submerged in sterile grief,
received the spattered salt on your mask,
and your eyes stowed the salty tears.
More than one poor life slipped through your
    arms
to the eternity of the mortuary waters
and the contact of the living and the dead
consumed your sea-wood heart.

Today we've retrieved your form from the sand.
At last, you were destined to my eyes. Perhaps
    you're
slumbering, sleeper, perhaps you've breathed your
    last, beloved:
at last, your movement has forgotten the murmur
and the roving radiance concluded its voyage.
Sea furies, sky blows have crowned
your haughty head with cracks and splinters,
and your face rests like a seashell
with wounds that scar your rocked brow.

For me your beauty harbors all the perfume,
all the roving acid, all the dark night.
And on your erect lamp or goddess breasts
—turgescent tower, immobile love—life lives on.
Retired, you navigate with me, until the day
when they let what I am fall into the foam.

XVI

The Man
Aboard
the Ship

Beyond the ship's line
spun by the salt in motion,
the dead grease that pierces dreams enters,
the crewman sleeps with naked fatigue,
a watchman drags a metal cable,
the world of the ship
rumbles, wind groans in the spars,
iron viscera pulse mutely,
the stoker stares at his face in the mirror:
in a piece of broken glass, he discerns
some eyes in that bony soot-stained mask:
those eyes that Graciela
Gutiérrez loved, before she died, without these
    eyes
that she loved being able to see her at her bedside,
to set sail together for the last time, within
the journey, amid the hot coals and oil.
No matter, with the kisses sealed
between those trips and gifts, now no one,
no one at home. On the sea night, love
touches all the beds of the sleeping, lives on
beneath the ship, like nocturnal
kelp drifting its branches upward.

Others are stretched out on the night of the
    journey,
in the void, without sea beneath their dreams,
like life, fragmented heights, bits
of night, rubble that removed
the torn net of dreams.
                 At night
land invades the sea with its waves and blankets
the poor sleeping passenger's heart

with a single syllable of dust, with a
spoonful of death that reclaims him.
Every oceanic stone is ocean, the minuscule
ultraviolet waist of the medusa, the sky
with all its starry emptiness, the moon

has abolished sea in its specters:
but man shuts his eyes, bites his footsteps
a bit, threatens his little heart,
sobs and scratches the night with his fingernails,
seeking earth, turning into maggots.

It's earth that the waters don't cover and kill.

It's pride of clay that will die in the jug,
breaking, scattering the drops that sang,
binding its indecisive stitchwork to the earth.

Do not seek this death in the sea, do not wait for
territory, do not save the fistful of dust
to integrate it intact and deliver it to the earth.

Deliver it to these infinite singing lips,
donate them to this choir of motion and world,
destroy yourself in the eternal maternity of water.

XVII

**The
Enigmas**

You've asked me what the crustacean spins
between its gold claws
and I reply: the sea knows.
You wonder what the sea squirt waits for in its
    transparent bell? What does it wait for?
I'll tell you: it's waiting for time like you.
You ask me whom the embrace of the alga
    Macrocystis reaches?
Inquire, inquire at a certain hour, in a certain sea
    that I know.
You'll doubtlessly ask me about the accursed
    ivory of the narwhal, so that I'll tell you
how the sea unicorn dies harpooned.
You'll perhaps ask me about the halcyonic feathers
    that tremble

in the pure origins of the austral sea?
And about the polyp's crystalline construction
  you're no doubt pondering
another problem, trying to unriddle it now?
Do you want to know the electric matter of the
  seafloor's barbs?
The armed stalactite that breaks as it walks?
The hook of the fisher fish, music stretched out
in the depths like a thread in the water?

I want to tell you that the sea knows this,
that life in its coffers
is wide as the sand, countless and pure,
and amid sanguinary grapes time has polished
the hardness of a petal, the medusa's light,
and it has plucked the bouquet of its coral fibers
from a cornucopia of infinite mother-of-pearl.

I'm nothing but the empty net that advances
human eyes, lifeless in that darkness,
fingers accustomed to the triangle, measurements
of an orange's shy hemisphere.

I lived like you probing
the interminable star,
and in my net, at night, I awakened naked,
the only catch, a fish trapped in the wind.

XVIII

Oceanics, you don't have the matter
that emerges from the vegetal lands
between springtime and the spikes of grain.

The blue touch of the air that navigates
between the grapes doesn't know the face
that flows to the ocean from solitude.

The face of the pummeled rocks,
that doesn't know bees, that has
nothing but the agriculture of waves,
the face of stones that accepted

361

the desolate foam of combat
in its pocked eternities.

Rough ships of hirsute granite
abandoned to the fury, planets
in whose motionless dimension
the sea's flags arrest their surge.

Thrones of cyclonic elements.

Towers of shaken wilds.

Sea rocks, you possess the victorious
color of time, matter spent
by an eternity in motion.

Fire brought forth these ingots,
which the sea shook with its pomegranates.

This wrinkle in which copper and brine
merged: this orange-colored iron,
these spots of silver and pigeon,
are the mortal wall and the frontier
of the depths with its clusters.

Stones of solitude, beloved stones
from whose hard cavities
the tumultuous cold of algae hangs
and to whose border embellished by the moon
solitude rises from the seashores.
From the feet lost in the sand
what aroma was lost, what motion
of nuptial corolla climbed up trembling?

Sand plants, fleshy triangles,
planed substances that came
to ignite their splendor on the stones,
marine springtime, delicate
wineglass raised above the stones,
little lightning bolt of amaranth faintly
lit and frozen by the fury,
grant me the condition that defies
the sands of the starry wasteland.

Sea stones, sparks stopped
in the combat of light, bells

gilded by rust, sharp
swords of grief, broken cupolas
in whose scars the toothless
statue of the earth is built.

XIX

From California I brought a spiny murex,
with silica in its barbs, its bristling elegance
of a frozen rose bedecked with mist,
and its pink palate interior burned
with the soft shade of a fleshy corolla.

And I had a cypraea whose spots fell
on its cape, embroidering its pure velvet
with burned rings of gunpowder or panther,
and another had on its back, smooth as a
    wineglass,
a branch of rivers tattooed on the moon.

But the spiral line, sustained
by air and sea alone, O
stairway, delicate *scalaria*,
O fragile monument of the dawn
coiled by a ring with kneaded
opal, exuding sweetness.

Clearing the sand, I fetched from the sea
the oyster bristling with bloody coral,
spondylus, enclosing the light of its
sunken treasure in its halves,
chest enveloped in scarlet needles,
or snow with assailing spines.

In the sand I gathered the graceful oliva,
wet wayfarer, purple foot,
moist jewel in whose form
fruit hardened its flame,
crystal polished its marine condition
and the dove rounded its oval nakedness.

The triton's shell retained
distance in the grotto of sound

and in the structure of its braided lime
its cupola sustains the sea with petals.

O *rostellaria*, flower impenetrable
as a sign raised on a needle,
minuscule cathedral, pink spear,
sword of light, watery pistil.

But in the heights of dawn the creature
of light, made of moon, peeps forth,
the argonaut propelled by a tremor,
kneaded by the tremulous contact of foam,
navigating on a wave
with its spiral ship of jasmine.

And so hidden in the tide,
undulant mouth of the purple sea,
lips of titanic violet,
the *tridacna* closes like a castle,
and there its colossal rose devours
the blue stirps that kiss it:
monastery of salt, immobile heritage
that imprisoned a hardened wave.

But I should name, barely touching,
O Nautilus, upon your winged dynasty,
the round equation in which you navigate,
plying your pearly ship,
your spiral geometry in which
seaclock, mother-of-pearl and line merge,
and I must run to the islands,
in the wind, with you, god of structure.

XX

**The
Battered
Birds**

High above Tocopilla lies the nitrous pampa,
the barrens, the stain of the salt marshes.
It's the desert without a leaf, without a beetle,
without a blade of grass, without shade, without
time.

There the sea gull made its nests,
long ago, in the solitary hot sand,

left its eggs, stripping flight
from the seacoast, in waves of feathers,
toward solitude, toward the remote
square of desert that they carpeted
with the downy treasure of life.

Beautiful river from the sea, wild
wilderness of love, wind feathers
rounded into magnolia globes,
arterial flight, winged pulse
in which all lives accumulate
in a reunited river, its pressures:
and so the sterile salt was colonized,
the plumed wasteland was crowned,
and flight incubated in the sands.

Man came. Perhaps those boughs
of billing that trembled like the sea
in the desert filled his misery
of a poor desert stray,
perhaps that crackling expanse
of whiteness dazzled him like a star,
but others followed in his footsteps.

They came at dawn, with clubs
and baskets, they robbed the treasure,
clubbed the birds, destroyed
the ship of feathers, nest by nest,
checked the weight of the eggs and smashed
those that had chicks.

They raised them to the light and threw them
against the desert floor, amid
flight and shriek and wave
of wrath, and the birds spread
all their fury in the invaded air,
eclipsing the sun with their banners:
but destruction pummeled the nests,
hoisted the club, and the city
of the sea in the desert was razed.

Then the city, in the evening
brine of fog and drunkards,
heard the baskets that passed selling
seabird eggs, wild fruits from
the wasteland where nothing survives,

365

except the solitude without seasons,
the assailed and bitter salt.

XXI

Leviathan   Ark, wrathful peace, slippery
bestial night, antarctic alien,
you won't pass by me displacing
your shadowy floe without my
one day entering your walls and raising
your armor of submarine winter.

Your black fire of an exiled planet
crackled South, the territory
of your silence that moved algae
shook the age of density.

It was just form, magnitude closed
by a tremor of the world in which
his leathery majesty glides by startled
by his own potency and tenderness.

Angry ark lit
with torches of black snow,
when your blind blood was founded
the sea's age slept in gardens,
and in its extension the moon dismantled
the tail of its phosphorescent magnet.
Life crackled
like a blue bonfire, mother medusa,
multiplied tempest of ovaries,
and all growth was purity,
pulsing of a marine tendril.

And so your gigantic rigging was
disposed amid the waters like the passage
of maternity over blood,
and your power was immaculate night
that slipped down engulfing the roots.
Deviance and terror shook
the solitude, and your continent fled
beyond the awaited isles:
but terror passed over the globes

of the glacial moon, and entered your flesh,
assailing wilds that harbored
your terrifying extinguished lamp.
The night went with you: it enveloped you,
bonded a tempestuous ooze to you
and your cyclonic tail churned
ice in which the stars slumbered.

O great wound, hot fountain
churning its thunder vanquished
in the region of the harpoon, stained
by the sea of blood, bled white,
sweet slumbering beast conveyed
like a cyclone of broken hemispheres
to the black longboats of grease
filled with wrath and pestilence.

O great statue murdered in the crystals
of the polar moon, brimming the sky
like a cloud of terror that weeps
and covers the oceans with blood.

XXII

Phalacro-
corax

Guaniferous birds from the islands,
multiplied will of flight,
celestial magnitude, countless
migration of the wind of life,
when your comets glide past
sanding the secretive sky
of silent Peru, the eclipse flies.
O leisurely love, wild springtime
that uproots its brimming cup
and navigates the ship of the species
with a fluvial tremor of sacred water,
transporting its torrential sky
toward the red islands of dung.

I want to immerse myself in your wings,
to head South sleeping, buoyed
by all the tremorous density.
To wing my way with a lost voice
in the dark river of arrows, to divide myself

in the inseparable palpitation.
Then, shower of flight, the whitewashed
islands open their cold paradise
where the moon of plumage falls,
the mourning tempest of feathers.

So man bows his head
before the billing of mother birds,
and scratches dung with blind hands
that raise the rungs one by one,
scrapes the clarity of the excrement,
collects the scattered feces,
and prostrates himself amid the islands
of fermentation, like a slave,
hailing the acid shores
that the illustrious birds crown.

XXIII

**Not Only
the
Albatross**

You're not expected, not by
springtime, not in the corolla's thirst,
not in the purple honey woven
fiber by fiber in vine stocks and clusters,
but in the tempest, in the tattered
torrential cupola of the reef,
in the crevice drilled by dawn,
and even more, on the green spears
of defiance, in the crumbling
solitude of marine wastelands.

Brides of salt, procellarian pigeons,
you lent your back wet by the sea
to every impure aroma of the earth,
and into the wild purity you plunged
the celestial geometry of flight.

You're sacred, not only the one that rode
the gale of the bough like a cyclonic
droplet: not only the one that nests
on the slopes of fury, but
the gull rounded off with snow,
the form of the cormorant upon the foam,
the silver-plated bundle of platinum.

When the pelican fell like a
clenched fist, plunging its volume,
when prophecy soared
on the vast wings of the albatross,
and when the petrel's wind flew
over eternity in motion,
beyond the old cormorants,
my heart took refuge in its cup
and extended the mouth of its song
to the seas and feathers.

Grant me the icy tin that you bear
in your breast to the tempestuous stones,
grant me the condition that collects
in the talons of the osprey,
or the motionless stature that resists
all growth and ruptures,
the abandoned orange-blossom wind
and the taste of the boundless homeland.

XXIV

**Marine
Night**

Marine night, white and green statue,
I love you, sleep with me. I roamed all
the streets burning and dying,
wood grew with me, man
conquered his ash and prepared
to rest enveloped by earth.

Night closed in so that your eyes
wouldn't see his miserable repose.
He wanted closeness, he opened his arms,
safeguarded by beings and by walls,
and fell into the dream of silence, sinking
into funereal earth with his roots.
Ocean night, I came with the love
that builds me to your open form,
to your expanse tended by Aldebaran,
to the wet mouth of your song.

I saw you, sea night, when you were born,
pounded by infinite mother-of-pearl:
I saw starry filaments woven

and the electricity of your waist
and the blue motion of the sounds
that besiege your consumed sweetness.

Love me without love, bloody bride.

Love me with space, with the river
of your respiration, with the increase
of all your brimming diamonds:
love me without the truce of your face,
grant me the rectitude of your exhaustion.

You're lovely, beloved, lovely night:
You tend the tempest like a bee
slumbering in your alarmed stamens,
and dream and water tremble in the cups
of your breast besieged by fountains.

Nocturnal love, I pursued what you elevated,
your eternity, the tremulous tower
that assumes the stars, the measure
of your vacillation, the communities
that the foam raises on your flanks:
I'm chained to your throat
and the lips that you shatter in the sand.

Who are you? Night of the seas, tell me
if your precipitous hair covers
all the solitude, if this space
of blood and meadows is infinite.
Tell me who you are, full of ships,
full of moons that the wind crushes,
mistress of all metals, rose
of the depths, rose wet
by the elements of naked love.

Tunic of the earth, green statue,
grant me a bell-like wave,
grant me a furious orange-blossom wave,
the multitude of bonfires, the ships
of the capital sky, the water in which I navigate,
the celestial fire's multitude: I want a single
minute of extension and, more than all
dreams, your distance:
all the purple that you span, the solemn
pensive starry system:

all your hair visited by
darkness, and the day that you prepare.

I want to possess your simultaneous brow,
to open it inside me in order to be born
on all your shores, to set forth now
with all the secrets inhaled,
with your dark lines harbored
within me like blood or flags,
bearing these secret proportions
to the sea of every day, to the combats
that in every door—loves and forebodings—
slumber on.
           But then
I'll enter the city with as many eyes
as you have, I'll sustain the vestments
with which you visited me, and may they touch
    me
to the total immeasurable water:
purity and destruction against all death,
distance that cannot be consumed, music
for those who sleep and for those who wake.

I AM

I

**The
Frontier
(1904)**

I first saw trees, ravines
adorned with flowers of wild beauty,
moist territory, forests aflame
and winter behind the world, in flood.
My childhood is wet shoes, broken trunks
fallen in the forest, devoured by vines
and beetles, sweet days upon the oats,
and the golden beard of my father leaving
for the majesty of the railways.

In front of my house the austral water dug
deep defeats, swamps of mournful clays
which in summer were yellow atmosphere
through which the ox carts creaked and wept,
heavy with nine months of wheat.
Rapid sun of the South:

stubble, clouds of smoke

on roads of scarlet earth, banks of rivers
of round lineage, corrals and pastures
in which the high noon honey reverberated.

The dusty world gradually inched into
the sheds, around barrels and twine,
into the storerooms stacked with the red résumé
of hazel trees, all the forest's eyelids.

I seemed to ascend the torrid dress
of summer, with the threshing machines,
over boldu tree slopes, on the varnished earth,
indelible, raised amid the southland beeches,
sticking to the wheels like mangled flesh.

My childhood journeyed the stations: amid
the rails, the stacks of fresh wood,
the house, with no city, protected only
by cattle and apple trees of indescribable perfume
I went, a slender child whose pale form
was impregnated with pristine forests and
    storerooms.

II

**The
Slingman
(1919)**

Love, perhaps indecisive, insecure love:
just a slap of honeysuckles in the mouth,
just some braids whose movement rose
toward my solitude like a black bonfire,
and the rest: the nocturnal river, the signs
from the sky, the fleeting wet springtime,
the possessed solitary brow, desire
raising its cruel tulips in the night.
I wounded myself stripping constellations,
sharpening my fingers on stars,
spinning fiber by fiber the frozen contexture
of a castle without doors,
          O starry loves
whose jasmine arrests in vain its transparency,
O clouds flowing on the day of love
like a sob amid hostile weeds,
naked solitude bound to a shadow,

to an adored wound, to an indomitable moon.
Name me, I said perhaps to the rosebushes—
they perhaps, the shadow of confused ambrosia.
Every tremor of the world knew my footsteps,
the darkest corner awaited me, the statue
of the sovereign tree on the prairie:
everything on the crossroad reached my delirium,
threshing my name upon springtime.
Then you, sweet face, burned lily,
who did not sleep with my dream, medallion
pursued by a shadow, fierce, unnamed
love, made of all the structure of pollen,
all the wind burning over impure stars:
O love, untangled garden that is consumed,
in you my dreams rose and grew
like a leaven of dark bread.

III

**The
House**

My house, the walls whose fresh,
recently cut wood still smells: dilapidated
homestead that creaked
with every step, and whistled with the warrior
   wind
of austral weather, becoming stormy
element, strange bird
beneath whose frozen feathers my song grew.
I saw shadows, faces that grew
around my roots like plants, kin
who sang songs in the shade of a tree
and shot amid the wet horses,
women hidden in the shadow
cast by masculine towers,
gallops that lashed the light,
                 rareified
nights of wrath, barking dogs.
To what lost archipelagoes
did my father slip away, with the land's
dark daybreak, in his howling trains?
Later I loved the smell of coal in smoke,
oils, axles of frozen precision,
and the solemn train crossing winter stretched

over the earth, like a proud caterpillar.
Suddenly the doors trembled.
                              It's my father.
The centurions of the road surround him:
railwaymen wrapped in wet ponchos,
steam and rain cloaked the house
with them, the dining room was filled with
hoarse stories, glasses were drained,
and from those beings to me, like a separate
barrier, inhabited by sorrow,
anguish arrived, sullen
scars, men without money,
the mineral claw of poverty.

IV

**Travel
Companions
(1921)**

Then I arrived in the capital, vaguely impregnated
with mist and rain. What streets were those?
The clothing of 1921 pullulated
in an atrocious smell of gas, coffee and bricks.
I circulated among the students bewildered,
concentrating the walls within me, seeking
every evening in my poor poetry the branches,
the raindrops and moon that had become lost.
I repaired to its depths, submerging myself
in its waters every evening, grasping impalpable
stimuli, gulls from an abandoned sea,
until I closed my eyes and wallowed in the core
of my own substance.
                              Was it darkness, was it
just hidden wet leaves from the subsoil?
From what wounded matter was death husked
until it touched my members, conveyed my smile
and excavated an ominous pit in the streets?

I set out to live: I grew and hardened
I pounded the miserable back streets,
without compassion, singing on the borders
of delirium. The walls were filled with faces:
eyes that didn't look at the light, twisted waters
illuminated by crime, patrimonies
of solitary pride, cavities
brimming with rent hearts.

I went with them: in their chorus alone
my voice recognized the wilds
where it was born.

I entered manhood
singing amid the flames, embraced
by companions of nocturnal condition
who sang with me in the dives,
and gave me more than one tenderness,
more than one springtime defended
by their hostile hands,
the only fire, true plant
of the crumbling barrios.

V

**The
Student
(1923)**

O you, sweeter, more interminable
than sweetness, carnal beloved
amid the shadows: from other days
you rise filling your wineglass with
heavy pollen, in pleasure.
                          From the violent
night, night like streaking
wine, rusty purple night,
I fell to you like a wounded tower,
and between the poor sheets your star
pulsed against me burning the sky.

O jasmine nets, o physical fire
nourished in this new shade,
darkness that we touch squeezing
the central waist, pounding time
with cruel bursts of spikes of grain.

Nothing but love, in the void
of a bubble, love with dead streets,
love, when all life died away
and left us kindling the corners.

I bit woman, plunged in fainting away
from within my strength, I treasured clusters,
and set forth walking from kiss to kiss,
tied to caresses, bound

to this grotto of cold hair,
to these legs ranged by lips:
hungering amid the earth's lips,
devouring with devoured lips.

VI

The
Traveler
(1927)

I plied the seas to the seaports.
The world amid cranes
and storerooms of the sordid shore
revealed stiffs and beggars in its chasm,
companies of the spectral hungry
alongside the ships.
                        Recumbent,
parched countries, in the sand,
resplendent robes, flaming mantles
emerged from the desert, armed
like scorpions, guarding the hole
of petroleum, in the dusty
network of calcined wealth.

I lived in Burma, amid cupolas
of powerful metal, and thickets
where the tiger burned its rings
of bloody gold. From my windows
on Dalhousie Street, the indefinable
odor, moss in the pagodas,
perfumes and excrement, pollen, gunpowder,
of a world saturated with human moisture,
rose up to me.
                        The streets summoned me
with their countless movements
of saffron fabrics and red spittle,
beside the filthy waves of the Irrawadhy,
soupy water whose blood and oil
ran down discharging its lineage
from the high lands whose gods
at least slept enveloped by its clay.

VII

**Far
from
Here**

India, I didn't love your tattered clothes,
your dismantled community of rags.
For years I walked with eyes that wanted
to scale the promontories of contempt,
amid cities like green wax,
amid talismans, pagodas
whose bloody pastry
sowed terrible spines.
I saw the miserable wretch heaped
atop the suffering of his brother,
streets like rivers of anguish,
tiny villages crushed
between the flowers' thick fingernails,
and I went in the throngs, a sentry
of time, separating blackened
scars, tribulations of slaves.
I entered temples, steps of stucco
and gemstones, dirty blood and death,
and bestial priests, inebriated
by the burning stupor, quarreling over
coins rolling on the floor,
while, O minuscule human being,
great idols with phosphoric feet
stuck out vindictive tongues,
or crushed flowers slipped over
a phallus of scarlet stone.

VIII

**The
Plaster
Masks**

I didn't love . . . I don't know if it was pity or
      vomit.
I rushed through the cities, Saigon, Madras,
Khandy, to the buried, majestic
stones of Anuradapurna, and on the rock
of Ceylon, like whales,
effigies of Siddhartha, I went farther:
in the powdery dust of Penang, along the banks
of rivers, in the jungle

of the purest silence, brimming
with the flock of intense lives,
beyond Bangkok, the dresses
of dancers with plaster masks.
Pestilential gulfs raised
roofs studded with gemstones,
and on wide rivers, dwelling
of the teeming indigents, crammed
in boats, and others, all
covered the infinite earth,
beyond the yellow rivers,
like the single skin of a broken beast,
skin of nations, hide humiliated
by one master or another.

       Captains and princes
lived above the damp death throes
of moribund lamps, bleeding
the lives of poor craftsmen,
and amid talons and whips, the concession
was higher: the European,
American petroleum,
fortifying aluminum temples,
plowing over the defenseless skin,
establishing new sacrificial slaughters.

IX

**The
Dance
(1929)**
In the depths of Java, amid territorial
shadows: here the palace is lit.
I pass between the green bowmen, glued
to the walls, I enter
the throne room. There's the monarch,
apoplectic pig, impure peacock
studded with gold braid, glittering,
between two of his Dutch masters,
scowling merchants who stand guard.
What a repugnant swarm of insects, how
conscientiously they cast spadefuls of filth
upon human beings.

      The sordid sentries
of faraway lands, and the monarch
like a blind bag, dragging

his heavy flesh and false stars
over the humble nation of jewellers.
                                    But suddenly,
from the remote depths of the palace
ten dancers entered, slow as a dream
underwater.
                    Each foot approached
sideways advancing nocturnal honey
like a gold fish, and their ocher masks
bore a fresh garland of orange blossoms
above their hair of oiled density.
                                    Until they stood
before the satrap, and with them the music, a
        fluttering
of crystal wing cases, the pure dance
that grew like a flower, their light
hands building a fleeting statue,
their tunics pounded on their heels
by surging surf or whiteness,
and in every movement of a dove
made in sacred metal, the whispering
air of the archipelago, aflame
like a nuptial tree in springtime.

X

**The War
(1936)**

Spain, shrouded in dreams, awakening
like a head of hair with spikes of wheat,
I saw you being born, perhaps amid brambles
and darkness, industrious,
rising amid oak trees and mountains,
traversing the air with open veins.
But I saw you attacked on street corners
by the ancient bandoliers. They
were masked, with their crosses made
of vipers, their feet mired
in the glacial swamp of corpses.
Then I saw your body extricated
from brushlands, broken
on the sand, bloody, opened,
without world, spurred in agony.
To this very day water from your crags
runs amid dungeons, and you bear

your barbed crown in silence,
to see who will last longer, your grief
or the faces that pass without looking at you.
I lived with your dawn of rifles,
and I want people and gunpowder
to shake the dishonored branches
until the dream trembles and the earth's
divided fruits are gathered again.

XI

Love

You gave me firm love, Spain, with your gifts.
The tenderness that I waited for joined me
and the one who brings the deepest kiss
to my mouth accompanies me.
                              Storms could not
separate her from me,
nor did distances add ground
to the space of love we conquered.
When before the fire, your clothing appeared
amid Spain's fields of grain,
I was double notion, duplicated light,
and bitterness rolled down your face
until it fell on lost stones.
From great sorrow, from bristling harpoons
I rushed into your waters, my love,
like a horse galloping amid
rage and death, and suddenly
a morning apple receives it,
waterfalls of wild tremors.
Since then, love, the wastelands
that created my conduct knew you,
the dark ocean that pursues me,
and chestnuts of the immense Autumn.

Who didn't see you, my sweet love,
struggling beside me, like a
vision, with all the signs
of the star? Who, if he walked
amid the multitudes to seek me
(for I'm a kernel from the human granary),
didn't find you, pressed to my roots,
raised in the song of my blood?

I don't know, my love, if I'll have the time
and place to write once more your fine shade
cast over my pages, my bride:
these days are hard and radiant
and from them we harvest sweetness
kneeded with eyelids and spines.
I no longer recall when you begin:
you were before love,

                          you came
with all the essences of destiny,
and before you, solitude was yours,
perhaps it was your slumbering hair.
Today, wineglass of my love, I only name you,
title of my days, adorable,
and in space you occupy like the day
all the light that the universe possesses.

XII

**Mexico
(1940)**

Mexico, from sea to sea I lived you, pierced
by your iron color, scaling mountains
where there are monasteries
bristling with thorns,

                        the venemous noise
of the city, the treacherous teeth
of the pullulating poetaster, and upon
the leaves of the dead the steps
built by unyielding silence,
like the stumps of a leprous love,
the wet splendor of the ruins.

But from the acrid encampment, sullen
sweat, spears of yellow kernels,
collective agriculture rises forth
distributing the nation's bread.

Other times calcareous cordilleras
blocked my path,

                       forms
of shell-pocked glaciers
riddle the dark cortex
of Mexican skin, and horses

it lives in ashen grains:
when—after the nocturnal shadow—
the vinestocks of dawn are stripped,
Cuauhtémoc's eyes open their remote light
over the foliage's green life.

I sing to Cárdenas. I was there:
I lived the storm of Castile.
Those were the blind days of lives.
Sorrows high as cruel branches wounded
our heartbroken mother.
It was abandoned mourning, walls of silence when
that country of dawn and laurel
was betrayed, sacked and wounded.
Then
only the red star of Russia and the gaze
of Cárdenas shone in the night of mankind.
General, President of America, I leave you in this
    song
something of the glow that I gleaned in Spain.

Mexico, you have opened your doors and hands
to the migrant, the wounded,
the exile, the hero.
I regret that this cannot be said in another way
and once again I want my words
to cling to your walls like kisses.
You left your combative door wide open
and your hair was filled with foreign offspring
and with your hard hands you touched
the cheeks of the child
who with tears birthed the world's tempest for
    you.

I end here, Mexico,
here I leave you this calligraphy
upon your temples so that time
can keep expunging this new discourse
of someone who loved you for freedom and for
    depth.
I'm saying good-bye to you, but I'm not leaving.
I'm leaving, but I cannot
say good-bye to you.

Because in my life, Mexico, you live like a little
lost eagle that circles in my veins

and only death will finally fold its wings
over my slumbering soldier's heart.

XIV

I returned . . . Chile welcomed me with the
    yellow face
of the desert.
              I wandered suffering
from an arid moon in a sandy crater
and encountered the planet's barren dominions,
unadorned light without tendrils, empty rectitude.
Empty? But without vegetation, without talons,
    without
manure the earth revealed its denuded dimension
    to me
and in the distance its long cold line where birds
and igneous breasts of smooth contexture are
    born.

But farther away men dug the borderlands,
gathered hard metals, some disseminated
like the flour of bitter grains,
others like the scorched heights of fire,
and men and moon, everything enveloped me in
    its shroud
until the empty thread of dreams was lost.

I embraced the deserts and man from the slag
    heaps
emerged from his hole, from his mute asperity
and I discovered the sorrows of my lost people.

Then I plied the streets and corridors of power
and disclosed what I'd seen, I revealed hands
that mined clumps charged with grief, dwellings
of forsaken poverty, miserable
bread and the solitude of the abandoned moon.

And elbow to elbow with my shoeless brother
I tried to change the kingdom of dirty coins.

I was persecuted, but our struggle continues.

Truth is loftier than the moon.

The men from the mines see it as if they were
gazing at the night from the deck of a black ship.
And in the shadow my voice is sown
by the hardest stock of the earth.

XV

**The
Wood
Line**

I am a blind carpenter, without hands.
$\qquad\qquad\qquad\qquad\qquad$ I've lived
underwater, consuming cold,
without building fragrant boxes, dwellings
that cedar by cedar raise grandeur,
but my song kept seeking forest threads,
secret fibers, delicate waxes,
and it kept cutting branches, perfuming
solitude with wooden lips.

I loved every material, every droplet
of purple or metal, water and shock of grain,
and I entered dense strata protected
by space and quaking sand,
until I sang with a ravaged mouth,
like a corpse, in the grapes of the earth.

Clay, mud, wine covered me,
I delighted in touching the hips
of the skin whose flower was poised
like a fire beneath my throat,
and in the stone my senses roamed
invading closed scars.

How did I change without being, not knowing
my trade before I came to be,
$\qquad\qquad\qquad\qquad\qquad$ the metallurgy
that was destined to my hardness,
or the sawmills scented
by horses in winter?

Everything turned into tenderness and springs
and I was but a creature of the night.

XVI

**Combative
Kindness**

But I did not have the kindness killed in the
    streets.
I rejected its purulent aqueduct
and didn't touch its contaminated sea.

I extracted good like a metal, digging
beyond the eyes that bit,
and amid the scars my heart
born in swords kept growing.
But I didn't pour forth, discharging
dirt or knife among men.
                    My trade
was neither wound nor poison.
I didn't subdue the helpless man in bonds
that scourged him with cold lashes,
I didn't go to the plaza to seek enemies,
stalking them with a masked hand:
I just grew with my roots,
and the soil that extended my rigging
deciphered the buried worms.

Monday came to bite me and I fed it some leaves.
Tuesday came to insult me and I kept on sleeping.
Then Wednesday arrived with irate teeth.
Building roots, I let it pass by.
And when Thursday came with a poisonous
spear black with nettles and scales
I waited for it in the middle of my poetry
and in the moonlight I broke off a cluster for it.

Let them come here to dash themselves on this
    sword.

Let them dissolve themselves in my dominions.

Let them come in yellow regiments
or in the sulphurous congregation.

They'll bite shade and blood from bells
beneath the seven leagues of my song.

XVII

**The
Steel
Gathers
(1945)**

I have seen evil and evil men, but not in their
    lairs.

Evil in a cavern is a fairy tale.

After the poor had fallen
into tatters, into the wretched mine,
they filled their road with spooks.
I found evil seated in the courtrooms:
in the Senate I found it dressed
and groomed, twisting debates
and ideas toward its pockets.
                        Evil and evil men
had just taken a bath: they were
bound in satisfactions,
and were perfect in the smoothness
of their false decorum.
                I've seen evil, and to
banish this pustule I've lived
with other men, adding lives,
becoming a secret cipher, nameless,
invincible unity of people and dust.

The proud man was fighting
fiercely in his ivory closet
and evil flashed by
saying: "His solitary
rectitude is admirable.
Let him be."

The impetuous man unsheathed his alphabet
and mounted on his sword he stopped
to perorate in the deserted street.
Passing by, the evil man told him: "How brave!"
and went to the Club to comment on the deed.

But when I was stone and mortar,
tower and steel, associated syllable:
when I joined hands with my people
and went to combat with the entire sea:
when I abandoned my solitude and put

my pride in the museum, my vanity in the
attic with broken-down carriages,
when I became party with other men, when
the metal of purity was organized,
then evil came and said: "Hit
them hard, let them rot in jail!"

But now it was too late, and the movement
of man, my party,
is the invincible springtime, hard
beneath the earth, when it was hope
and common fruit for the future.

XVIII

Wine Spring wine . . . Autumn wine, grant me
my friends, a table where the equinoctial
leaves can fall, and the great river of the world,
let it pale a little, moving its sound
far from our songs.
                              I'm a good friend.

You didn't enter this house to have me seize
part of your being. Perhaps when you depart
you'll take something of mine—chestnuts, roses or
a security of roots or ships
that I've tried to share with you, friend.

Sing with me until the wineglasses
overflow leaving purple decanted
on the table.
                    This honey comes to your mouth
from the earth, from its dark clusters.

So many are missing, shadows of my song,
                                                       friends
that I loved sincerely, taking from my life
the incomparable virile science I profess,
friendship, woodland of furrowed tenderness.

Give me your hand, meet me,
simply, seek nothing in my words

but the emanation of a bare plant.
Why ask more of me than of a worker? Now you
    know
that blow by blow I kept forging my buried
    ironworks,
and that I only want to speak as my language is.

Go look for doctors if you don't like the wind.

We'll sing with the thundering wine
of the earth: we'll strike the Autumn wineglasses,
and the guitar or silence will keep bringing
love lines, the language of rivers that don't exist,
revered stanzas that have no meaning.

XIX

**Fruits
of the
Earth**

How does earth rise through corn seeking
milky light, hair, hardened ivory,
the exquisite net of ripe tassels
and the entire kingdom of gold that's husked
    away?

I want to eat onions, bring me one from
the market, a globe brimming with crystalline
    white,
that transformed the earth into wax and balance
like a ballerina arrested in flight.
Give me some quail from the game bag, smelling
of moss from the forests, a fish attired
like a king, distilling wet depths
on the serving dish,
                opening pale gold eyes
beneath the multiplied nipple of lemons.

Come, and under the chestnut tree the campfire
will leave its white treasure on the coals,
and a lamb with all its gifts will keep gilding
its lineage until it's amber for your mouth.

Give me everything from the earth, recently
fallen pigeons, inebriated with wild clusters,
sweet fluvial eels that, on dying,

pay out their diminutive pearls,
and a tray of acid sea urchins
will give their submarine orange
to the fresh firmament of lettuce.

And before the marinaded hare
fills the lunch air with aroma
like a wild flight of flavors,
my kiss goes soaked in the substance
of the earth that I love and journey
with all the roads of my blood
to the oysters of the South, freshly opened,
in their sheaths of salty splendor.

XX

**Great
Happiness**

The shadow that I probed is no longer mine.
I possess the enduring happiness of the mainmast,
the forest legacy, the wind of the road
and a determined day beneath the earthly light.
I don't write so that other books can imprison me
or for passionate apprentices of lilies,
but for simple inhabitants who request
water and moon, elements of the immutable
     order,
schools, bread and wine, guitars and tools.

I write for the people, even though they cannot
read my poetry with their rustic eyes.
The moment will come in which a line, the air
that stirred my life, will reach their ears,
and then the farmer will raise his eyes,
the miner will smile breaking stones,
the brakeman will wipe his brow,
the fisherman will see clearly the glow
of a quivering fish that will burn his hands,
the mechanic, clean, recently washed,
smelling of soap, will see my poems,
and perhaps they will say: "He was a friend."

That's enough, that's the crown that I want.

At the gates of factories and mines I want
my poetry to cling to the earth,
to the air, to the victory of abused mankind.
In the hardness that I built, like a box,
slowly and with metals, I would like
the youth who opens it, face-to-face, to find life,
and plunging his soul in may he reach the gusts
that spelled my happiness, in the stormy heights.

XXI

Death

I have resurrected many times, from the depths
of defeated stars, reconstructing the thread
of eternities that I filled with my hands,
and now I'm going to die, without more ado,
      with earth
on my body, destined to be earth.

I didn't purchase a parcel in heaven sold
by the priests, nor did I accept the darkness
that metaphysicians manufactured
for the carefree affluent.

In death I want to be with the poor
who had no time to study it,
while those who have the sky
divided and deeded beat upon them.

My death is tailor-made, like a suit
that awaits me, of the color that I love,
of the dimensions that I sought in vain,
of the depth that I need.

When love spent its evident matter
and struggle husks its hammers
in other hands of joined strength,
death comes to expunge the signs
that kept building your borders.

XXII

Life Let others worry about ossuaries . . .

The world
is colored like a naked apple: the rivers
dredge a torrent of wild medals
and sweet Rosalía and her mate Juan
live everywhere . . .

The castle is made
of rough stones, and my house was made
of clay smoother than grapes and straw.
Wide lands, love, slow bells,
combats reserved for the dawn,
tresses of love that awaited me,
dormant deposits of turquoise:
homes, roads, waves that build
a dream-swept statue,
bakeries at daybreak,
clocks trained in sand,
poppies of the circulating wheat,
and these dark hands that kneaded
the matter of my own life:
for life the oranges are aflame
over the multitude of destinies!

Let the gravediggers pry into ominous
matter: let them raise
the lightless fragments of ash,
and let them speak the maggot's language.
I'm facing nothing but seeds,
radiant growth and sweetness.

XXIII

Testament I leave my house by the seaside
(I) in Isla Negra to the labor unions
of copper, coal and nitrate.
Let them rest there, those abused children
of my country, plundered by axes and traitors,
dispersed in its sacred blood,
consumed in volcanic tatters.

I want the poor to rest in the clean
love that ranged my dominion,
let the obscure be seated at my table,
let the wounded sleep in my bed.

Brother, this is my home, enter the world
of sea flower and spangled stone
that I raised struggling in my poverty.
Here sound was born in my window
as in a crescent conch
and then it established its latitudes
in my disorderly geology.

You come from burning galleries,
from tunnels bitten by hatred,
here I will you peace,
the water and space of my oceania.

XXIV

Testament
(II)

I leave my old books, collected
in corners of the globe, venerated
in their majestic typography,
to the new poets of America,
                         to those who'll
one day weave tomorrow's meanings
on the raucous interrupted loom.

They'll have been born when the rough fist
of dead woodcutters and miners
has given a countless life
to clean the crooked cathedral,
the demented kernel, the filament
that entangled our avid plains.
Let them touch hell, this past
that crushed the diamonds, and let them defend
the granary worlds of their song,
whatever grew on the tree of martyrdom.

Upon the chieftains' bones, far
from our betrayed legacy, in the open
air of nations that stand alone,

they'll fill the statute
of a long victorious suffering.

Let them love as I loved my Manrique, my
    Góngora,
my Garcilaso, my Quevedo:
                   they were
titanic guardians, platinum
armor and snowy transparency,
who taught me precision, and let them seek
in my Lautréamont old laments
amid pestilential agonies.
In Maiakovsky let them see how the star climbed
and how spikes of grain were born of his
    thunderbolts.

XXV

Dispositions

Comrades, bury me in Isla Negra,
facing the sea that I know, every wrinkled area
of stones and waves that my lost eyes
won't see again.
              Every ocean day
brought me mist or pure tumblings of turquoise,
or simple extension, rectilinear water, invariable,
whatever I requested, the space my brow
    devoured.

Every grieving passage of a cormorant, the flight
of great gray birds that loved winter,
and every dark circle of sargassum
and every solemn wave that shakes its cold,
and more, the earth that a secret hidden
herbarium, offspring of mists and salts, gnawed
by the acid wind, minuscule corollas
of the coast clinging to the infinite sand:
all the wet keys of the seaboard
know every state of my happiness,
                know
that I want to sleep there amid the eyelids
of sea and earth . . .
             I want to be swept

down in the rains that the wild
sea wind assails and shatters
and then to flow through subterranean channels,
toward the deep springtime that's reborn.

Open beside me the hollow of the one I love, and
  may she
one day accompany me again in the earth.

XXVI

I Am
Going
to Live
(1949)

I am not going to die. I'm departing now,
on this day full of volcanoes,
for the multitudes, for life.
Here I've settled these matters
now that the gangsters strut
with "western culture" in arms,
with hands that murder in Spain,
and the gallows that swing in Athens
and the dishonor that governs Chile
and I bring my story to a close.
     I'm staying here
with words and people and roads
that await me again, and pound
on my door with their starry hands.

XXVII

To My
Party

You have given me fraternity toward the
  unknown man.
You have joined the strength of all the living.
You have given me the country again as in a
  birth.
You have given me the freedom that the loner
  cannot have.
You taught me to kindle kindness, like fire.
You have given me the rectitude that the tree
  requires.
You taught me to see the unity and the difference
  among mankind.

398

You showed me how one being's pain has
  perished in the victory of all.
You taught me to sleep in beds hard as my
  brothers.
You made me build on reality as on a rock.
You made me adversary of the evildoer and wall
  of the frantic.
You have made me see the world's clarity and the
  possibility of happiness.
You have made me indestructible because with
  you I do not end in myself.

XXVIII

**I End
Here
(1949)**

This book ends here. It was born
of fury like a live coal, like territories
of burned forests, and I hope
that it continues like a red tree
propagating its transparent burn.
But you found not only rage in its
branches: its roots sought
not only sorrow but strength,
and I'm strength of pensive stone,
happiness of joined hands.

At last, I'm free within beings.

Amid beings, like live air,
and from corralled solitude
I set forth to the multitude of combats,
free because my hand holds your hand,
conquering indomitable happiness.

Common book of mankind, broken bread
is this geography of my song,
and a community of peasants
will one day harvest its fire
and will again sow its flames
and leaves in the ship of the earth.

And this word will rise again,
perhaps in another time free of sorrow,
without the impure fibers that adhered

black vegetation in my song,
and my burning and starry heart
will flame again in the heights.
And so this book ends, here I leave
my *Canto general* written
on the run, singing beneath
the clandestine wings of my country.
Today, 5 February, in this year
of 1949, in Chile, in "Godemar
de Chena," a few months before
I turned forty-five.

NOTES TO INTRODUCTION

1. *Canto general*, edición especial y limitada al cuidado de Miguel Prieto, con guardas dibujadas por Diego Rivera y David Alfaro Siqueiros (Mexico: Talleres Gráficos de la Nación, 1950). Biographical information is drawn from Pablo Neruda, *Memoirs*, tr. Hardie St. Martin (New York: Farrar, Straus, and Giroux, 1976), original Spanish, *Confieso que he vivido: Memorias* (Barcelona: Seix Barral, 1974), and from Emir Rodríguez Monegal, *El viajero inmóvil: Introducción a Pablo Neruda* (Buenos Aires: Losada, 1966). A more prolyx account is provided by Velodia Teitelboim's *Neruda* (Madrid: Libros del Meridion, 1984), which discusses in detail the poet's political life as well as his poetry. The best introduction in English to Neruda's life and works is *Earth Tones: The Poetry of Pablo Neruda*, by Manuel Durán and Margery Safir (Bloomington: Indiana University Press, 1981).

2. *Poesía y estilo de Pablo Neruda: Ensayo de interpretación de una poesía hermética* (Buenos Aires: Losada, 1940). I am quoting from the 1977 Sudamericana edition (Buenos Aires), 34.

3. An interesting testimony of their lives together, and particularly of Neruda's last years, is her *Mi vida junto a Pablo Neruda (Memorias)* (Barcelona: Seix Barral, 1986).

4. A moving account of Neruda's final months, as well as a perceptive analysis of his very last poems, can be read in Fernando Alegría's "Reminiscences and Critical Reflections," in *Pablo Neruda*, ed. Harold Bloom (New York: Chelsea House, 1989), 61–68. A more prosaic but detailed report is contained in Matilde Urrutia's *Mi vida*, op. cit.

5. James E. Miller, *The American Quest for a Supreme Fiction* (Chicago: University of Chicago Press, 1979).

6. Octavio Paz, "A Literature of Foundations," in *The Siren and the Seashell, and Other Essays on Poetry and Poetics*, tr. Lysander Kemp and Margaret Sayers Peden, illus. Barry Moser (Austin: University of Texas Press, 1976), 179.

7. See my anaylsis of this phenomenon in *Myth and Archive: A Theory of Latin American Narrative* (Cambridge: Cambridge University Press, 1990).

8. "Mito e historia: Dos generadores del *Canto general*," *Revista Iberoamericana*, 39, nos. 82–83 (1973): 111–135.

9. "The book [the *Canto*] was born the day in which José del Carmen Reyes died, the harsh railroad worker who never wanted his son to be a poet." *El viajero inmóvil*, 236. In Rodríguez Monegal's analysis, the father is associated with the Spanish conquistadors. *El viajero inmóvil* continues to be the best overall interpretation of Neruda's poetry, one that the poet himself endorsed in his *Memoirs*.

10. John Felstiner's superb book, *Translating Neruda: The Way to Macchu Picchu* (Stanford: Stanford University Press, 1980), details the relationship between the trip to the site and the composition of the poem. It is

the best introduction to the *Canto general*, both in terms of Neruda's life and the relationship between life and poetic creation.

11. Pablo Neruda, *Para nacer he nacido* (Barcelona: Seix Barral, 1977), 309–310. This useful collection of prose was compiled by Neruda's widow (Matilde Urrutia) and Miguel Otero Silva.

12. *Para nacer*, 338.

13. Enrico Mario Santí's unsurpassed reading of the *Canto* as a prophetic book, drawing on Neruda's numerous biblical allusions, is proof that the poet's political vision was mediated by a Christian conception of history. See Santí's *Pablo Neruda: The Poetics of Prophecy* (Ithaca: Cornell University Press, 1982).

NOTES TO THE CANTO GENERAL

"Bío-Bío," p. 20

"Dividing into mouths and breasts" (dividido en bocas y senos). The Spanish "senos" means "breasts" as well as "bays," "inlets," "gulfs." My choice of "breasts" is motivated by both the erotic imagery and the fact that the two promontories at the river's mouth are called "las tetas" (the tits) of the Bío-Bío.

"Man," pp. 24–27

"At the bottom of America without name / was Arauco." Today, Arauco and Araucania are a province and a territory, respectively, in the south of Chile. Historically, the names were used interchangeably for the entire area south of the Bío-Bío River inhabited by the indomitable Mapuche or Araucanian Indians, who for three centuries successfully opposed domination, first by Inca forces, later by the Spaniards, and finally by the Chileans, after they acquired independence from Spain. The struggles that took place there during the wars of conquest are the subject of Alonso de Ercilla's *La araucana* (1590), an epic foundation myth for modern Chile, the subject of sixteen poems in Parts III and IV of the *Canto*, and also important to Neruda for its Americanism and nature descriptions.

"Among the cypress trees a cry." Misnamed "larch" (*alerce*) by Europeans who observed that it was used for shingling in Chile, just as the larch is used in Europe, this millennial coniferous tree (*Fitzroya cupressoides*) native to southern Argentina and Chile is in fact related to the cypress.

"They Come Through the Islands (1493)," pp. 43–44

"Guanahaní" is the original name given to the island of San Salvador (today, Watling), where Columbus arrived in 1492.

"De las gredas mayorales / y el ramaje de Sotavento" (From the greater clays / and the branches of Sotavento). The word *mayorales* is a reference to both the "Greater" Antilles and the exploitation of slave labor on the sugar plantations, inasmuch as *mayoral* also means "overseer." The "branches of Sotavento" are the Sotavento or Leeward Islands, the northern group of the "Lesser" Antilles in the West Indies.

"Land and Man Unite," p. 61

"Araucania, cluster of torrential southland beech." *Roble* is the Spanish word for "oak," but in Chile, it is one of the common names for several species of *Nothofagus* ("southern" or "false" beech), of which there are ten different species—some deciduous, some evergreen—whose appearance and chemical properties vary greatly. This is most likely a reference to the common *pellín* or *roble pellín* (*Nothofagus obliqua*).

"Advancing in the Lands of Chile," pp. 77–78

"The forest of maytens" (*maitenes, Maytenus boaria*). The Chilean mytenus or "mayten," (*leña dura* in Argentina), a highly desirable tree for gardens, looks remarkably like a small evergreen weeping willow.

The flowery topa-topa (slipperwort) is a flowering plant of the genus *Calceolaria*.

"Lautaro Against the Centaur (1554)," pp. 84–85

"Watching from behind the copihues" (Chilean bellflowers). The copihue (*Lapageria rosea*), Chile's national flower, was named in honor of Josephine de La Pagerie, Napoleon's first wife, who took it to Europe from Martinique, where it also grows wild. There is also a white copihue, which is less common than the red.

"Pedro de Valdivia's Heart," pp. 85–86

"The cinnamon laurel raised its language." The *canelo* (*Drymis winteri*), a tree of the magnolia family named after Captain W. Winter, who took its bark to Europe as an effective remedy against scurvy. It is also the sacred tree of the Araucanian Indians, who revered it for its numerous medicinal properties and attributed magical properties to it. Its branches were considered to be a peace symbol, and important treaties were made in its shade.

"Commoners from Socorro (1781)," pp. 91–92

"The commoners / shook the viceroyalty." The rebels claimed that they represented the towns or "communes" (*comunas*) and so called themselves *comuneros*, just as the Paraguayans had fifty years before. The Spaniards who rose against Charles V in 1520 first established this principle of popular sovereignty in their challenge to government policies (see Mina, 100).

"Bernardo O'Higgins Riquelme (1810)," pp. 94–97

"You're Chile, between patriarch and *cowboy*." In Chile, the *huaso* is in fact a cross between cowboy and farmhand but with the social status of a peon. Mariano Latorre correctly asserts that whereas the Argentine gaucho has been a popular hero and the subject of great epic literature (*Martín Fierro*, for example), the huaso is seen as a country bumpkin and is the subject of popular jokes. In Argentina, a *gauchada* refers to a generous trait, a personal sacrifice for a friend, but in Chile, a *huasería* is something done crudely or in bad taste, and a *huasamacada* is stupidity (*Memorias y otras confidencias*, [Santiago: Editorial Andrés Bello, 1943], 29, 30). Neruda gives the huaso the heroic stature he justly deserves.

"Manuel Rodríguez," p. 108

Composer Vicente Bianchi put the words of this poem to music in the mid-1950s. Now known as "La tonada de Manuel Rodríguez," it has been taught in all Chile's grammar schools and has become a nationally popular song. According to Chilean poet Raúl Zurita, most Chileans are not aware that the words are Neruda's or that the song was initially a poem published in the *Canto*.

"Castro Alves from Brazil," pp. 115–116

Castro Alves (1847–1871), Brazil's great abolitionist poet, is still read and revered for his burning sympathy for liberty and justice and his campaigns for the abolition of slavery.

"To Emiliano Zapata with Music by Tata Nacho," pp. 125–127

Tata Nacho is the pseudonym of Ignacio Fernández Espolón (1894–1968), a songwriter from Oaxaca and one of Mexico's leading cultural personalities in postrevolutionary Mexico. Also active in films and radio, he is most remembered for songs such as "Adiós mi chaparrita," and "La borrachita," an enormously popular song taken from oral tradition.

"Prestes from Brazil (1949)," p. 141

"Pursued by the pale-eyed tyrant." The reference is to Getúlio Vargas, president of Brazil from 1930 to 1945 and from 1951 to 1954.

"And deliver / his consort to Germany's brown-shirted executioner." In 1936, Graciliano Ramos, Brazil's most prominent modern protest novelist, was held in the same prison as Carlos Prestes's wife Olga when she and other Jewish leftists of German descent were turned over to the Gestapo in Brazil and returned to Germany. Pregnant at the time of her imprisonment, she and her baby daughter disappeared forever. Ramos refers to these events in his posthumously published prison memoirs (*Memórias do Cárcere*, 1953), which also constitute a scathing indictment of the abuses and iniquities of Vargas's "New State."

"Rosas (1829–1848)," p. 152

"Puñales, carcajadas de *mazorca*" (Daggers, government thugs' guffaws). *Mazorca* (ear of corn, corncob) was the name given to the political party formed by Argentine dictator Juan Manuel Rosas, which he called "*de la mazorca*," because it was symbolically represented by an ear of corn to indicate the close-knit union of its members. The mazorca was also used as an instrument of torture and repression; today, it has come to mean (1) a tyrannical government, or group of people who constitute it or execute its orders, or (2) a gang of hired thugs (*Diccionario ejemplificado de chilenismos*, Vol. 4 [Valparaíso: Universidad de Playo Ancha de Ciencias de la Educación, 1986], 2880).

"The Oligarchies," p. 161

"Los libros de *Bilbao*" (Bilbao's books). Francisco Bilbao (1823–1865), a Chilean sociologist persecuted for his liberal ideas, died in exile in Buenos Aires.

"Promulgation of the Funnel Law," p. 163

The "ley del embudo" (funnel law) is a one-sided agreement or an unequal law.

"Los amables yanaconas" (the friendly lackeys). *Yanacona*, a name of

Quechua origin used by the Incas to mean the servants of the great states, was later used to designate the personal servants of the Spaniards.

"The Cream," p. 165

"Salteadores de banca y bolsa" (bank and bourse robbers). As *bolsa* means both "stock market" or "exchange" *and* "purse," the additional meaning of "purse snatcher" would also apply.

"Fops," p. 168

"Los mugrones enterrados" (the buried suckers). *Mugrón* means both "plant sucker" or "shoot" and "filthy pig."

"The Nitrate Men," p. 187

"Las vinchucas" (the bedbugs), winged insects (Reduvius infestans) about two centimeters long, hide in the roofs by day and at night draw the blood of the sleeping.

"The Man Buried in the Pampa," p. 209

"O kill me, Vidalita." The *vidalita* is an Argentine love song, generally of a sad nature, sung with guitar accompaniment.

"Quila Bamboo," p. 225

Quila (Chusquea quila), one of two species of bamboo native to southern Chile, grows in dense, often impenetrable thickets; its leaves and shoots provide an important source of fodder for livestock, and it is used as well for basket weaving, pens and cages, furniture, fencing, and construction in general.

"Botany," pp. 228–229

"The sanguinary litre and the beneficent boldo tree." Both trees are native to southern Chile. The litre (*Lithaea caustica*) is called "sanguinary" because contact can cause serious allergic reactions such as nettlerash and smarting of the skin. The boldo (Peumus boldus) is "beneficent" for its ornamental beauty, its edible fruit, and the medicinal value of its leaves; grama grass (*chépica, Anthoxanthum adoratum*) provides a dense ground cover that grows in bright yellow clusters; "artemisa" (*Ambrosia artemisaefolia*) grows in clusters of yellow flowers; "quelenquelén" (*Polygala stricta* and *Monnina linearifolia*), a plant of the milkwort family, grows in clusters of pink flowers; the "dedal de oro" (literally, "golden thimble"), translated here as "golden foxglove," is in fact the California poppy, which now covers Chile's central valley in springtime; in summer, the ubiquitous *ulmo* (*Eucryphia cordifolia*, heartleaf eucryyphia) blankets the south with clouds of fragrant white flowers; "doca" (*Mesembrianthemum chilense*), a plant of the fig-marigold family which grows in coastal regions of southern Chile, has flowers that range from pink to purple, and its fruit bears resemblance to the strawberry; the "patagua" (*Crinodendron patagua*), called "evident" for its dense green foliage, elegant shape, and abundant flowers, is a tree found in ravines, riverbanks, and wet areas in general; the leaves of "paico" (*Chenopodium chilensis*), a plant of the wormseed family, are valued for their medicinal properties.

LATIN AMERICAN LITERATURE AND CULTURE

General Editor
Roberto González Echevarría
R. Selden Rose Professor of Spanish and
Professor of Comparative Literature
Yale University

1. Manuel Bandeira, *This Earth, That Sky*, trans. Candace Slater
2. Nicolás Guillén, *The Daily Daily*, trans. Vera M. Kutzinski
3. Gwen Kirkpatrick, *The Dissonant Legacy of* Modernismo: *Lugones, Herrera y Reissig, and the Voices of Modern Spanish American Poetry*
4. Pablo Neruda, *Selected Odes of Pablo Neruda*, trans. Margaret Sayers Peden
5. Rosamel del Valle, *Eva the Fugitive*, trans. Anna Balakian
6. Jean de Léry, *History of a Voyage to the Land of Brazil, otherwise called America*, trans. Janet Whatley
7. Pablo Neruda, *Canto General*, trans. Jack Schmitt